GET-A-CLUE

DEVOTIONS

GET-A-CLUE

DEVOTIONS

THE CASE OF
THE HOWLING DOG

AND 51 MORE MYSTERIES

BY MARK LITTLETON

Standard®
PUBLISHING

Cincinnati, Ohio

Published by Standard Publishing, Cincinnati, Ohio
www.standardpub.com

Published in association with the literary agency of Schiavone Literary
Agency, Inc. 236 Trails End, West Palm Beach, FL 33413-2135.

Printed in: United States of America
Project manager: Carla Crane
Project editor: Dawn Korth
Cover design: Scott Ryan
Interior design: Dale Meyers

ISBN 978-0-7847-2378-4

Library of Congress Cataloging-in-Publication Data
Littleton, Mark R., 1950-
 Get-a-clue devotions : the case of the howling dog and 51 more mysteries /
by Mark Littleton.
  p. cm.
 ISBN 978-0-7847-2378-4
  1. Christian children—Prayers and devotions. 2. Devotional calendars—
Juvenile literature. 3. Detective and mystery stories, American. I. Title.
 BV4870.L58 2010
 242'.62--dc22
                    2009040659

15 14 13 12 11 10   2 3 4 5 6 7 8 9 10

DEDICATION

To Gardner, first and only son
May God use you all your days
May you love him all your hours

TABLE OF CONTENTS

TABLE OF CONTENTS

You can read these stories in any order you want, but here's a suggestion based on the calendar.

During this month	Read these stories
January	Weeks 1–4
February	Weeks 5–8
March	Weeks 9–13
April	Weeks 14–17
May	Weeks 18–21
June	Weeks 22–26
July	Weeks 27–30
August	Weeks 31–34
September	Weeks 35–39
October	Weeks 40–43
November	Weeks 44–47
December	Weeks 48–52

INTRODUCTION

These stories are all fiction. Some involve robberies, others kidnapping and people missing, still others a lie or something else. All were made up by the author. Most are just stories to entertain you as you hopefully learn something through them about the Bible.

I hope you enjoy them. I hope you learn from them. Most of all, I hope they draw you closer to the Lord, move you to serve the Lord better, or just love him all the more, which are the only reasons to do anything in this world in my estimation.

This is one way for me to "delight in the Lord," as Psalm 37:4 says. I've thought a lot about that verse, and one way I think we might miss delighting in him is simply enjoying doing what we do for the Lord. I love to make up stories and share them with others. It's just fun to me. But that fun involves something deeper because it gives me a chance to say to God, "I like being with you, around you, knowing that you're watching me, listening to me, being part of my life."

So I hope you will delight in these stories and just have a little fun being a Christian.

If for some reason you want to contact me, please e-mail me at mlittleton@earthlink.net.

Mark Littleton
May 19, 2009

GOT A CLUE?

As you read the devotions in this book, you'll need to do some investigating on your own. When you see this symbol —◉, search God's Word to discover the facts. You can write what you find out in the section called, "I've Got a Clue About . . ." in the back of the book, starting on page 376.

Josh heard the dog before his father. But clearly, his father was upset.

"Can't anyone shut that dog up?" his father said, pacing and looking out the window.

"That family just moved in," Josh's mother said. "Maybe their dog is lonely, or scared."

Josh went to the window and looked out. He couldn't see over the fence, but the dog had a distinct howl: *Arrr-oooo. Arrr-oooo.* Maybe it was a full moon.

Josh smiled and stepped into the family room. "What if I run over and ask them if something's wrong?" he said to his parents.

"Good idea."

Josh went out the door, but was back in a minute. "There's no one home," he said.

"Put a note on the door then," his father said. "Maybe that will wake them up."

Josh printed a neat note—"Please take care of your dog"—and taped it to the front door.

As he walked away, the dog howled even louder. It sounded more upset than ever. "I hope they come home soon," Josh half-said, half-prayed as he walked away.

Do you believe God has a plan for your life? Many Christians do, and they live by the truth of Jeremiah 29:11: "'For I know the plans I have for you,' says the Lord. 'They are plans for good and not for disaster, to give you a future and a hope.'" That's one reason Josh responded to the dog the way he did. He saw that even this little event had a purpose from God.

Will you let God lead you today into all the plans he has for you?

MYSTERY OF THE
HOWLING DOG

The next morning, Dad complained of a fitful night. The dog howled for most of it. Josh traipsed next door to see if anyone had come home. His note hung in its place on the door, undisturbed.

He glanced at the mailbox. It was stuffed full. "They're gone somewhere," Josh said, thinking fast. "Maybe that's why the dog is howling. He's lonely and scared without them."

As he started down the stairs he noticed a sign: "Beware of Dog."

Great, and it's vicious too, Josh thought. At 11 years old, he was no coward. But a mean dog could tear you up.

He walked back alongside the house to the fence. Looking over, he saw the dog in the middle of the yard. It lifted its head and yowled again. But clearly it had run out of steam. For a while.

The dog was big, perhaps a mixed breed of rottweiler and pit bull. "Now that's a great combination," he said. But actually, the dog didn't look nasty, just fearful.

He decided to open the gate and look closer.

Fear is something we all must face. Whether it's a big dog, a tough test, a school bully, or some other challenge, we cannot run away. Paul wrote to a fearful young man named Timothy, advising him to have courage despite his fears. He said, "For God has not given us a spirit of fear and timidity, but of power, love, and self-discipline" (2 Timothy 1:7). When you are afraid, refuse to back down or back away. Decide to do what's right even if it hurts. What do you fear today?

Josh crept into the yard, watching the dog. The dog glared at him for a second, and then threw his head back and howled.

"Nice dog," Josh said, holding out his hand. He left the gate open in case he needed to make a fast exit. "You're not mean. You're lonely, aren't you fella?"

As he neared the dog, he saw it was chained to a doghouse. Obviously, the dog wasn't going anywhere.

"Nice dog," Josh said again and the big lummox stood, wagging his tail.

Carefully Josh let the dog sniff his hand. He moved slowly, and in another minute, Josh sat down next to the dog and hugged him. "You're OK," he said. "You're doing fine." He paused and looked around the yard. "So what's the problem?"

Everything seemed in order. Nice, clipped grass, some trees for shade, fresh water, and two bowls filled to overflowing with dog food. Josh studied them a little closer. One was smaller than the other, and there were two different kinds of dog food in them.

"You a gourmet?" Josh asked, and stepped over to the bowls. Each had a distinct kind of crunchy dog food. He examined them closely, and picked up a couple pieces from each.

The dog howled again. Josh turned around to see him poking around at the back of the doghouse.

Josh backed away. "Be right back," he said.

Taking risks in the name of Christ is what life is all about. Jesus knew the risk he faced in the Garden of Gethsemane. There he prayed about his coming death on the cross: "Father, if you are willing, please take this cup of suffering away from me. Yet I want your will, not mine" (Luke 22:42). Josh was taking a big risk going into that yard. Danger, fear, and worry intrude, but the person of faith and courage takes the risk. Are you that kind of person?

MYSTERY OF THE
HOWLING DOG

Josh showed his mom the two different kinds of food. "Why would they give him two kinds?"

Mom studied the pieces of food, one in small, dark, marble-like balls. The other was shaped like fish and stars. It was lighter in color.

"I think it's obvious," she said. "The big pieces are for the dog. The little ones are for a cat."

Josh's eyes went wide. "Ah, that explains a lot."

He went back to the dog and found him rolling in the dirt and about to howl again.

"So there's a kitty?" he said to the dog.

It looked back at him with big, brown, unhappy eyes.

"Well, where is it?"

The dog didn't move or flinch.

"Cat? Kitty? Kitten? Is there one around here?"

The dog gazed mysteriously back at him.

Josh began walking around the yard, looking under the bushes and in the trees. No sign of a cat.

He went back to the dog. "Well, you'll have to tell me something. I'm stuck."

Josh may have looked a little crazy talking to a dog. But he was doing something important at that moment. The apostle Paul told us in Galatians 6:2, "Share each other's troubles and problems, and in this way obey the law of Christ." Helping a hurt person or animal lifts heavy loads. It helps overcome the problem. It also shows God's love through you. Whose burden can you help lift today?

MYSTERY OF THE
HOWLING DOG

As the dog howled once more, Josh sat and squeezed a piece of the dog food between his fingers. *How sad it must be to eat the same thing every day,* he thought.

The dog did seem lonely. But maybe he and the cat were friends. After all, the bowls sat right next to each other. But why was the cat gone? Surely the people wouldn't leave a roaming cat out there alone. Cats that traveled the neighborhood often got into trouble, including getting squashed flat on the street.

Josh shuddered. "I hope that's not what happened," he said, and prayed, "Help me find this cat, God."

"OK, I'll be right back," he said, getting up. "Let me get something first."

He went back to the house and soon found his flashlight. He wasn't sure what he needed it for, but he might have to look into dark spots.

He said to his mom, "Don't we have some cans of cat food around from when we had Bennie?" Bennie was their cat who died the previous winter.

"In the pantry," Mom said. "What for?"

"I think the dog is howling because his cat friend is missing."

No matter how big or small the problem in your life, God wants to be involved. Praying is the way to begin. Jesus told us, "Keep on asking, and you will be given what you ask for" (Matthew 7:7). For Josh to pray for help finding the cat was not foolish, nor a pain to God. God wants to be involved in everything in our lives. So learn to pray about everything. Whom or what can you pray for today?

1
Day 6

MYSTERY OF THE
HOWLING DOG

Josh stepped back into the yard. The dog looked like he was waiting for him. Josh gave him a friendly pat and then sat down. He opened the cat food. The dog clearly wanted a bite, but Josh set it out of his reach.

"Now let's just listen for a minute," he said.

Silence reigned as he and the dog sat very still. The wind riffled the leaves in the trees. Traffic whizzed by on the street. Dogs barking in the distance and other sounds intruded. But it was quiet in the yard.

Josh stood and took the cat food to another spot. He set it down and listened again.

Nothing. "I guess it went out of the yard," he said to the dog. "I don't think I can do anything about that." He was about to leave when he heard something, and the dog howled again.

"Be quiet," Josh said. As if he understood, the dog stopped and peered at Josh.

Josh listened hard, and then he heard it: a tiny *mew, mew,* from somewhere near the house. Josh hurried over to the place the sound came from.

Listening to the world around you opens up important doors in life. When we become listeners, we give other people a great compliment: "I care so much that I'm willing to hear whatever you have to say." Listening comes from a loving heart.

When Jesus gave a sermon or told a story he often said, "Anyone who is willing to hear should listen and understand!" (Matthew 13:43). There is a time to speak, and a time to listen. We all have to learn to do both. Who can you listen to today?

The dog really howled now, but Josh waved his arm at him. "You'll have to be quiet, or I'll never find your friend!"

The dog stopped and gazed at him. "OK," Josh said, "speak up, cat, or forever hold your mew."

He listened again. Nothing happened.

He picked up the cat food can and started walking around the back of the house.

"Mew, mew, mew," came the little voice.

Josh looked closer. He cocked his head.

"Mew, mew."

In a moment, Josh found a drainpipe with a wire mesh over it. He turned on the flashlight and shone it inside. Two wide green eyes gazed back at him. "Mew."

Josh saw what happened. The mesh hung in place, but it only opened in, not out. The cat had crawled in, but couldn't get back out.

He pushed back the mesh and the cat shot out. In a moment, she cuddled with the big dog, lying between his paws.

Josh walked over and set the cat food down in front of her. "I bet you're hungry after all that," he said, and the cat began scarfing down the food.

That night, everyone in Josh's house slept soundly.

When we love God, his people, and his creation, and step in to be a friend, a helper, or a listener, we build God's kingdom. It's the little things that make outsiders believe God is there, and in us. By Josh's concern for this dog and cat, he showed real love. Even if no one else saw it, God did. And one day God will thank Josh for his faithfulness.

The Bible says, "This is the message we have heard from the beginning: We should love one another" (1 John 3:11). Whom can you love today?

MYSTERY OF THE
BLOODY SWORD

Katie's mother sat down on the couch and patted the seat next to her. "Come, I have to tell you something."

Katie sidled over.

"Nana is sick," Mom said. "She had a stroke."

"What's a stroke?"

"A blood vessel in your brain breaks. There's bleeding. Sometimes after one, you can't walk or talk or do much of anything."

Katie eyes filled with tears. Nana was her favorite grandparent. Of course she loved them all, but Nana lived nearby. So she saw Nana more than any of the others.

That afternoon they visited Nana in the hospital. She slept the whole time.

Afterwards, Mom drove to Nana's house. Inside everything looked as it usually did, except for one thing: a long, shiny, metal object on the living room floor. "What's that?" Katie asked.

God never said bad things won't happen to good people in this world. In Heaven, there will never be pain, or tears, or hurt again. But here, we have trouble. The apostle Peter wrote, "Dear friends, don't be surprised at the fiery trials you are going through, as if something strange were happening to you" (1 Peter 4:12). We will all face trouble in this world. The great truth for Christians is that God will be with us through all of it. No matter how much Nana suffers, Katie can be sure God is with her. And that is great comfort.

What struggle are you facing right now that you can trust God about?

On the floor lay Grandpa's military sword. He had been a marine years before. The sword normally hung over the fireplace. But now it lay on the floor, out of its sheath.

"Why is this here?" Katie asked her mom.

Mom walked into the living room. She gazed at the sword. "I don't know."

Katie stepped closer. "There's blood on it," she said with a gasp.

Mom stooped down. "Nana's hand was cut when they found her," she said. "Maybe this was how."

"But why would Nana put this sword here?"

Mom shook her head. "Maybe you can find out."

Katie studied it a moment. She tried to think of when Nana might have spoken about the sword. She remembered Grandpa telling her about it, how every marine received one at his commissioning. He told her how the marines made a double line at their wedding and held their swords crossed above the bride and groom. Grandpa said, "Nana thought it very romantic. But I was worried one of them might cut my head off."

Katie always found the story funny. But Nana rarely spoke of such things. Why had she put the sword there? Surely there was some reason.

Everything in life has purpose, at least from God's point of view. One of Solomon's proverbs says, "The Lord has made everything for his own purposes" (Proverbs 16:4a). People don't always understand the reasons for certain events and situations in life. However, it's always good to remember that God has reasons for everything.

Katie's idea that Nana put the sword on the floor for a purpose is a good one. When we find out what God is doing in the world, we grow in respect and love for him.

What purpose can you see in a situation in your life today?

MYSTERY OF THE
BLOODY SWORD

The next time Katie visited Nana in the hospital, she was awake. Katie brought up the sword right away. "Why was the sword on the floor? How did it get bloody? Did you cut your hand?"

Nana still couldn't talk. She couldn't even move her hand. Her eyes just blinked, and she seemed to be trying to nod her head.

Katie sighed. "I'll pray that God makes you better." And she bowed her head and prayed.

Back at Nana's house, Katie walked around looking for clues. Mom had cleaned the sword and put it back in its sheath. It now hung back over the fireplace.

Why would Nana take down the sword like that? She looked out the windows and studied things in the room. Suddenly it hit her: Nana had not tried to commit suicide, had she?

"No way," Katie whispered. "She is happy. She loves everyone. She would never do that."

She stood over the spot on the floor where the sword had lain. "What were you trying to tell us, Nana?"

When a person has a problem, others are affected. For example, when an elderly person like Nana has a stroke, loved ones hurt too. They must be patient and show concern for the person, especially if their loved one can't tell them what's wrong.

Jesus told his disciples, "Your love for one another will prove to the world that you are my disciples" (John 13:35). Love is the greatest thing we show in life. Who can you show love to today?

Looking around more closely, Katie remembered Nana had kept a diary every year. Where was the latest one?

"Mom, where did Nana keep her diary?"

"In the end table by her bed, I think."

Katie went to it. She found the little purple book in the drawer. It was not locked, so Katie picked it up. She walked into the kitchen. "Mom, do you think Nana would mind if I read her diary?"

"Under the circumstances, I don't think so."

Katie opened to the first page. "January 1. Cold, blustery day. No snow yet. Birds at the feeder all day. Saw a bluebird and a cardinal."

She turned the page. "January 2. Mildred called. Very lonely. I wish I could do something. Filled the feeder again. Lots of birdies. Mrs. Nelson next door is sick. Took her some lasagna. She said, 'Being a widow is awful. I wish I could just die.' I told her to think about her family and friends, but she didn't want to hear about it. I feel bad for her. Will pray."

Katie sighed. "Just regular stuff, I guess." She turned to the next page.

Reading the writings of others is a good way to explore their hearts and minds. In the Bible, God tells us that reading his Word will bless us. In Revelation 1:3, the apostle John writes, "God blesses the one who reads this prophecy to the church, and he blesses all who listen to it and obey what it says." Many times the Bible tells us that God will bless us as we learn and obey his Word.

Katie hoped to find out more about her Nana through her diary. Similarly, we learn much about God through the Bible. What have you learned about God from his Word?

MYSTERY OF THE
BLOODY SWORD

Katie kept reading. More stuff about Mrs. Nelson, lasagna, and birds, birds, birds. "I'm beginning to think birds are her best friends," Katie muttered as she read.

It seemed to her that Nana had a happy, full life. She had plenty of interests, she cared about people, and she seemed upbeat. She would never try to commit suicide. That was not why she had taken out the sword.

"One more page," Katie said, and she began to read: "I must show Katie the new bird feeder. I'm sure she'll love it. It has three different kinds of feed and a place for some suet. Now every bird in the area will come to my feeder. I really should start taking pictures. Maybe I could write a book about it, telling stories about the different birds. That would be fun. Katie would love it. She's such a great reader. How I love it when she comes to visit."

Katie couldn't read on. Her eyes filled with tears as she thought about Nana's loving words.

Then it hit her. The birds. That was what Nana was interested in. Maybe she should go look at them right now. Perhaps that was a clue.

She went to the window and looked out. There was the feeder, on a pole that Grandpa installed years earlier. Who put the new feeder on it for Nana? Someone had to have helped her.

Katie gazed at the feeder, thinking. Then she noticed something: no birds fluttered around it!

Could God have been leading Katie through this mystery? Proverbs 3:6 tells us that if we look to God in all we do, "he will direct your paths." While we don't always get the hints and clues God may leave in life, we can be sure they're still there. Just as Katie found ideas from Nana's diary, so God puts "marks" in life, and in his Word, to lead us in the right path.

Katie hurried back to the book. She read through several more pages until she came to the one that was written on the morning of Nana's stroke. Katie read eagerly.

"I hope Katie comes by today. Must show her the feeder. Alas, it's empty. I'll have to go out and fill it. It's such a big job, and my arms ache. But the birds are so funny, and lovely. Little spats. Whole families sitting there. Chasing off intruders. Good thing the squirrels can't get at it anymore. They would ruin everything."

That was it, Katie thought. She hurried to the window again. Yes, no birds there. Why? Because the feeder was empty. Nana had meant to fill it that day. But the stroke stopped her.

But what about the sword?

Katie went to the fireplace and took down the gleaming sword. She pulled it out of the sheath and walked over to the window. She was about to lay it down on the floor when her mom walked in.

"Katie, what are you doing? That could be dangerous."

"Mom, I think I figured it out."

"Figured what out?"

"What Nana was doing."

One of the things Katie learned from her adventure with Nana's sword is to be patient and wait. A great truth is found in Psalm 27:14: "Wait patiently for the Lord. Be brave and courageous. Yes, wait patiently for the Lord." Many times in the Christian life we must wait: for God to open a door, or to show us the way, or to give us the clue. God doesn't do everything the minute we ask him to.

What might you pray about now, and then wait on God?

Katie put the sword in the exact position she remembered seeing it. Then she followed it to its point. It directed your eyes right to the bird feeder. How Nana had loved those birds! How she wanted to refill the feeder that day. But the stroke hit, and all she could think of doing was to use the sword to point to the bird feeder . . . in case she died.

Tears filled Katie's eyes. What compassion and love Nana had—for Katie, for her family, and for the hungry birds.

"We have to fill it, Mom. That's what Nana wants."

Mom stood nodding her head. "Well, you figured it out," she said.

They both went into the pantry and found the sacks of bird food. Then they went outside and filled each of the three slots and hung a big piece of suet.

Later, they went to the hospital and told Nana what they had done. Her eyes teared and Katie knew she'd been right.

When they pulled into Nana's driveway in the car, Katie looked at the bird feeder. There, about a million birds fluttered around, ate, fought, and chirped merrily.

The birds would never be hungry again!

Solving that mystery must have been a great relief to Katie. Even better, though, was her knowing that she had done a good thing—for the birds, for Nana, for herself, and for God.

The apostle Paul tells us in Galatians 6:9, "So don't get tired of doing what is good. Don't get discouraged and give up, for we will reap a harvest of blessing at the appropriate time." Doing good is a big part of Christian living. How can you do good? God has put opportunities in your life this very day to help others, to love, and to give. Look for them, and then step up to take the right action. In what way can you do some good today?

Barrie stood at the front door watching for his bus. Normally he'd wait outside, but on the coldest winter days he stayed inside where it was warm. Sometimes the other boy at his stop came in and waited with him.

His breath condensed on the window. When he looked down, he noticed it—a letter, on the floor just inside the door. He picked it up.

There was no mailing address, no return address. All it said was, "To the Jensen family."

"Mom!" Barrie called, and stared at the handwriting. He didn't recognize it. "Mom!"

"What?"

His mom stepped out of the kitchen with a towel in her hand. "This letter was pushed under the door. Do you know about it?" Barrie asked.

"No. Who's it addressed to?"

"The Jensen family."

"Well, open it. You're one of the Jensens."

Still watching for the bus, Barrie tore the edge of the envelope. Inside was a card. On it was written, "I am coming soon."

Barrie stared at it. "Are we expecting some company?"

"No." Mom took the letter and studied it. "It must be a joke."

"It's a plot!" Barrie said.

You need clues and other information to solve a mystery or discover a secret. Yet there is one from whom you can never keep secrets—God. He knows everything. That's why the Bible says, "But when you pray, go away by yourself, shut the door behind you, and pray to your Father secretly. Then your Father, who knows all secrets, will reward you" (Matthew 6:6). What secret thoughts do you want to talk to him about today?

MYSTERY OF THE
UNSIGNED
LETTERS

Barrie took the letter to school and showed it to some of his friends. James said, "I bet it's Finkel. He does those things."

Barrie didn't know John Finkel very well, though. Since they weren't good friends Barrie doubted that John would go to all the trouble to do this. Instead, he spent a little time watching kids in his class and observing their handwriting. He looked for anyone whose writing was similar to the letter. He found no one.

When Barrie arrived at home, he went right to his mother's bedroom, where she was cleaning.

"No one at school knows anything," he said to her.

She looked up, her hair damp with sweat. "Well, don't worry about it. The note said, 'I am coming soon.' I'm sure the trickster will reveal himself in time."

"Yeah, but I want to figure out who he is before he comes. That's even more fun."

"Fine. But first, you can clean the toilet in your bathroom."

Barrie moaned, but quickly got the brush and gave the toilet some swishes.

Then the doorbell rang.

Why do you think it's important for a person who may be coming for a visit to announce it beforehand? What does an announcement do in the hearts of the people who are to be visited?

Think of some of the prophecies in the Bible in which God announced the coming of Jesus. Here's one from Micah 5:2: "But you, O Bethlehem Ephrathah, are only a small village in Judah. Yet a ruler of Israel will come from you, one whose origins are from the distant past." God announced through the prophet that Jesus would be the Messiah and would come from Bethlehem. And that's exactly where Jesus was born. If you had lived in Bethlehem at the time of the prophecy, how might you feel?

UNSIGNED LETTERS

Barrie hurried to the front door and opened it. No one was there. He looked up and down the street, but saw no one. He stepped out the door and yelled, "Who's there?"

No one answered. Then he looked down at the doormat. There lay another letter. On the cover were the words, "To Barrie, who is curious."

He quickly opened it and read, "Be watching. I'm coming quickly."

Barrie sighed and went inside. "Mom! This is getting weird!"

Showing the letter to her, she studied it a moment. "Yep—I think you have a genuine mystery on your hands."

"What on earth could it be? What would be the purpose?"

Mom shook her head. "The person seems to know a lot about us."

Barrie mulled this over. "Yeah, he says I'm curious. He must have seen me at school today."

"OK, let's call your dad at work. He might have a suggestion."

They called Dad, but he was as flummoxed as they were. "It's happened twice now, huh?" he asked.

"We showed you the first one."

"Of course, but—"

"Could it be a friend here in town?" Barrie asked. "Could it be someone you know?"

"I doubt it, since the second one was addressed just to you."

"I wonder," Barrie said, "if he's going to bring something for me." That afternoon, Barrie made a list of all the birthday and Christmas presents that he'd requested but never received.

Why this person is making such a commotion about his coming is crucial. When Jesus told his disciples he would be coming back, he assured them there was a purpose for it. We read about that purpose in John 14:1, 2: "Don't be troubled. You trust God, now trust in me. There are many rooms in my Father's home, and I am going to prepare a place for you. If this were not so, I would tell you plainly."

MYSTERY OF THE
UNSIGNED LETTERS

The next morning Barrie found still another letter pushed under the door. This one said, "Are you watching? Are you ready?"

He tried to think of what he could do to answer these questions. Yes, he was watching. It was driving him crazy. Yes, he thought he was ready. But what could he do to prepare for this? He knew nothing about who this person was. Was he supposed to fix up his room, or the house, to welcome this person?

Then he turned to the list of things he wanted that he'd made up the day before: a Wii game, a new basketball, and tickets to see the Yankees. But what did this mystery person have to do with any of those things?

Barrie was really stumped. But he decided to wake up early the next day, crack the door, and watch to see if anyone came to slide another letter under it.

He did that very thing, waking up at 5:00 AM. He crouched behind the front door and cracked it open just enough so that he could see anyone who approached. Gradually, his head sank down and he dozed, until a sound jolted him awake. It was 6:15, but there was no letter on the stoop.

He watched for awhile, then dozed again, his head against the door. Nothing woke him till his mother came in and roused him for school. "Time to get up," she said.

"Rats, I fell asleep." He immediately looked out the door to the doormat. Nothing was there.

Waiting is hard. Watching and waiting may be even harder. When Jesus ascended to Heaven, Luke described the scene. His disciples watched Jesus as he was taken up to the sky, and two angels said, "Someday, just as you saw him go, he will return!" (Acts 1:11).

Do you long for Jesus to come back, just as Barrie longed for the mystery person to show himself?

Barrie climbed on the bus, his heart a little heavy. Why no note today? Had the mystery person given up because Barrie was too close to finding out who he was?

He went down the aisle and his friend Jerry called out, "Hey, Barrie! Come here. I have something for you."

Barrie looked up and went to the empty seat beside Jerry. "We found this in front of our door this morning," he said, and held out another letter.

Barrie took it, rolling his eyes. The mystery person certainly could be creative! The envelope said, "Give this to Barrie Jensen, please."

He said to Jerry, "Did you see anyone?"

"No, it was just lying there. What is it?"

Barrie explained about the letters.

"Well, open it," Jerry said. Barrie did so. This time the note said, "Not much longer. Prepare to be amazed."

Barrie sucked in air. So did Jerry. "Wow," he said, "that's incredible."

"Yeah," Barrie said. "I just hope I don't die from curiosity. I can't stand this much longer."

> The Bible tells us what it will be like when Jesus comes again: "For the Lord himself will come down from Heaven with a commanding shout, with the call of the archangel, and with the trumpet call of God. First, all the Christians who have died will rise from their graves. Then, together with them, we who are still alive and remain on the earth will be caught up in the clouds to meet the Lord in the air and remain with him forever" (1 Thessalonians 4:16, 17). How do you feel when you imagine the scene on that day? Are you looking forward to being there?

MYSTERY OF THE
UNSIGNED
LETTERS

3

Day 6

Barrie could make no progress solving the riddle on Friday. He talked to both his mom and dad about it, and they were equally confused. Barrie tried checking the door the next morning at various times, but nothing appeared. He even set a little trap with a trip string tied to a small alarm that would go off if anyone hit it. But nothing happened.

That evening Barrie got a phone call. A strange voice said to him, "The secret will be revealed." The person then hung up.

The next day, Sunday, he went to church as frustrated as ever. He took all the letters with him with the intent to ask his Sunday-school teacher, a young man named Zeph Walters, what he thought of them.

The service was fine, and the sermon was on the second coming of Christ. As the minister talked about not knowing the day or time Jesus would come back, Barrie thought about his experience that week. He had heard sermons like this one before, but this time Barrie understood it in a new way.

After worship he walked downstairs to meet his small group. Zeph stood in front of the five boys and asked, "So, did anything weird happen to anyone this week?"

All five boys raised their hands at once.

For God's children, being watchful and ready is what it's all about. In 1 Thessalonians 5:4-6, Paul wrote, "But you aren't in the dark about these things, dear brothers and sisters, and you won't be surprised when the day of the Lord comes like a thief. For you are all children of the light and of the day; we don't belong to darkness and night. So be on your guard, not asleep like the others. Stay alert and be sober."

It turned out that every boy in the class had gotten notes just like Barrie. When they all compared theirs to the others, the handwriting was the same. Zeph was smiling the whole time.

"Who do you think might have done it?"

Everyone looked around. Then it hit Barrie. "The sermon was about the second coming of Christ. So maybe one of the teachers—"

Instantly he knew. "You!" he cried, pointing to Zeph.

"The very one." Everyone had a good laugh.

"But why?" Barrie asked.

Zeph nodded reflectively. "I wanted you guys to experience something important—anticipation, the desire to look forward to an event, watchfulness and readiness. Weren't you all on the edges of your seats all week?"

Everyone agreed they were.

"That's the kind of attitude God wants us to have about Jesus' coming. The Bible tells us that we should always be ready. We don't want to be caught doing something bad when he comes, right? And when we're watchful for him, we're also watchful about what we do in life. So I wanted each of you to experience that by my little trick."

Barrie nodded and grinned. "It was good. It made me realize that when I'm expecting something, I do get excited. And I guess getting excited about Jesus is the most important thing of all."

"Exactly," Zeph said. "Now let's look at some Bible passages."

In a parable, Jesus warned his disciples about being ready for his return. Read Luke 12:39, 40. Every day we should live as if he might come in the next minute. That's strong motivation, don't you think?

MYSTERY OF THE
BACKPACK SECRET

Day 1

Lukas was up. He was known to roof a kickball now and then, he was that good. Johnny Holmes moved back in his position in left field. He bent down, hands on knees, ready to move in whatever direction Lukas kicked it. Behind him—he took a quick look—sat Katie Johnson, the girl with the blue backpack.

Backpack Girl, everyone called her. She always had that stuffed blue backpack on her back. *What's in it?* Johnny thought for the millionth time. *What on earth is so important that she has to always have that backpack on?*

Two sixth-grade girls, Tess and Tina, approached Katie. "So, what's in the backpack?" Tess asked sarcastically.

Johnny glanced her way, but kept his eye on the ball.

"Pitch!" someone yelled.

"Can we see?" Tina added, leaning down and reaching for the backpack.

Katie drew back, saying nothing. That was so strange about her. She hardly spoke a word to anyone.

Johnny yelled, "Leave her alone!" just as Lukas kicked. The ball soared high into left field. Johnny watched the ball and backed up . . . farther.

It whacked into his hands just as he tripped and fell backward into Katie. Tess and Tina laughed and walked away. Katie was under him, but he had the ball. He jumped up, holding it up, then looked down at her.

"Your knee is bleeding!" he said.

There are always kids who are rejected by others. What does Scripture say about such people? Take a look at Romans 15:7: "So, accept each other just as Christ has accepted you; then God will be glorified." Is there anyone in your school who needs acceptance?

Johnny stooped down. Katie held her knee and moaned. "Let me take you to the nurse," he said.

Katie shook her head.

"You're bleeding. Come on. I'll carry your backpack."

Katie pulled it onto her back. "I'm OK," she said. "I can take care of it."

She got up and walked toward the school. Johnny hesitated. Everyone was still cheering about his catch, which had ended the game and won it. But he knew he should help Katie no matter how strange she was.

He threw the ball back to the gym teacher and sped after Katie. He caught up to her. "Look, you're limping. Let me help you."

"I don't need your help," Katie said between clenched teeth.

Johnny touched her shoulder and stopped her. "Everyone needs friends."

Katie sighed and stopped. She looked away at the playground. Suddenly, Johnny noticed everything was quiet and the kids were staring at him. "Don't worry about them," he said.

He looked back at Katie. She was cute for all her weird presence. Maybe he could help her lose the backpack.

"OK," she said. "But I'll carry my backpack."

"Great."

Many times a simple nice gesture like reaching out, being friendly, or saying kind words can connect with someone who has been rejected. Jesus said in Matthew 5:7, "God blesses those who are merciful, for they will be shown mercy."

Remember a time when you felt rejected, and reach out to someone else.

Johnny left Katie with the nurse and headed back to his class. About 15 minutes later, Katie stepped back into the science class and sat down, still wearing her backpack. The teacher said, "Please, Katie, take off the backpack. It's safe in here."

When one of the girls reached toward Katie to help her take off the backpack, Katie swiped at her hand like a lion raking prey. Katie recoiled, falling off the chair into a heap. Everyone laughed. Except Johnny.

"Shut up, people," Johnny said. "That's not nice."

Katie dusted herself off and took off the backpack, setting it at her feet. She sat back down. Tess glared at Johnny.

Johnny watched Katie during class. She took notes and seemed like she understood what the teacher was talking about. He wondered what she was really like. At home, with people who cared about her, was she weird then? Did she take off the backpack?

After class, he waited for her at the door. As she passed him he said, "I'm willing to bet you're pretty smart."

She stopped and glared at him. "Why are you doing this?"

"What?" he said, pretending he had no idea.

"Following me? Helping me? No one else does. You have a group of friends."

Johnny stared at her, not sure what to say.

The Bible tells us that God values people who don't fit in. Psalm 68:5 says, "Father to the fatherless, defender of widows—this is God, whose dwelling is holy." Johnny was being a friend and defender of Katie. What more could he do to show Katie he cared?

As Johnny gazed at Katie, he thought of something and smiled. "I believe in being friendly."

"Why? Because I'm some sort of project for you? Help the weird girl? Maybe she'll be less weird?"

Johnny felt the red run up his neck. "No, you're not my project. If you don't want to be friends, fine. I can live with it."

"What do you want?" she asked, looking frustrated.

"Look," he said, "I just think people should give you a chance. I'm willing to—"

"Why?"

He sighed heavily. "Do I have to have some great reason?"

She turned to go. "OK. You want to be friends? Then don't treat me like I'm weird, like everyone else does."

Johnny said, "I can do that."

"Good," she said, and hurried down the hall.

Clearly, Katie was not going to respond easily to his attempts at friendship. Maybe he should just give it up, he thought. Why should he make the effort? Besides, some of his friends might call him an idiot or avoid him because he went out of his way like this to help the school weirdo.

As he walked along, he prayed in his mind, *Please, God. I don't mean to be weird myself. But maybe something happened to Katie, and that backpack is a clue. If I get to know her a little better, I can figure out a way to do something good for her. I'll wait to see what you do.*

Sometimes people have wounds that cause them to alienate others. About such people, the Bible offers direction: "Pay all your debts, except the debt of love for others. You can never finish paying that! If you love your neighbor, you will fulfill all the requirements of God's law" (Romans 13:8). Love can heal wounds of the past.

MYSTERY OF THE
BACKPACK SECRET

After school, Johnny walked to the bike rack to grab his bike and head home. At another rack, he saw Katie unlocking her bike. When she rode off, he followed at a distance and just watched her.

Suddenly she stopped and waved, and he rode up.

"What are you doing now?" she asked fiercely. "Don't stalk me."

Johnny took a breath. "I just wanted to tell you something."

"What?"

"If you didn't wear that backpack like body armor, a lot of people would probably think you're normal."

"You don't know anything!" Katie said, shaking.

"I don't want to hurt your feelings. But think about it. You never let that backpack out of your sight. What's with you?"

Katie stared straight ahead. "Why do you want to know?"

He reached into his pocket and took out a small object. He held it out to Katie. "See this? It's Han Solo. You know, from the *Star Wars* movies. He's like my good luck charm. I mean, I'm a Christian, and I believe in God, but I always carry Han around. It's a secret nobody knows about and—"

"Nobody knows about it?"

"Not really."

"Why did you show it to me?"

Johnny shifted his weight. "If I tell you, will you tell me something about the backpack?"

A friendship is a two-way relationship. Give a little, offer more than words, and sometimes people will lighten up. Jesus told his disciples in Luke 6:38, "If you give, you will receive. Your gift will return to you in full measure, pressed down, shaken together to make room for more, and running over. Whatever measure you use in giving— large or small—it will be used to measure what is given back to you."

Katie took the Han Solo figure out of Johnny's hand. She turned it over and over. He watched her, wondering what she was thinking.

After a minute, she handed it back to him. Suddenly, she took off the backpack. She opened the top, but he didn't try to look in. He would let her go at her own pace. Perhaps this was very emotional for her, and he didn't want to step all over that.

She rummaged in the backpack. Finally, she pulled out a little bag. She opened it, and dropped the contents out into her hand. Johnny looked at them closely and realized they were military medals.

She took them one by one, showing him several ribbons. "These represent battles a soldier has been in." She took two sets of silver bars and handed them to him. "These are a captain's insignia," she said. Then she handed him two metal tags. He knew instantly what they were.

Johnny was entering Katie's world in a way that perhaps no other person ever had. This was a sacred moment, and you can bet Johnny knew that's exactly what it was. What should he offer her as she did this? Respect. First Peter 2:17 says, "Show respect for everyone. Love your Christian brothers and sisters."

Note that God doesn't say here, "Just respect those you like," or, "Show respect to people who deserve it." He says, "Respect everyone." Being respectful to people is an essential element of good relationships. When you respect others, usually they will respect you. Many fights have broken out because someone "dissed" another, which means "disrespected." So show respect, even if you're not sure why.

37

MYSTERY OF THE
BACKPACK SECRET

Katie handed the last items to Johnny. "Do you know what these are?"

He nodded, the emotion swelling. "Dog tags. What a soldier wears in case—"

He stopped there and she continued staring at him. She went back to her backpack, then drew out something else. It was folded into a triangle, but he knew instantly it was an American flag.

"When my father was killed in Iraq, the officers who came to the funeral gave my mom this. These are the only things I have left of my father, except for some pictures. So that's why I carry this backpack around . . . so I can feel like my father's still here with me wherever I am."

She didn't blink, but Johnny's eyes filled with tears. "I'm sorry," he said. "I—I don't know what else to say."

She nodded. "Losing my dad was the hardest thing I ever went through."

Johnny said, "People say and do mean things and they don't know what they're doing. That's what Jesus said on the cross about the people who put him there: 'Father, forgive them, for they know not what they do.' I guess in a way that's what you have to do—forgive."

Katie nodded. "And I do."

He helped her gather her things and they both rode off.

When people treat you badly, think about Jesus' words in Luke 23:34. When you're rejected, realize Jesus endured the same treatment. He understands completely. Is there someone you need to forgive? Why not bow your head right now and tell God about it?

When Grant was younger, he loved the kids' videos on YouTube. He had learned to make his own videos to put online. In one, he showed some shots of his family, his house, his dog Bleu, and his bike. Finally he panned around his room. He showed his trophy shelf with four trophies from the swim team; a signed picture of Hank Aaron, one of his favorite baseball players; and the picture of the ship that his grandmother had given him. He also took shots of his desk, and one outside his window.

Finally, he posted it on YouTube, not thinking much more about it. He got a few e-mails about it telling him what a good job he'd done. One asked if the Hank Aaron signed picture was real, and who the painter of the ship was. He answered that yes, the photo was real and the painter was G. Seminole. Eventually he got a little bored with the whole YouTube thing and stopped making videos altogether.

One night, the family came home to a bad scene. The front door had been jimmied, and someone had broken in and made a mess in all the rooms, clearly looking for valuables. From Grant's room, the Hank Aaron photo was gone, but Grant didn't notice anything else . . . until that night. As he lay in bed, he stared at the wall.

"My painting!" he cried. "It's gone too."

You never know when thieves might strike your home. It happens sometimes. And God sees when it happens.

In the Bible Satan objected to how God protected Job and his property. You can read about it in Job 1:9. Many people today believe that in the same way God protected Job he protects his people's homes and property from harm, including theft. For some reason, though, God allowed thieves to break into Grant's house. What might be the reason?

Grant's dad reported the theft to the insurance company. They decided to do an investigation because several things taken, including silverware, a knife collection, and some coins, were quite valuable.

Grant decided to check out some places in town, mainly pawn-shops, where he'd heard you could sometimes find items that had been stolen. He rode his bike out to Good Cents Pawn on Vivion Road and stepped inside. It seemed to have everything, from guns and knives to watches, coins, and even some paintings. He asked the man behind the counter, "Do you ever get signed pictures of baseball players in here?"

The man led him over to a box with many pictures in it. "Some are signed," he said.

Grant looked through and even found a couple of Hank Aaron. But neither was signed like his had been.

"Have you had anyone come in with some gold coins?" he asked again.

"Yes, we have a few over here."

When the man showed him the display, Grant's jaw went slack. "Sixteen hundred dollars for a coin?" he cried.

"Gold is selling nicely now," the man said.

Grant went to the door, then stopped. "Are there any other pawnshops around here?" he asked.

"Ace Pawn, down on 48th," the man said.

Theft causes trouble and sadness. Ephesians 4:28 says this: "If you are a thief, quit stealing. Begin using your hands for honest work, and then give generously to others in need."

Most thieves probably wouldn't pay much attention to this verse. But if they feel any guilt and want to get right with God, it's a good place to start.

Grant asked his dad where he might find a place that sold paintings like his little ship picture by G. Seminole. "I don't know," Dad said. "You might try one of the galleries in the city. If you want, we can drive down to a couple this Saturday."

They hit two stores that Saturday, Griff's Gallery, and another called The Art Place. It was interesting to walk around and look at the many paintings that hung on walls and were stacked upright in long lines on the floors. Grant didn't see anything that even resembled his painting.

He and his father talked to the owner. "Who are some famous painters of ships?" Grant asked the man.

"William Coulter, for one," he answered. "And James Tyler. Of course, Rembrandt did some, but you won't find him in a gallery around here." He laughed. "Why do you ask?"

Grant described the painting. "Have you ever heard of G. Seminole?"

"Native American, perhaps?" the man asked.

"I don't know."

"No, never heard of him."

Dad said, "Why don't we look him up in a history book or something? Maybe we'll find him."

Grant couldn't wait to get home.

Whenever you need to find out about a person or subject, research is the first step. The Gospel writer, Luke, even mentioned his research at the beginning of his book on Jesus: "Having carefully investigated all of these accounts from the beginning, I have decided to write a careful summary for you, to reassure you of the truth of all you were taught" (Luke 1:3, 4). How do you search for truth?

MYSTERY OF THE
YOUTUBE VIDEO

Grant and his dad stopped at the library, but found no reference to G. Seminole. When they got home, Grant decided to Google the painter. Only one site came up, but it was a big one.

G. Seminole had been a painter in the early 1900s who mostly painted ships and sea scenes. Grant learned that today one of his paintings, even a small one, could sell for thousands of dollars.

Grant ran into his parents' bedroom with the news.

His father said, "But how would anyone know that we had a Seminole painting? I've never told anyone, or even talked about it."

Grant remembered his video. He asked his parents. "Do you think someone might have seen the YouTube video of my room and came to our house to get it?"

Everyone agreed it was worth figuring out. Dad called the insurance people that Monday, and they assured him they would check up on it. Meanwhile, Grant prayed, asking God to help him recover the stolen painting.

"What about eBay?" Grant asked his mother. "Wouldn't the thieves try to sell to the highest bidder?"

They went to the computer and began searching eBay. First they tried "Original art works."

Millions of them came up. It was hopeless wading through the screens.

"Wait!" Grant cried. "Let's just try G. Seminole."

Suddenly a painting came onto the screen, with seven others listed. Grant's heart took a leap.

Many times in life it's necessary to ask for God's help. When we ask for his guidance, he promises he will. Read 1 John 5:14, 15. We can be sure that if we ask for God's will, he will show us the way to success.

There on the screen was a painting that resembled Grant's gift from his grandmother. They looked at the price: "Starting bid: $6000."

Everyone gasped. "Six thousand dollars!" Grant cried. "I had a painting like that, and I just thought it was worth ten dollars?"

"Let's get our insurance people on it," Dad said. "They can track down this person and find out how he came to have the painting."

The next morning, before Grant left for school, his dad called the insurance people. They said they'd get the FBI right on it. Grant was amazed. "The FBI?"

"I think it has something to do with the laws about taking something out of state," his dad explained. "Anyway, they'll get to the bottom of it."

Grant was on pins and needles all day. What would happen? Would the crooks be found out? Would he ever get the painting back?

People who do evil things think they will escape without being caught. It's too bad they don't know God, or care, because he has some strong things to say about such people. To his followers God says, "Don't worry about the wicked. Don't envy those who do wrong. For like grass, they soon fade away. Like springtime flowers, they soon wither" (Psalm 37:1, 2).

You can be sure that God will not let you do evil things without consequences. He will discipline you, and possibly allow you to be caught and humiliated in public for what you've done. But how should Grant handle what was about to happen next?

"We have them," the FBI agent told Dad. It turned out that the thieves who broke into Grant's house were high school kids in his area. They watched YouTube videos to find out about places that had valuable treasure. None of them knew how valuable the little painting was until they did some research. It was the most valuable item they'd ever taken.

Unfortunately, they were also stupid. They put the painting on eBay where people with knowledge and skill could see it and buy it . . . and also track it down, as Grant had done.

When the insurance man, Mr. Stevenson, came by with the painting, as well as the Hank Aaron picture, the gold coins, and the silverware, everyone was elated. Grant put the picture back up, but this time he had a new appreciation for its worth.

At dinner that night Grant ate in silence. Then he said, "The boys who stole the stuff—I'd like to meet them."

Everyone turned to stare at Grant. Then Dad said, "Why?"

The Bible is clear about how we are to treat our enemies. You find the passage in the Sermon on the Mount, Matthew 5:43-45: "You have heard that the law of Moses says, 'Love your neighbor' and hate your enemy. But I say, love your enemies! Pray for those who persecute you! In that way, you will be acting as true children of your Father in heaven. For he gives his sunlight to both the evil and the good, and he sends rain on the just and on the unjust, too."

Grant, his mom, dad, and sister all stepped into the detention center where the boys were being held. Guards led them into a room and they sat down. Then the four boys were brought in.

All of them had long, disheveled hair, tattoos, piercings, and nasty glints in their eyes. It made Grant nervous just to look at them.

When the boys sat down, one of them, probably the leader, said, "Say what you gotta say, then get out."

Everyone looked at Grant. "OK, this is it. I want you to know that I forgive you for everything, and so does my family. But the most important thing is that you know that God forgives too."

"God? Whaddayou know about God?" the leader asked.

"He is love," Grant said. "He forgives." He fixed each boy with his eyes. "I hope you will go to God through Jesus, admit all the bad things you've done, and get right with him."

The boys all shook their heads with contempt.

"That's all," Grant said.

The boys were taken out. The family returned home. On the way, Dad said, "That took guts, Grant. I'm proud of you."

"I just feel bad that they have to live like that," Grant said. But deep down he felt God was at work. And maybe one or two, maybe all four, would find eternal life in Jesus.

It's important to forgive your enemies, and it's important for them to know what God offers everyone. He says in Isaiah 1:18, "Come now, let us argue this out. . . . No matter how deep the stain of your sins, I can remove it. I can make you as clean as freshly fallen snow. Even if you are stained as red as crimson, I can make you as white as wool."

Telling the lost the gospel is one of the reasons God saved you. Take that responsibility in hand.

The first valentine appeared in Neva's mailbox several days before Valentine's Day. She opened it on the way back to her house from the box by the side of the road. It read, "I hope you feel loved, because I love you."

Neva's dad was in Iraq with the Marines, but it didn't look like his handwriting. It wasn't like Grandma's writing, either; hers was tiny and had lots of curlicues and flourishes. Not Aunt Darcie. She usually printed, and this was cursive. But who could be sending this to her? A girlfriend? She chuckled nervously. A boy?

She didn't know. When she showed the valentine to her mother, Mom just said, "How nice. A secret valentine. Sounds like fun."

"Fun?" responded Neva. "I'm not so sure. What if it's some weird boy from school who's trying to soften me up?" She shuddered. "Yuk! Is there such a thing as a *bad* surprise?"

"Not exactly. I think that's called suspense," said her mother.

"Well, I'm in suspense all right." Neva looked into her mother's eyes. "It's not you, is it? Pretending to write differently from the way you usually write?"

"No, darling," said her mother. "I don't do things like that."

Neva tore up the note.

Life is full of the unexpected, good and bad. Have you ever been in suspense, or dreaded some surprise? Read Psalm 37:3-7. You can be sure that God has a plan for your life, and he is in control. You can trust your future to him. Talk to him about what you dread today.

The next day, Neva's mom called her from the bottom of the stairs. "Neva, there's a letter here for you."

Neva hurried downstairs and took it. It didn't look at all like the last one, so she opened it without hesitation. Sure enough, it was another valentine. This time the note said, "I hope you'll be happy when you see me."

She shook her head. "I can't believe this, Mom. Why would someone do this to me?"

"You just have an admirer."

"I wish he or she would tell me who it is now. I don't like not knowing. It's creepy."

"Maybe the person wants you to stretch yourself a little. Perhaps you should do some investigation."

Neva thought about it, and the more she thought, the more she liked the idea of nailing this person. Where would she start? The post office seemed like the logical place.

She decided to ride down there on her bike the next day and see if they could give her any information. As she wheeled out her bike after school, her heart beat a little more rapidly than usual.

When people care about you, they do nice things. How do you think Neva's admirer would feel if he or she knew Neva thought the valentines were more disturbing than flattering?

With God in your life, you need never fear the future. In Proverbs 23:18, he has a message for those who love him: "For surely you have a future ahead of you; your hope will not be disappointed."

Neva stopped her bike in front of the post office and went in. There was a short line, and soon she stood at the front desk. She pulled out the envelope from the letter she'd received. "Can you tell me how I could trace this?" she asked the man at the window.

He took the letter and looked at it. "Well, young lady," he said, "the postmark says it's from our town, and the time it was mailed was two days ago. But that's all I can tell you."

"Can't you go back into your office and find out more?"

He laughed. "No, that would be a breach of privacy. Besides, it's impossible. Remember that anthrax scare that happened after 9/11? Maybe you're too young. But we had a very hard time figuring out who that was, and the FBI was involved in that one."

"I don't think this is a terrorist," Neva said.

The man laughed. "Me neither. What did the letter have in it?"

"A valentine."

"Was there a note?"

"Yes."

A gentle smile came onto his lips. "That message would probably tell you more than anything. I'd work on that."

"Thanks," said Neva, disappointed. But as she left she had another idea.

"There is a God in heaven who reveals secrets" (Daniel 2:28). When you have a mystery to solve, the Bible is a great source. Daniel revealed mysteries to kings because of God's help. Read how he described God in Daniel 2:19-22. Then you can say with Daniel, "He reveals deep and mysterious things and knows what lies hidden in darkness, though he himself is surrounded by light."

The next day, another valentine arrived: "I am here, there, and everywhere, and I know all about you. I love you."

Neva shook her head and went to her mom. "Who on earth could be like that?" she said, after reading the note to her.

"Honey, I don't know what to tell you. What happened at the post office?"

Neva told her what the postman had told her.

"He's probably right. Have you studied the notes?"

"I've been doing it. But I don't remember ever seeing this handwriting before."

Mom took the note and studied it. "You know, I don't remember ever seeing anyone write like this either. That could mean that the notes were written by someone you don't know but who knows you. It could also mean that it's someone you do know who's trying to disguise their identity. Why don't you compare all the notes?"

"I can't compare all of them. I tore one up. But I have two left."

Her mom shook her head. "See if you can spot any differences or inconsistencies in the handwriting. That might indicate someone is trying not to be identified."

Neva took the notes up to her bedroom, laid them out on her desk, and hunkered down. Suddenly, she jumped up: "Mom!"

Too many young people today think parents can't tell them anything. Mark Twain once said, "When I was sixteen, I thought my father was the stupidest person I ever met. But when I turned twenty-one, I was amazed at how much he'd learned in five years." Twain didn't mean his father had really learned anything, but that he had come to grow up and recognize his father's wisdom.

God's wisdom is beyond human understanding. Read about it in Job 11:7-9. Give thanks to God for his wisdom that "is broader than the earth and wider than the sea."

The next morning, Neva went to school with a mission: to find the person who was the source of her suspense, and let him—or her, if it was a her—know just how much they'd messed up her life.

She sat down at her homeroom desk and looked around. There was Dink Morson. Not very smart. And always making nasty noises when no one was looking. "Don't let it be him," she whispered, half in hope, half in prayer.

To her left sat Shellie Small. They had been friends once, in about second grade. But Shellie started this big rumor about how Neva had a crush on someone—who was it?—she couldn't even remember. And that was the end of that relationship.

She glanced at several others, but no one seemed to be the type to send her love notes, or the type to play pranks on her.

She went to first period and made a similar effort. No one seemed likely. As the day wore on, she prayed constantly, "Don't let this be a prank. No prank, please."

By the end of the day, Neva turned her attention to Henry Watts. He was cute, very polite, and had once held out her chair for her. But did he have the creativity for something like this? And could he really like her if he hardly seemed to notice her?

Walking home, she worked it over and over in her mind. When she walked in the door, she went to the kitchen and found Mom making a cake. "It's Henry Watts, Mom."

It's human nature to make assumptions about others. Neva assumed that Henry Watts was the letter-writer because she knew he was a kind person.

The Bible says, "Even children are known by the way they act, whether their conduct is pure and right" (Proverbs 20:11). When others look at what you do, what can they assume about your character?

The next day Neva smiled several times at Henry to see how he'd respond. He seemed not to really notice, and treated her just like he treated everyone else. By the time the school day ended, she was having serious doubts about Henry. If he loved her enough to write her notes, surely he could show a little more interest.

She went home that afternoon with a heavy heart. Maybe it really was a cruel prank. Someone wanted her to think she had a special secret friend so she'd get all excited, and then be devastated when no one came forward. Why had she wasted so much time and energy this week over those stupid notes?

As if to make her more miserable, there was another note waiting for her with the mail. "Tomorrow is the day!" it said. Neva tore it up and threw it away.

Her mom noticed her moping around. "What's the matter, honey?" she asked at dinner.

"I think it's a horrible joke," Neva said. "Somebody's messing with my mind. I can't imagine anyone who would write those notes just to torture me."

"Oh, Neva." Her mom had a pained expression on her face. "It can't be that bad. I wish I could convince you not to be so pessimistic. Can't you try to think of something good about the mysterious notes?"

"I've tried. I can't." As Neva went upstairs to her room, she thought her mom looked like she was about to cry.

David the psalmist knew what it felt like to be discouraged and sad. Read his words in Psalm 42:5-8. How did David answer the question, "Why am I discouraged? Why so sad?"

Are you discouraged or sad? How about someone you know? Take those feelings to God in prayer. He will pour "his unfailing love" on you.

MYSTERY OF THE
VALENTINES

Neva woke up with a little bit of a hitch in her heart. Would this be a good day, or a bad one?

She went to school and nothing exceptional happened. She tried to notice if anyone was watching her.

Finally, after what seemed like forever, the school day was over and she went home. When she stepped inside, she saw her mom at the kitchen table. "Anything happen?" her mom asked.

"Nothing."

"I'm sorry, honey. Still think it was just a cruel prank?"

Neva shrugged. "Condition of my life," she said, and walked up to her bedroom. After all the suspense, she felt pretty bad.

The doorbell rang. Neva heard her mother answer it, and then call up the stairs, "Neva, you have a visitor."

Neva went to the head of the stairs and looked down. Then she ran down and crushed herself in the arms of her father. "What are you doing home?"

"I wanted to surprise you. But from what Mom tells me, you weren't exactly thrilled with my letters."

"You? You sent me those letters? But your handwriting?"

Dad held her close. "I had someone in my unit help me write and send them. I wanted it to be fun. I guess it backfired, and caused you a lot of stress. I'm sorry for that. But I'm home on leave now. Do you think that will help you feel better?"

Neva looked at her mom and they both laughed. "You bet it will, Dad!"

Sometimes God surprises his children by turning bad things into good. Read what David wrote in Psalm 30:11, 12 about God turning mourning into dancing. For what can you thank God this week?

MYSTERY OF THE
NOISES IN THE ATTIC

Mason and Alissa listened to the radio as their mom drove them home. "It'll be a great party," Alissa said.

Mason agreed. "I hope all the kids are there from the fifth grade."

The radio crackled and then the announcer came on. "Strange situation going on in Clark County," he said. "An escapee from the local prison psychiatric ward has come up missing at the daily count. This person is likely to be confused and may act unpredictably. He is identified by his false teeth, which make a clacking noise when he talks, eats, and laughs. He is probably not armed, but keep your doors locked and do not let him in. He is wearing blue overalls and a Steelers cap."

Mason glanced at Alissa knowingly. The prison was just a couple miles from their house.

Their mother said, "We'd better make sure all the doors and windows are locked when we get home. I'll give Dad a call."

If you listen to the news much these days, you know that bad things happen. If you're tempted to worry about your safety, read these words from the Bible: "The name of the Lord is a strong fortress; the godly run to him and are safe" (Proverbs 18:10). Does this verse give you confidence about the many dangers this world brings into our lives?

MYSTERY OF THE
NOISES IN THE ATTIC

Mason, Alissa, and their mom pulled into the driveway at their house. "Hurry inside, kids," their mom said.

Mason ran up to the door with Alissa. They both stopped and stared.

"What's wrong?" Mom asked.

"The door," Mason said with a shudder. "It's open. Did you forget to lock it?"

"No," Alissa said. "You had the keys, remember?"

Mom gripped her cell phone. "OK, I'm pulling out my pepper spray. You hold the phone, Alissa. Be ready to call 911."

Mom held up the spray in front of her, and the three entered the house. They went from room to room on the main floor, but didn't see anything unusual. Nothing appeared amiss. They heard no strange noises, and everything seemed fine.

"Where would a robber go, anyway?" Mom said. "They'd take the valuables, maybe look in our bedroom closets. It doesn't look like anyone's been here. Maybe we left the door unlocked by mistake. Let's use this as a reminder to always think about house security whenever we come and go. For now, I don't think there's anything to worry about."

"I'm just gonna watch some TV," Mason said.

God promises to protect us in this life, but that doesn't mean bad things won't happen. Read Proverbs 3:21-26. These verses instruct us to live and act wisely, knowing we can depend on God to protect us. Remember this: "the Lord is your security." Give him thanks for that.

Mason settled down and Alissa curled up on the sofa. They watched a rerun of an ancient *Beverly Hillbillies*. Nothing seemed out of the ordinary.

Mom came into the den with her car keys in her hand. "The lettuce I was counting on using for dinner is spoiled. I've got to run to the store for more. Are you two OK to stay here alone until I return?"

Mason didn't move. "Sure," he grunted.

"Um—" Alissa looked worried. She glanced at Mom, then at Mason. "Well, uh, OK." She paused. "We'll keep the house locked, and you won't be gone that long."

Mom left, and they continued watching TV, laughing when Jed Clampett swatted Jethro Bodine with his hat. The sound of the laugh track on the show filled the room with laughter.

Suddenly Alissa grabbed the remote and pressed the mute button. "What was that?" she cried, her eyes wide.

Sometimes danger is very clear: the county issues a warning that a tornado has been sighted in the area; the lights flash and the gates swing down at a railroad crossing; the house is filled with the high-pitched shriek of a smoke alarm.

Other times danger isn't so obvious, but it's danger just the same. The Bible tells us that no danger of any kind can separate us from the God who loves us. Read Romans 8:35-39 to find out about the "overwhelming victory" that is ours because of Jesus.

MYSTERY OF THE
NOISES IN THE ATTIC

"What's with you?" Mason asked. "Turn the sound back up."

Alissa's face was pale. "I heard a creaking sound . . . and it came from the attic."

Mason scoffed. "Aw, come on. It's nothing. The wind blew in or something."

Alissa went to the front window and looked out. "Everything's still. The trees aren't blowing. There is no wind."

"I hear that kind of noise in the attic all the time," Mason said.

"No," Alissa said. "Not like that. The only time I hear that noise is when someone's walking around up there."

Mason sat up. They both listened. *Creeeeee-ak. Creeeee-ak.*

"Should we call the police?" Alissa asked.

"Let's just go upstairs and listen for a second," Mason said, starting for the stairs.

They both went upstairs to the main bedroom. Everything was quiet.

"See?" said Mason. "There's no one up there. I told you it was just the wind."

As they turned to leave there was another sound: *Clackety-clack.*

"What was that?" Alissa asked, her voice trembling.

Mason's eyes grew wide. "The radio said the guy has false teeth, and they clack!"

It's not wise to search out danger, but sometimes in life danger finds you. That's why the Bible says, "A prudent person foresees the danger ahead and takes precautions. The simpleton goes blindly on and suffers the consequences" (Proverbs 27:12). While we can be confident that God will be with us in dangerous situations, we should not act rashly or impulsively.

What are precautions kids should take when they're home alone?

"Should we call the police?" Alissa asked for the second time.

"Let's think about this for a minute," Mason said. "Is this a real emergency? All we know is that we've heard funny noises."

"Yeah, but on the radio they said—" Alissa started.

"Look," Mason went on. "If we go look in the attic and see something, we can easily run down the stairs and lock the door behind us, right? Or we can wait on the front lawn till Mom comes home." Mason felt as though he should be brave. He never liked to be shown up by his sister.

He shook his head. "Let's just take a look first."

Creak! Creak! Clack!

"It doesn't sound loud enough to be a person moving up there," Mason told Alissa. "Maybe it's a bird that got in through a crack and can't get out."

"Oh, poor bird!" Alissa said. She had a heart for animals.

Mason placed his hand on the door, then turned to Alissa. "Leave the door open," he whispered. "Do not shut it."

"I've got an idea," Alissa said suddenly. She wheeled and ran down the stairs.

God created the human body with a wonderful defense in times of stress. It's called the "fight or flight" response. When people are in danger or afraid—even if they don't know why—their bodies prepare for action. Heartbeat and breathing come faster, and nutrients rush to the arms and legs in case they're needed for protection and escape. A person's body does this automatically, without conscious thought.

But thinking is essential in a potentially dangerous situation. Keeping a clear head can be the difference between safety and harm. Read Proverbs 2:1-8 to discover how God "grants a treasure of good sense to the godly."

Alissa returned a second later with the cordless phone in her hand. "Good idea," Mason said and grinned. "Now we've got him."

Alissa kept her fingers right over the buttons on the phone.

Mason pulled the door open a crack. He listened.

Creeeee-ak.

He slowly pulled the door all the way open. It made a loud thud as small wooden steps dropped down.

"I hate this door," he said, and stuck his foot out to mount the first step.

They took it one stair at a time. *Creak-creak-creak* went the stairs. Every few stairs, they both stopped and listened.

Now there was nothing. No sound at all.

The top of the stairs was just ahead. Alissa grabbed the handrail, her heart beating so hard she almost fainted. Without thinking, she dialed the phone. A voice answered: "Nine-one-one. What's your emergency?"

"We're in our house," whispered Alissa. "We think there's someone here in our attic."

"The police are on the way," the voice on the phone said.

"Hurry." She hung up.

It's never a mistake to ask for help. Police officers and emergency responders will tell you that they'd much rather be called to an emergency that turns out to be nothing, than for someone to wait until it is too late. Don't feel embarrassed if a situation is too much for you to handle.

God is the ultimate source of all help. Isaiah told people who followed God and repented of their sins, "When you call, the Lord will answer. 'Yes, I am here,' he will quickly reply" (Isaiah 58:9). Read the whole message in Isaiah 58:8-11.

Mason and Alissa stood in the middle of the attic. There before them was a rocking chair—rocking. *Creak-creak; creak-creak.*

They looked closer. Next to the rocker stood a small table. On the table was a little glass of water—with false teeth in it! Sitting in the chair was a man wearing a blue jumpsuit and a Steelers hat.

"Wh-who are you?" Mason stammered.

"A friend," the man said. From somewhere deep in his mind, Mason thought he recognized that voice, though it was kind of raspy.

"What do you want?"

"To have you two for dinner. But I can't eat without my teeth." The stranger reached into the glass of water and took them out. *Clack, clack . . . slurp.* He put the teeth in his mouth.

Suddenly, Mason knew who this was. "Grandpa! You tricked us!"

Alissa's knees buckled. "We were scared to death! It's not funny!"

In the distance they could hear police sirens as they approached.

"Uh-oh," Grandpa said sheepishly. "I guess I've got some explaining to do to those officers. I wonder if they'll go easy on an old man playing a practical joke?"

"Don't worry," Mason said. "We'll tell them we're all right."

Alissa smiled slowly. "Yeah, we'll tell them, Grandpa. But just wait! Sometime when you least expect it, we're going to play a practical joke on you!"

Grandpa gave her a hug. "I can't wait."

A loving grandparent can be one of God's most wonderful blessings. Proverbs 16:31 says, "Gray hair is a crown of glory; it is gained by living a godly life." Grandparents and other older people can be examples to you of how to live as a Christian. Thank God for those people.

MYSTERY OF THE
CABIN-BREAKERS

"I think I might do it," Crista Mayfield said to her sixth-grade friend, Jeff Pallaci, as they both gazed out over the still frozen lake. It was a Saturday in late February. They sat on Jeff's grandfather's dock where it had been pulled up onto the beach for the winter. Crista mused, "She's really a nice kid and I know she wants to learn. She's just having some trouble reading, that's all. The plan is for me to read with her, so she gets extra practice."

Jeff, always fidgeting with something, drew back his slingshot and fired a pebble out onto the ice. "I think you'd be good at it, Crista."

"I would?" She was pleased Jeff encouraged her.

"Yeah, you're good at that kind of stuff," Jeff answered. He began fitting another pebble into the sling pouch. "Watch this! It'll bounce all the way to the other side."

Crista watched as the stone arced upward, then struck the ice. It skittered across toward the other shore, about a half mile away.

Because Jeff's parents were in the middle of a divorce, he was staying with his grandparents in their lake house. Crista's mother had been killed in a car accident almost two years before. She and her father, Dr. Jason Mayfield, continued on in their cabin.

Jumping down from the dock, Crista brushed snow off her jeans.

"What's her name?" Jeff said, pushing himself off the dock behind Crista.

Crista has a chance to help a little girl learn to read. Have you ever helped a little kid like that? We know God values little children because of something Jesus said. He said people have to be like little children to enter God's kingdom. How are adults to be like children? Read Luke 18:15-17 to find out.

"Lindy Helstrom," Crista answered. She bent down to tighten her figure skates. She and Jeff frequently skated together, even going as far as the small island about a mile down from their cove.

"What grade is she in?" Jeff said. He began pulling on his skates, too.

"Second. Mrs. Walters. I had her in second grade too. She can really scare you the way she slaps down her ruler for quiet. And she has these big bulgy eyes." Crista frowned. "Well, I shouldn't say that, but she does. Kids always talked about her bulgy eyes, even though I didn't think it was nice."

Jeff made a funny face. "Bulgy eyes? I think I saw her in a movie. It was called—what was it? *Night of the Bulgy-eyed Teachers.*"

"That's gross, Jeff!" Crista gave him a shove. "Anyway, Mrs. Walters was good for me. I had to learn to keep my mouth shut when it should be shut, and also to listen to directions carefully." She jumped off the dock and ran down to the lake in her skates. "Race you to the point, meatball!"

Calling people names, especially in play, can be harmless fun. However, if calling someone a name comes from a heart of disrespect or contempt, God does not approve. Jesus said that the feelings of hate that cause murder are rooted in feelings of anger and disrespect that result in name-calling: "But I say, if you are angry with someone, you are subject to judgment! If you call someone an idiot, you are in danger of being brought before the high council. And if you curse someone, you are in danger of the fires of hell" (Matthew 5:22). It's not the name you call someone, like "idiot," that is sinful; it's the thoughts and feelings behind the name. Are you guilty of verbal disrespect for others?

MYSTERY OF THE
CABIN-BREAKERS

"Meatball?!" Jeff yelled, as he dropped to the ground. "If I'm a meatball, you're a—a—"

In three minutes, they were both panting and laughing after a hard race to the little jut of land that separated the end of the cove from the body of the lake. "Want to go to the island?" Jeff wheezed, as he grinned at Crista.

For once she'd beaten him, but Crista decided not to rub it in. Sometimes Jeff was sensitive about things like that.

"Sure, but no more racing. I'm gonna die!"

They skated off leisurely toward the island. As they loped along, Jeff said, "They still haven't caught the cabin-wreckers, have they?"

That winter, a number of summer cabins had been broken into and literally destroyed. The robbers stole computers, home theater equipment, and anything else of value they could find. They wrecked the first two or three because they hadn't found anything worth stealing in them.

Most of the cabins on the lake were occupied only in the summertime, when their owners boated, swam, and skied on the lake. During the winter, most were empty, even though a few people—like Jeff and his grandparents and Crista and her father—remained on as residents.

"No," Crista answered. "I haven't read anything about it lately."

An empty house is a target for trouble because there is no one to guard it. Jesus used the image of an empty house to describe a person: "When an evil spirit leaves a person, it goes into the desert, searching for rest. But when it finds none, it says, 'I will return to the person I came from.' So it returns and finds that its former home is all swept and clean" (Luke 11:24, 25). Jesus explained that a person is like an empty house when he is not on guard to keep evil from his heart.

"Yeah, I think the newspapers are downplaying it," Jeff answered. "They don't want to get people in an uproar."

"Have you heard something?"

"Just that two of the cabins were broken into on our side of the cove two weeks ago."

Crista turned to Jeff with sudden fear. "Do you think they'd actually come to our section?"

"Well, you remember about Mrs. Holmes?" Jeff said. "That's why I'm working on my aim with my slingshot."

Mrs. Holmes lived several doors down from Crista. Her home had been broken into, but nothing had been stolen. The police thought it was kids. In fact, some had even accused Jeff, though he had not been involved.

"Well, if you didn't go around with that slingshot everywhere, people wouldn't think you were up to no good."

Jeff pulled it back and sent a stone clattering toward the point. "I should have been named David. Didn't he slay a giant with a slingshot?"

Crista chuckled. "It was a sling—not exactly the same thing." Jeff was good with the slingshot, even if she didn't approve of it the way Jeff wished she did. Anyway, she knew very well that stopping several robbers with a slingshot was foolish. She went on: "What would you do if they really did come into one of the houses?"

You may know how David defeated the giant Goliath with a sling, a weapon sort of like a slingshot. But when David came before Goliath, he didn't mention the sling. What did he say as he faced the giant? Read 1 Samuel 17:45-47 to find out. Then answer this: When you face giants, do you have the same power David did?

Crista trusted Jeff in ways she didn't trust other kids her age. He was reliable and loyal and definitely brave. Being around him made her feel courageous too. But continuing news of the cabin-wreckers had already given her a nightmare or two in the past month.

"Well, first, I'd get them in my sights," Jeff said, a little twinkle in his eye.

"Yeah?"

"Then I'd pull back my stone . . ."

Crista rolled her eyes.

"Then I'd tell them to turn on the music."

"Turn on the music?" Crista asked.

"Yeah—rock music! Then I'd shoot them all!" Jeff's face lit with a huge grin, but Crista only groaned.

As they neared the island, Crista noticed the air was slightly warmer, and she sensed spring would arrive soon.

After several minutes of silence, simply enjoying their glide across the lake toward the island, she said seriously, "No, really, Jeff, what would you do if they came to your house?"

"I'd call you up and sic you on them."

"Jeff!"

He slowed down and stared at her with sudden urgency. "You're really worried about this, aren't you?"

When you hear of crimes that occur in your town, are you afraid that something bad may happen to you? Talk to your parents or other trusted adults about how you feel. But also, and more important, remember that the God who created everything is in control, and he cares for you. Say with David, "But as for me, how good it is to be near God! I have made the Sovereign Lord my shelter, and I will tell everyone about the wonderful things you do" (Psalm 73:28).

She turned to look away to the island. "Well, kind of."

"Look," Jeff said solemnly. "What you do is call the police: 911. That's all I'd do. They'd be there in two minutes. Besides, the thieves are cowards. They only break into vacant cabins. If they encountered anyone, they'd probably run like rabbits."

They skated on, and as they did, Crista looked up at the houses. Suddenly she stopped. "What's that?"

Jeff halted next to her. "What?"

"There." She pointed to a house where she could clearly see two men walking around the back and looking in windows.

"Couldn't be," Jeff said.

"Let's get closer."

They skated in nearer to the house, crept to the edge of the frozen lake, and watched. The two men kept looking around, but didn't see Jeff and Crista. Then, suddenly, one of them swung a hammer and smashed a window.

"I think I've seen enough," Crista said.

They waited till the men disappeared into the empty house, and then sped off. When they reached Crista's house, Crista dialed 911 and told the operator what she had seen. The operator told her they'd send out a cruiser.

"Let's go out to the road and tell them which house it is. I couldn't give them the number."

They both went out to the road and waited.

When you know someone has done wrong, do you want to see him or her punished? That's a desire for justice. While sometimes in life people get away with crime without being punished, we can be sure that God knows the truth, and that he is always just. A Scripture to remember is, "But I am trusting you, O Lord, saying, 'You are my God!' My future is in your hands" (Psalm 31:14, 15a).

MYSTERY OF THE
CABIN-BREAKERS

In a few minutes the cruiser appeared and turned down their part of the long beachfront road. Crista waved them down.

"Officer, I'm the one who called this in. We thought you might need us to show you which house it is."

"Good," the policeman said. "Hop in."

Crista and Jeff climbed into the back seat and directed the officer to the house. When they got there, he told them to wait in the car.

He walked around to the back, and reappeared a few minutes later.

"I'm calling for backup," he said.

He climbed into the cruiser and got on the radio. In a matter of minutes three cruisers parked outside the house. Two policemen went around back while a third guarded the front.

In only seconds, the front door burst open as the two robbers tried to escape, but the guarding officer had his gun on them.

"Freeze!" he cried.

For the next hour, Crista and Jeff talked with the police officers and gave witness statements. Then they were dropped off at home.

"I can't believe we did that," Crista said to Jeff as they ate dinner together with Crista's father.

"You guys are heroes," her dad said. "You can be proud of what you did."

Even at your age you can do good for your community. God says this about being a good citizen in Romans 13:1, 2: "Obey the government, for God is the one who put it there. All governments have been placed in power by God. So those who refuse to obey the laws of the land are refusing to obey God, and punishment will follow." How might you apply this truth to your life now?

Alline and Jerusha looked up at the clock tower with everyone else. The hands were stopped at 8:15, either from that morning or last night. No one had noticed till this afternoon. There had been a storm the night before, and people said it was just like in that movie where the tower was struck by lightning and stopped.

"*Back to the Future,*" Alline said. "One of my favorites."

"Was there lightning in this area last night?" Jerusha asked.

"I don't really know."

They asked people in the crowd, and several said there was lightning, but it had been miles away. "I don't think anything struck around here," an older man said.

Another added, "And the clock tower has a lightning rod. It isn't even the tallest building around here."

"Come on," Alline said. "Let's see if we can go up."

"What do you know about clocks?" Jerusha said, as they both hurried across the lawn.

"I know what I see," Alline said.

They reached the courthouse building and went inside.

Have you ever seen a tree or building damaged by lightning? Lightning is a powerful force of nature that can cause fires and damage to property. Worse yet, it can cause injury or death to people. The Bible describes how God controls thunderstorms: "He draws up the water vapor and then distills it into rain. The rain pours down from the clouds, and everyone benefits from it. Can anyone really understand the spreading of the clouds and the thunder that rolls forth from heaven? See how he spreads the lightning around him and how it lights up the depths of the sea" (Job 36:27-30). The next time it storms, use it as an opportunity to praise God for his power.

When they got inside, Jerusha found the front desk. "Mind if we go up to the tower?" she asked the security guard.

"Go ahead. Better hurry. They're gonna rope it off. The clock stopped."

"We know. Thanks."

The girls climbed the stairs and were soon huffing and puffing as they mounted the 50 steps that went up to the clock. It had a bell above it too, but that was still working. Jerusha just hoped she could see into the mechanism and check it out.

They reached the top, and above them was a little ladder to a trap door.

"Should we open it?" Alline asked. "Won't someone be mad?"

"The guard said we could come up. There's nothing that says we can't open that trap door."

"OK, but if we go to jail I'm confessing that this was all your idea."

"Right. Good. Then I'll get the glory too, when I fix it."

Alline gave Jerusha a shove. "Go to it, eager beaver."

Jerusha mounted the ladder. At the top, she pushed open the trap door slightly and looked inside. There was just another floor and she couldn't see the clock, so she lifted the trap all the way. Moments later, she climbed into the loft.

Climbing a tower can be physically challenging. Have you ever climbed an observation tower, lighthouse, or tall building? What's the greatest number of steps you've ever climbed?

Does it seem strange to think of God as a tower? Read this verse from the book of Psalm: "For you have been my refuge, a strong tower against the foe" (Psalm 61:3, *NIV*). God is powerful and protective. Will you thank him for being your tower?

Alline was about to climb the ladder, but she heard footsteps on the stairs. "Someone's coming," she called up to Jerusha.

Seconds later, Jerusha's head appeared in the trap doorway. "Should I come down?"

"Yeah, better."

Jerusha quickly climbed down the ladder and both girls walked to the railing to look out over the town. Seconds later, a man with a toolbelt appeared. It was Mr. Fitch, the handyman who worked in the courthouse. Jerusha knew him because he also fixed things at her junior high school, and she often said hello to him.

"Hi, Mr. Fitch."

"Oh, hello, Jerusha. What are you doing here?" Mr. Fitch had a long handlebar mustache and a big dimple on his chin.

"We wanted to see the clock. I thought we might see how to fix it."

He smiled. "Well, you can come up with me, but I just realized I forgot my flashlight. If you'll run down and get it for me, I'll let you come up. You might also grab my sandwich on top of the box. It's right inside the front door."

"You really would?"

"Sure. I don't want to do all those steps again. Besides, I know you're good girls. Maybe you'll see something I don't."

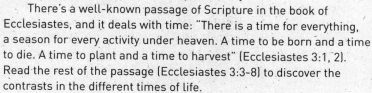

How many times a day do you look at a clock? Do you wear a watch? Is being on time important to you?

There's a well-known passage of Scripture in the book of Ecclesiastes, and it deals with time: "There is a time for everything, a season for every activity under heaven. A time to be born and a time to die. A time to plant and a time to harvest" (Ecclesiastes 3:1, 2). Read the rest of the passage (Ecclesiastes 3:3-8) to discover the contrasts in the different times of life.

Jerusha and Alline found the sandwich and the flashlight just where Mr. Fitch had said. The security guard walked over to them. "Hey, those belong to Mr. Fitch."

"He sent us down here to get them."

"Oh, really? Well, I'll just check that."

He spoke into his pager: "Mr. Fitch, did you send these two girls down here to get some things?"

The voice crackled on the other end. "Yeah. Send them up."

The security guard nodded to the girls. "You never know what some people steal around here. Last week I—"

Jerusha wanted to be polite, but she didn't want to be detained. "Tell us when we come down," she said.

Looking a little deflated, the guard smiled tightly and waved them off. They quickly mounted the stairs again. Because they went so fast, their breath came hard, and by the time they reached the top, they were seriously out of breath. Mr. Fitch took the flashlight and the sandwich gratefully.

"Didn't have breakfast this morning because of that storm."

"Do you think lightning hit the clock?"

"Guess we'll see."

"Even a stopped clock is accurate two times a day." Have you ever heard that old saying? Do you understand why it's true? It applies to clocks with hands—not digital clocks that just go dark when they're not working.

The Bible tells about one time when time stood still. Joshua prayed that nightfall would not stop a battle the Israelites were fighting. Joshua 10:13 records how God answered Joshua's prayer: "The sun stopped in the middle of the sky, and it did not set as on a normal day." Read more about the battle in Joshua 10:9-15, and think about how God has control over time.

While Mr. Fitch finished his sandwich, the girls waited impatiently. He seemed to take all day, but then he wiped his chin and motioned to them to follow. He began climbing the ladder, pushed open the trap door, and moved up inside.

Jerusha was next. "You must take care of this clock all the time," she said to Mr. Fitch.

"Actually, that was Shank's job. But he retired so they called me in. Don't know a thing about it. It's pretty complicated, you ask me."

Soon all three of them stood underneath the large mechanism. It was about five feet wide and had lots of gears, drives, and other parts. Mr. Fitch shined the light up into it and moved it around. "I need to see inside, but I'm too big to fit." He looked at Jerusha. "Mind if I hoist you up, and you can take a closer look?"

"No, I'd love to do that," Jerusha said.

"She's smart, and handy too," Alline said.

"Good. We need that," said Mr. Fitch.

He held his hands together. "Just set your foot in there," he said.

Jerusha placed her right foot in the hand-step. Her heart began pounding, she was so excited. If she fixed this thing, maybe she would write a report on it for school.

How do you feel when you know you've done a good job? You can be proud of yourself, and you may want to tell others about your accomplishment. The writer of Ecclesiastes describes that feeling of satisfaction as a gift: "I know that there is nothing better for men than to be happy and do good while they live. That everyone may eat and drink, and find satisfaction in all his toil—this is the gift of God" (Ecclesiastes 3:12, 13, *NIV*).

MYSTERY OF THE
CLOCK TOWER

As Jerusha looked into the clock gear area, it was hard to see things. There were many big and small gears, at least 50 or so, and there were other mechanisms within and around the whole area.

"Don't stick your hand into it," called Mr. Fitch. "You might jar something, and if the clock starts again, it may crush your hand."

"Hand me the flashlight," Jerusha said.

"See anything?" Mr. Fitch asked.

"Be careful," said Alline.

Jerusha reached down for the flashlight and grabbed it. Mr. Fitch was panting.

"You OK?" she asked him.

"Look fast," he said.

Jerusha shined the light all around. She could see around to the right but not to the left. "Can you move me around to the left?" she asked.

"Sure, move with me."

Mr. Fitch shifted to the left and Jerusha kept up with him. She put down the flashlight while she moved, and then picked it up.

Suddenly, above her, she heard a chattering noise.

Planning your moves and acting cautiously is always wise. Did you know that God has a plan for the world, and you are a part of it? Ephesians 1:11, 12 describes God's plan: "Furthermore, because of Christ, we have received an inheritance from God, for he chose us from the beginning, and all things happen just as he decided long ago. God's purpose was that we who were the first to trust in Christ should praise our glorious God." Ask God today to help you fulfill his purpose.

Jerusha picked up the flashlight and shone it inside the gears. "I don't see anything yet."

She leaned as far as she could look, then she thought she saw something brown in one of the golden gears.

"Shift me around to the other side," she said to Mr. Fitch.

Slowly, Mr. Fitch moved her around to the other side. Jerusha shined the light on the area where she thought she saw something. "I see it."

"What is it?"

"I'm going to reach in."

"Careful! Be careful!" Mr. Fitch said.

Jerusha lifted her arm with the flashlight in her left hand. As she lighted the spot, she reached with her right hand and grabbed it. "It's an acorn. There's a squirrel's nest up here."

"Can you get it?"

"I think."

She pulled it, but it wouldn't budge. "Here, try this," Mr. Fitch said, handing her a pair of pliers.

She got it that time.

Mr. Fitch let her down and she held up the acorn. "Let's see what happens now." He pulled a lever and the clock clanged into gear.

"You did it!" Mr. Fitch cried, and they all hugged.

A tiny acorn caused a huge clock to stop working. Can you think of other examples of small things that have big effects? The Bible gives several examples: a small bit controls a big horse; a tiny rudder makes a huge ship turn; a little spark causes a massive fire. In addition, the Bible talks about a small part of the body that can change the entire course of your life. What is it? Read James 3:2-8 to find out.

Jill stalked down the hall toward the girls' bathroom. What you had to do to get Miss Johnson to allow you to get a pass! *Honestly,* she thought, *you'd think the lady never had to go herself!*

She pushed open the door and looked in. Empty. She headed for a stall. The first one was closed. She walked into the second one. Suddenly, two quick sniffles cut the silence from the stall next to hers.

Someone was there.

Jill waited. More sighs and moans broke the quiet, then muffled crying.

She wondered what to do. Should she just ignore it and leave? She started to say something, then stopped. What if whoever-it-is didn't want help?

She concentrated, but the muffled sobbing made it hard to think. *Please, God, help me know what to do,* she prayed silently. *And help this girl with whatever she's upset about.*

She waited again for a moment. If she stayed away from class too long she would get in trouble with Miss Johnson. She didn't have time to wait. It was now or never.

"Are you all right?" she asked. She could feel her heart jumping in her chest.

No answer. More sniffles. More muffled crying.

She took a breath. "Can I help?"

There was a choked reply. "No one can help."

Someone needs real help. What do you do? If you're like Jill, the first thing you do is pray. You may recall a Scripture you've memorized, such as 2 Corinthians 1:4, which reminds you of the blessings you have through following the Lord: "He comforts us in all our troubles so that we can comfort others. When others are troubled, we will be able to give them the same comfort God has given us." How are you able to comfort someone else?

Jill thought she recognized the voice. It sounded like Eva Martin, one of the girls in her English class who was frequently absent. Jill didn't know her well.

Jill stepped out of the stall and knocked on the door of the second one. "Can I do anything? Are you all right?"

There was a long sigh. "I don't know," the voice said.

Jill stammered, "Look, if you just want to talk, we'll talk. You don't even have to open the door."

There was a long, uneasy silence. Then, "My dad—he . . ."

Jill waited.

"My dad beat me up this morning."

Jill gulped. She knew things like that happened, but she'd never known anyone to whom it had. What should she say now?

"I think my eye is swelling up."

Jill asked, "Do you want me to look at it?"

There was an even longer silence. Then the latch turned and the door came open slowly. It was Eva Martin. Her left eye was black and blue.

"Your eye looks bad," she said. "Maybe you should see the nurse." Jill put her arm over Eva's shoulder.

Eva jerked away. "No!" she seethed. "She won't do anything." She began to close the stall door. "Forget you even saw me."

Jill prayed momentarily for wisdom. She waited, thought, prayed, and waited again. Finally, she said, "Will you tell me what happened?"

Often a person who is in pain feels better just by talking about it. In his letter to the Colossians, Paul described the attitude Christians should have: "Since God chose you to be the holy people whom he loves, you must clothe yourselves with tenderhearted mercy, kindness, humility, gentleness, and patience" (Colossians 3:12). Ask God for his help to do so.

Jill listened as Eva poured out her story. Her father had beaten her that morning, and it wasn't the first time. She'd snuck into the girls' room after being dropped off by her mother and stayed there the whole day.

"Look," Jill said, after listening to Eva's story, "I'd like you to talk to a friend of mine. He might help. He's helped me before."

"Who is he?" Eva eyes flickered with a glimmer of hope.

"His name is Ken. He's one of our pastors at church."

Eva bit her lip and looked away. "He's not going to preach at me, is he?"

Jill shook her head. "I'll call him. We can meet you in back of the cafeteria after school."

Eva looked down and sighed. "I don't know. I just don't know what to do."

Jill smiled at her. Eva seemed calmer now. But Jill had a lump in her throat as she thought of her own dad and what a friend he was to her. What would it be like to have a dad who beat you? And what if that wasn't all? What if Eva held back the worst?

"I promise," Jill said. "We won't force you into anything. Just talk."

Eva looked up. There were tears in her eyes. Then she bowed and nodded her head. "OK. I have to talk to someone."

You need to know this: It is not your job to solve other kids' problems. That's not what God has called you to do at your age. The very best thing you can do—and what you should do—is to get help from a trusted adult. A wise and mature person can give you good and godly counsel. The Bible says, "Plans go wrong for lack of advice; many counselors bring success" (Proverbs 15:22).

Jill took a last look at Eva's bowed head and her pretty auburn hair. Eva was a striking girl, prettier than most of the girls in school. In a way Jill envied her. It was so incredible the way things happen in this world, she thought. Someone with all the looks gets beat up by her father. And someone like me gets blessed all the time. She couldn't understand it.

Jill's youth pastor, Ken Stoner, met her after school behind the cafeteria. Eva wasn't there. They waited for 30 minutes.

"I really thought she would come," Jill said.

"Maybe she's just not ready," Ken answered. "Or maybe she decided to talk to someone else, like a teacher or the school nurse. But since I'm here, why don't we pray for her, and spend a little time talking about what you can do for Eva?"

Jill and Ken prayed, and then Jill pulled out a piece of paper and listed several of the ways she could help Eva: praying for her, going out of her way to talk to her, listening when she needed to talk, and inviting Eva to her house for dinner or a sleepover.

Over the next two weeks, Jill reached out to Eva, but it was as though Eva didn't remember their little talk in the bathroom. She seemed to have shut down. But Jill continued to pray.

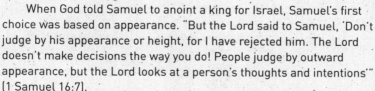

Who are the good-looking kids at your school? Are you ever tempted to envy them?

When God told Samuel to anoint a king for Israel, Samuel's first choice was based on appearance. "But the Lord said to Samuel, 'Don't judge by his appearance or height, for I have rejected him. The Lord doesn't make decisions the way you do! People judge by outward appearance, but the Lord looks at a person's thoughts and intentions'" (1 Samuel 16:7).

Jill waited. She knew she'd have to move at Eva's pace, not her own. She continued to reach out to Eva, but usually Eva didn't respond. Until one day.

"We both have to do reports on John Donne," Jill told Eva. "I've found some good references. Would you like to study together one afternoon?"

Eva cleared her throat and looked away. Then she said, "OK," barely audibly.

Jill smiled. "Well, I'm going over to the library this afternoon. Would you like to do it today?" She tried to make it sound casual, like it was all right if Eva didn't want to.

But Eva nodded. "All right. I'll meet you in the library."

After English, Jill had two other classes, and she wondered if Eva would really show up. She waited at the library door for several minutes, then went in.

A few minutes later, Eva walked in. Jill felt relieved and even a little excited. She hoped that just by spending time with Eva she could show her Jesus' love.

Reaching out to others is sometimes risky. But it is the heart of Christianity, and it pays off in great ways. John the apostle wrote, "Dear children, let us stop just saying we love each other; let us really show it by our actions" (1 John 3:18). How do your actions show others Jesus' love?

Jill showed Eva the reference books she'd found and they read passages together. They read Donne's famous words: "No man is an island, entire of itself; every man is a piece of the continent, a part of the main . . ."

After awhile, Jill felt a little playful and read in a deep masculine voice. The librarian immediately shushed them. But both girls laughed. For the first time, Jill saw Eva smile genuinely.

Afterwards, they had soft drinks at the nearby cafe. Jill told her about her family and her dog, Ripple. But when Eva's eyes welled with tears, she stopped. "I didn't mean . . ."

"No." Eva waved her hand. "It's all right. I just wish my life was like that." She told Jill about her own home situation. She lived with her father and stepmother. Her own mother had died when she was six. Her stepmother drank a lot.

Jill felt a lump forming in her throat. As they were leaving, she said, "Some kids from my youth group at church are going to the basketball game tomorrow night. Would you like to come with us?"

Eva smiled. "Sure. I'd like that."

Through Jill's patient and determined efforts, Eva began to open up. She was still absent frequently, and Jill worried that those were days when her father had become abusive. But she and Eva slowly built a friendship. After the basketball game, on another weekday evening Eva came to Jill's house for dinner. Then it was a Saturday they visited museums and went to a movie in town. Then one Sunday Eva came to church.

Sometimes love takes time before it sees results. But because we have experienced God's love, we can show it to others. "We love because he first loved us" (1 John 4:19, *NIV*). Who needs to know God's love through you?

MYSTERY OF THE
PRIVATE TEARS

Eva began coming to church regularly. Finally, a year after that first encounter in the bathroom, Eva's parents came for counseling. It was to be a long battle out of the darkness for them. But it wasn't a battle without hope.

One afternoon, nearly two years later, Eva and Jill were freshmen in high school. Eva rushed up to Jill in the hall one day outside her locker. "Guess what?" she said. "I did it."

"Did what?" Jill asked.

"I accepted Jesus as my Lord and Savior."

Jill stared with wonder into her friend's eyes, then hugged her with tears.

"How did it happen? How did you come to decide?"

Eva fixed her eyes on Jill's. "Because of you. You were my friend, even when I had little to give back to you. You changed my life by showing me God's love."

Jesus told his disciples that their love would bring others to him. "So now I am giving you a new commandment: Love each other. Just as I have loved you, you should love each other. Your love for one another will prove to the world that you are my disciples" (John 13:34, 35). Will you continue to show God's love, even when you don't see results?

Zack and Shooter sat in their tree house with soft drinks playing duels with their baseball cards. Zack had won a couple of big ones, taking away an A-Rod card and losing his Sammy Sosa card. But it was fun and relaxing.

Finally they stopped playing and lay back on the pillows they kept up there for just such an occasion. "Did you hear that Lennox is going to prove he can arm wrestle Bogan out of the running?"

"Bogan'll win," Shooter said. "He always does."

"Lennox has been working out. Have you seen his biceps?"

"Not as big as Bogan's."

Zack took a sip of the soda. "It'll be fun to see him try."

"When is it?"

"Tomorrow. Before school in the cafeteria."

"I'm there."

Suddenly, something crashed through the flimsy roof of the tree house. Zack and Shooter rolled to the side just in time.

A heavy yellow plastic bag sat on the floor of the tree house.

A heavy plastic bag fell from the sky! Can you imagine? Where do you think it came from?

The book of Joshua in the Bible records the story of Joshua and the Israelites in battle against the army of Gibeon. God gave the Israelites victory and routed the enemy army by dropping objects from the sky. What were they? Read Joshua 10:11 to find out.

Zack and Shooter stared at the bag, then looked up at the roof.

"It's ruined," Shooter said. "It took us weeks to build this thing."

Zack flipped the bag over, looking for an opening. "Look, it's locked," he said. "What could it be?"

"Let's go find a hammer," Shooter said.

They both climbed down the rope ladder to the ground, then headed off to Zack's house to get a sledgehammer. In a few minutes, they retrieved one from Zack's dad's workshop. They climbed the ladder back into the tree house.

They stood over the big bag. Zack turned it over, looking for markings. On one corner was a stamped address. It said, "US BANK." Below it was an address for nearby St. Louis, about a hundred miles away.

"You think it could be money?" asked Shooter.

"Finders keepers, losers weepers." To most people, that means if you find something, it's yours to keep. Do you believe that's true?

In the Bible God gives instructions about how people are responsible for items they find, specifically a "lost object that they claimed as their own" (Leviticus 6:4). Read all those instructions in Leviticus 6:3-5.

Zack grabbed a brick and draped the lock over it. Then he lifted the hammer over his head.

"Don't miss," Shooter said.

Zack swung. He landed square on the brick and broke it in half. "OK, I'll hit it right this time."

He moved the lock so it hung on the half brick. He swung the sledgehammer again, this time striking the lock. It didn't budge.

"You think this'll work?" he asked Shooter.

"Try again."

Three tries later, the lock broke. Both boys stared at the open padlock like it was a rattlesnake baring its teeth.

"I guess now we find out what's inside," Zack said.

He pulled off the padlock and pulled the cover off the latch. The bag was open. He reached in and felt around.

"What is it?" Shooter asked.

Zack pulled out a handful. He held it up to the light. The two boys gasped at the same time.

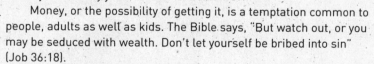

Since there was the name and address of a bank on the bag, do you think Zack and Shooter should have opened it? Why didn't they just contact the bank first?

Money, or the possibility of getting it, is a temptation common to people, adults as well as kids. The Bible says, "But watch out, or you may be seduced with wealth. Don't let yourself be bribed into sin" (Job 36:18).

MYSTERY OF THE
BAG OF MONEY

It was a wrapped stack of one-hundred-dollar bills.

"How much is it?" Shooter whispered.

"It says $10,000 on this side. And there are more."

Zack grabbed the bag and dumped it out onto the floor of the tree house. At least 50 packets of hundred-dollar bills fell out. Zack shook the bag until all came out.

"Let's stack them up, see how much this is," said Zack.

They put them in piles of ten. Soon they had eight and a half piles. "That's—that's—"

"Eight hundred fifty thousand dollars," said Zack, his eyes as big as apples.

"What should we do?" Shooter said, his voice trembling.

"How on earth did it get here? It fell from the sky—from a plane, maybe? Why would they dump it out?" Zack held up a stack of bills and grinned. "We could buy a boat with this, and a dirt-bike, and a pellet gun."

"Or a hundred pellet guns!" Shooter added. "But it belongs to someone, doesn't it?"

"US Bank, I guess. Maybe it was stolen from them."

"How can we find out?"

Both boys sat very still. "The news. It would be on the news, wouldn't it?"

"Let's go. It's almost six o'clock," Shooter said.

In his Word, God is very clear when it comes to taking as your own what doesn't belong to you: "Do not trust in extortion or take pride in stolen goods; though your riches increase, do not set your heart on them" (Psalm 62:10, *NIV*). *Extortion* is taking something through the use of force or threats. It's related to stealing, and equally wrong.

They put all the money back into the bag, then covered it up with the pillows and other things in the tree house. They climbed down the ladder.

"No one can see it from below, right?" Zack asked.

They both looked up. "But you can see the roof is broken through," Shooter said. "If someone came looking for it, they might notice."

"Let's just go listen to the news."

The boys hiked home quickly and went inside. Zack's mother was in the laundry room. "Hi, boys," she said.

"Mom, can we watch the news?" Zack said.

She stared at both of them. "Since when are you interested in the news?"

"No reason. Just thought we'd watch it."

"Maybe there's something interesting," Shooter added. "Like somebody shot somebody. You know."

"I recommend channel six."

The boys went into the family room and turned on the TV.

Why are Zack and Shooter concerned that nobody else finds out where the bag of money is? Do you think it's for their own safety, or because they don't want to share the money with anybody else?

If it's because they don't want to share the money, there's a Scripture they should read: Job 34:21, 22. It says, "For God carefully watches the way people live; he sees everything they do. No darkness is thick enough to hide the wicked from his eyes."

Though they watched the whole news program, no mention was made of a robbery or a plane. Zack kept thinking about it. Finally he said to Shooter, "I wonder if there is some way we could keep the money."

"What do you mean?"

"Maybe there's some kind of limit on it, like you get to keep any found money after 10 weeks or something."

"Let's call the police," Shooter said.

"Or maybe a lawyer."

Shooter shrugged. "I guess."

Zack looked up lawyers in the phone book. He found one that advertised a "free consultation for any legal problem."

"Him," he said. They called the number and a man answered.

"I have a question," Zack said to him. "If you find some money, how long do you have to wait for someone to claim it before you can keep it?"

"It depends," the man said. "Normally 90 days, unless it was stolen. Why do you ask?"

Zack hung up quickly.

It seems as though Zack's conscience is at work in this story. There's no honest way to keep stolen property, and he's beginning to deal with that. A Bible verse that is appropriate in this case is Proverbs 12:20: "Deceit fills hearts that are plotting evil; joy fills hearts that are planning peace!" If Zack and Shooter want peace in their hearts, what should they do?

Zack looked at his friend. "What if some bad guys are out there right now looking for it? They could find it and kill us."

Both boys sat quietly for awhile. When Zack's father came home, Zack didn't hesitate. He told his parents the whole story.

"I think we need to go to the police station," his dad said. "That's the honest thing to do."

They retrieved the money and drove to the station. There Zack and Shooter presented it to a couple of officers. They told all they knew.

One of the policemen nodded. "We just got word of a robbery in Kansas City. They took off in an airplane. In the sky, they ditched the plane and four bags of money, each nearly a million dollars. Then they parachuted to safety. A massive manhunt is on right now. You're very lucky the bad guys didn't find you first."

A week later, Zack got a call from US Bank. "Are you the guys who brought in the money?" asked the bank representative.

"Yeah," Zack answered. "It broke through our tree house."

"Well, we're happy to give you a reward for your part in this."

Zack stood there, shaking. "H-how much is the reward?"

"A thousand dollars."

Zack fell over right there.

Sometimes in life you will receive some prize or award for doing a good job. But sometimes you will do the right thing and not be rewarded. In that case, doing the right thing will be its own reward.

You can be sure that God knows when you've done the right thing, and he will reward you in his way and in his time. He says so in Jeremiah 17:9, 10. Read those verses to find out how God rewards people.

MYSTERY OF THE
GREAT WISH

Judd sat on the bench watching Craig Morgan bring the ball up from the back court. Being second string was hard. But knowing that Dad was in the stands was comforting. For two years now, Judd had been the only guy on the basketball team whose father attended every game of Jefferson Middle School's calendar. It was something of a funny story around the locker room that Judd's dad was so loyal. Why? Because he was blind.

"I mean, he can't even see you sitting on the bench," Judd's friend Lee often said.

Judd thought a lot about it. Would his father ever see him play? For years, he prayed that God would heal his dad. But it had never happened. Now Judd just hoped that medicine would one day restore his dad's sight.

Besides that, he had been working hard. He and Craig had battled it out in scrimmages and practice, and Craig had edged Judd out of first string by only one free throw. Judd had gone 12 for 20; Craig had gone 13. Otherwise, Coach Pellerend said, "They're equals."

This was the game Judd might get into, if Craig messed up. Not that Judd wanted him to mess up, or get hurt, or anything else. He wanted first string fair and straight. But it was hard sitting on the bench.

"Put Lezerian in!" a voice behind yelled. It was his sister Suzy, who usually drove his father to the games.

Getting into the game, being on the field or floor, making your shots—sports can be a thrill. Consider this verse from 2 Timothy 2:5: "Follow the Lord's rules for doing his work, just as an athlete either follows the rules or is disqualified and wins no prize." Whatever sport you play, however good you are, one thing is important to God: play according to the rules.

The whistle blew: foul. The ref raised his arm, ran over to the timekeepers and ref's bench and asked, "How many fouls on 16?"

Craig Morgan. Judd hadn't been counting. Craig rarely fouled.

"Three," the foul keeper said.

A second later, Coach Pellerend called out Judd's name. "Lezerian, get up here."

The coach called Morgan. "I'm putting in Judd. You have three fouls, Craig."

"Yeah, I know, Coach. I'm off tonight."

"All right. Take a seat and rest."

"Judd!"

A split second later, Judd stood at the coach's arm. "Watch that number 12 that Craig was covering. He's pulling fouls whenever he can."

"All right."

"GO LEZERIAN!" Judd's dad yelled as the boy ran out onto the court amid much cheering from the stands.

Sports are good for physical development. But spiritual development is more important. Look at what Paul says in 1 Timothy 4:8: "Physical exercise has some value, but spiritual exercise is much more important, for it promises a reward in both this life and the next." What rewards come from "spiritual exercise"?

MYSTERY OF THE
GREAT WISH

It had been a tough half. With only two minutes left, Judd didn't have a chance to get in much. As a forward, five-seven, tall for a seventh grader, he set up posts, ran some picks for the guards, and was alert for the center's rebounds. Judd ran the plays expertly. After 40 seconds of play, he had his first chance at a shot.

It was a steal by Jeremiah, one of the guards. He caught the Coldwell team off balance and Judd, being fresh and ready to run, took off down the court. The pass was right on. Judd dribbled twice, then went airborne. He laid the ball up against the left backboard. It sank in for two.

Judd had his only other two-pointer on a single hand feint and leap shot from the point. It sank for two in the final seconds of the half. The crowd roared. Judd heard his dad's voice and wondered if his father could visualize what had happened.

Morgan went in at the second half and played the rest of the tight game. But with four points in only two minutes of play, Judd had done well. The coach said to him as they exited the court, "You do well in practice this week, and I might start you on Wednesday."

In sports, a lot of coaches talk about winning, how it's "everything." Listen to what Paul says in 1 Corinthians 9:24, 25: "Remember that in a race everyone runs, but only one person gets the prize. You also must run in such a way that you will win. All athletes practice strict self-control. They do it to win a prize that will fade away, but we do it for an eternal prize." What prizes have you won in sports? What spiritual prize do you hope to win?

Judd's father had gone blind at the age of 14 as a result of scarlet fever. In his community in Communist Poland, he didn't have access to cutting-edge medical care. He'd come to the U.S. in the sixties on a special student exchange, and had stayed after he graduated. His family in Poland was gone and he'd managed to defect.

It was a well-known story in Judd's community. His father had become a rocket scientist, a mathematician working out the complex geometries of rocket science, and a computer enthusiast. Even without his sight, the man excelled.

On the way home from the game, Judd told his father and sister, "Coach said I might start next week if I play well in practice on Monday and Tuesday."

Suzy added, "You were great, Judd. I told Daddy about every move."

Suzy picked up their mom on the way home. She was a lawyer, and though she normally made the games, she had a heavy caseload at the moment and wasn't able to come.

When they were all together in the car, Mr. Lezerian had an announcement. "I'm going under the knife next week, Judd," he said.

All of us have wishes and hopes so deep we can barely speak of them out loud. Sometimes we're just afraid if we utter the words, the hope will be dashed and we'll never see it happen. But did you know God is in the business of making your dreams come true? Read these verses from Psalms: "The steps of the godly are directed by the Lord. He delights in every detail of their lives. Though they stumble, they will not fall, for the Lord holds them by the hand" (Psalm 37:23, 24). Do you believe God wants to make your wishes come true? Why, or why not?

MYSTERY OF THE
GREAT WISH

"What for?" Judd asked. His heart began beating hard. His father was healthy, but he was in his sixties—older than most of his friends' dads.

"It's experimental, so insurance won't pay for it. But we can afford it, and for the chance to see I'm willing to take the risk."

"What will they do?" Judd exclaimed.

"An eye transplant," Mr. Lezerian said.

Judd couldn't speak for a few seconds. "I didn't know they could do that."

"They're not really sure. Surgeons have tried it many times before, but there have been new advances. Anyway, I'll be the first success, if it works out."

Judd was speechless.

As they got out of the car, Mr. Lezerian took Judd's arm. "I'm real proud of you, son. You did well tonight. After this surgery, who knows? Maybe I'll see you play."

Judd said nothing. His heart was too full of hope to think.

A father's approval is one of the best things a young man or woman can gain in this world. When you know your dad supports you, is on your side, and is proud of you, you feel great, like you're on top of the world. These are the words of Solomon, who knew what it was to have a son in need of encouragement: "Listen my child, to what your father teaches you. Don't neglect your mother's teaching. What you learn from them will crown you with grace and clothe you with honor" (Proverbs 1:8, 9). What valuable lessons has a parent taught you?

Mr. Lezerian went into the hospital the next week. While Judd tried to stay focused at basketball practice, he was preoccupied with the hope that the surgery would work.

The donor was a young man who had been killed in an auto accident. He had donated all his organs, and several people had already been helped. Both eyes were going to Mr. Lezerian because the tissue match was so good. They would do one at a time, three weeks apart.

The family sat in the waiting room during the operation. It seemed as though Judd never stopped praying. They ate three meals in the cafeteria, and Judd napped several times out of boredom. He awoke each time praying.

Finally, about midnight, after a 14 hour surgery, the doctor stepped out into the waiting room.

"Everything looks great," he said. "It went well. Now we have to wait for him to wake up, and then it'll be a few days before we can take the bandages off. And then—well, maybe he'll see."

Before they left for the night the family prayed around Mr. Lezerian's bed. Judd didn't want to leave, but he was exhausted. He needed to talk to the team too, since they were all very concerned about all that was happening.

A successful eye transplant has not yet occurred. However, with advances in transplant surgery, God may allow humans to gain the skill, knowledge, and techniques necessary to accomplish it. Already, cornea transplants have saved the sight of people, so eye donors are needed today.

Physical sight is a wonderful blessing of God. But human sight won't be adequate to experience the glory of Heaven with God someday. Read 1 Corinthians 2:9 to discover how human sight fails.

MYSTERY OF THE
GREAT WISH

The day the doctors took off Mr. Lezerian's bandages, Judd had another game, and the coach allowed him to start. When he took the floor, Judd heard his father's familiar voice: "Go, Lezerian!" He looked and saw his father with the white cane he always used. His heart sank. The operation hadn't worked.

But Judd played the best he could. The coach never took him out, and even Craig Morgan congratulated him at the end. He received the game ball and a special plaque. Suddenly, his father was at his side, the cane in his hand. He put his arm around Judd.

A voice came over the loudspeaker. "Mr. Lezerian, father of Judd Lezerian, would like to say a few words." They brought up a microphone.

"You all know that I have been blind for many years. This past week, I had an operation to try and give me a new eye. And I want to announce here and now that I saw my son play basketball for the first time in my life tonight."

There was wild cheering. Judd just looked at his dad, astonished. "But why do you have the cane?"

"So I could do this." Mr. Lezerian took the cane in both hands and broke it over his leg. "From now on, you'd better play really well, because I'll be watching every move."

As they all drove home that night, Judd prayed over and over, "Thank you, God. Thank you."

Not many people have gone from complete blindness to restored sight, but it does happen. The Bible tells of several people who miraculously received sight at the hand of Jesus: a man in Bethsaida (Mark 8:22-26); Bartimaeus (Mark 10:46-52); two men (Matthew 9:27-31); a man born blind (John 9:1-34). Read one of these accounts, and find out how the blind person reacted to receiving his sight. How would you respond if it were you?

Quentin, at 12 years old, didn't get all excited about his Easter basket anymore, but he did like the chocolate. Mom knew what he liked, and she always got him a couple of solid chocolate bunnies and other pieces of chocolate. Along with his little brother James and sister Clara, they made quite a haul.

Quentin quickly stashed his basket on top of his dresser after Easter. That first night, he bit off the big bunny's foot. "What a chunk of chocolate!" he whispered as he chomped into it. "Delish," he said, but this time he would make those bunnies last till Halloween. One big bite per day, that was all he'd have. Well, maybe not. Maybe one big bite in the morning, and one after dinner at night. Yeah, that would work.

He went to sleep dreaming of giant chocolate bunnies scampering in a field and scaring the big bull from Farmer Goodenough's field next door.

The next morning he arose bright and early. He brushed his teeth, washed under his armpits, and put on some deodorant. Then he rushed into his room to get that first huge bite. Today, he thought, he'd do one of the big ears.

He picked up the bunny and stared at it in horror.

It's fun to receive candy treats on Easter. The most important thing about Easter, though, is celebrating Jesus' resurrection from the dead. Because of Jesus, we receive a far greater gift than anything we can imagine. Read 1 Peter 1:3, 4 to find out what the gift is, and where it is kept. —⊙

"Who ate my bunny ear?" Quentin yelled and went to James's bed. He was still asleep. Quentin rustled him awake. "Did you eat my bunny ear?" he shrieked into James's nose.

"Wh-what?" James said, rubbing his eyes.

"Did you eat part of my chocolate bunny?" he screeched again.

"No. I have my own," James said, coming more fully awake.

Quentin studied his eyes a moment, then decided he was probably telling the truth. Quentin ran downstairs. "Mom, someone ate my bunny ear," he told her.

Mom looked up from frying eggs. "Bunny ear?"

"My big chocolate bunny—from Easter—in my Easter basket," he cried.

"Are you sure you didn't eat it in your sleep?" she said with a laugh.

"I'm sure. Do you think Clara would have done it?"

Clara sat at the table eating cereal. "No," she said. "I can't even reach the top of your dresser." She was only six, and short. But she could have pulled up a chair. "Anyway, I have my own."

Quentin was furious. Who could have done this? Who would? He looked down at Aussie, their Australian sheep dog. "Did you do it?" he said to Aussie.

Quentin had no clear evidence that either his brother or sister had taken his chocolate without permission, but he accused them anyway. Have you ever been falsely accused of something you didn't do? How did it feel?

Jesus was falsely accused when he went on trial for his life. And he was found not guilty by two different judges. Read who they were in Luke 23:13-15. Even though Jesus was found not guilty, what was his sentence? Read Luke 23:23, 24.

Aussie cocked his head and looked back at Quentin innocently. How could the dog have gotten up there?

"Well, who did it?" he asked.

"I couldn't tell you, honey," his mom said, "but I think if you'll just be reasonable about it, you'll figure it out."

Quentin screwed up his face with anger, then stomped back up the stairs. In his bedroom, James was just climbing out of bed. Quentin looked at him again. He was 10, but fully capable of stealing chocolate bites off his bunny. He marched over to James again. "Did you do it?"

"Do what?" James said with irritation.

"My bunny? Eat a bite of its ear?"

"Not this again," James said and walked past him to the bathroom.

"You better not have," Quentin called after him. "I'll pound it out of you."

James stopped in the bathroom door and stuck out his tongue. "Here, you can lick it off my tongue."

"So you did do it!" Quentin roared as he hurried to confront James in the doorway.

"Go jump in the lake," James said, and shut the door.

Quentin stood there, seething. He looked down at Grandmom's room, but she was taking a nap. She napped most of the day.

All right, maybe people were going to play games. But next time, he'd catch the person chocolate-tongued.

When things go wrong, it's human nature to look for someone to blame. Even the very first people, Adam and Eve, looked to blame someone else when they were in trouble with God. Who did they blame? Find out by reading Genesis 3:12, 13.

MYSTERY OF THE
CHOCOLATE THIEF

That night, Quentin fought off sleep as long as he could. He made sure no one got the other bunny ear by chomping it off himself that night. But eventually, he simply could not keep his eyes open. He fell asleep.

Sure enough, the next morning Quentin found a large part of the bunny's foot missing, more than he'd taken before.

"You're doing it! I know!" Quentin said to James.

James shook his head and went to his Easter basket. "See this," he said, holding up a bunny just like the ones that Quentin had gotten. "Take a bite if you're so mad about it."

Quentin did, an extra big one. James complained about it, but things seemed to be settled with him. What good did it do James if he took bites from Quentin's and then had to give up extra big ones the next morning to Quentin himself?

"Even?" James asked.

"Fine," Quentin said, and stormed out. "Mom, another bite was taken."

"I'm sorry, honey," his mom said. "Maybe you ought to hook up an alarm system."

Quentin stared at her. "How much would that cost?"

"I don't know. But don't they have kids' alarm kits at the electronics hobby store?"

"Right," Quentin said and left, new ideas coming into his head.

Have you ever wanted to take revenge on someone who had wronged you? While you may feel like hurting someone who has hurt you, the Bible teaches that we should leave revenge up to God, and not take it on ourselves. In addition, the Bible has startling instructions for those who feel like taking revenge. Read them in Romans 12:19-21.

That afternoon Quentin studied the teeth marks on each of the places where the bunny had been bitten. He didn't see anything special except that his tooth marks were flatter and straighter. Was the chocolate thief even a human?

All afternoon he thought about how he might put an alarm on the chocolate bunny to go off when someone touched it. He finally figured out a way to fix a small buzzer to the bunny. If someone picked the bunny up, the buzzer would fall away and sound.

Quentin went to bed that night proud about his little invention. Now he would nail that thief, and good.

He lay in bed listening. At one point his mother came into his room and tucked him in better. But he pretended he was asleep. After awhile, though, he drifted off. Several times he woke up, thinking he heard the buzzer. But it was undisturbed.

He went back to bed, and promptly had another dream. But each time it was a false alarm.

Finally, he stayed asleep, but when he woke up in the morning, he jumped up and ran to his basket on the dresser. Amazed, the bunny was undisturbed. The person hadn't struck.

Then he looked at the other bunny, the one he had done nothing with.

"Awwwwww," he cried, disappointed. Both ears were gone. How could it have happened? Who was doing this?

The Bible describes the situation Christians are living in today: "We know that we are children of God and that the world around us is under the power and control of the evil one" (1 John 5:19). Even though God is all-powerful, bad things still happen in the world. It's frustrating, but it also causes us to look forward to Heaven someday, when bad things will never happen again.

MYSTERY OF THE
CHOCOLATE THIEF

That afternoon, Quentin devised a second alarm to go on the second chocolate bunny. He also counted the chocolate kisses scattered on the fake grass in the basket. He couldn't alarm each of them, but he would at least know if anyone had taken a few. His dad came home from a trip that evening, and Quentin asked him for a theory about the bunnies. But Dad was tired, and just made jokes about how it could be mice, army ants, or chocolate cougars.

Quentin fidgeted all evening wondering if this would be the day he would nail the thief. But the more he thought about it, the more he realized the thief had to be pretty smart to avoid those buzzers. How could someone have done it?

Finally, he went to bed, somewhat discouraged, but still determined to catch the chocolate thief. For tonight he had two buzzers on each of the bunnies, and one on the base of the basket. If anything was moved, surely he'd know.

As he slept he dreamed about buzzers. He was in a room surrounded by microwaves and dryers, and they were all going off at the same time. There was a band at a circus—but everyone was playing kazoos, and they all sounded like buzzers. He was on a game show, and when he gave a wrong answer—*Buzzzzz!*

No, wait! That one's real! Quentin startled awake and opened his eyes, and at that moment he saw a dark figure whisk out of the room.

Most of the time you can believe what you see, but sometimes you can be wrong. In the Bible, God gave his people instructions about eyewitness testimony: "Never convict anyone of a crime on the testimony of just one witness. The facts of the case must be established by the testimony of two or three witnesses" (Deuteronomy 19:15). God is concerned with justice, and he always judges fairly.

Quentin crept over to the dresser. The whole basket was gone. The buzzer lay there, the battery dead.

He stepped cautiously out of his room and went across the hall. He looked toward the stairs and could see a beam of light coming from the kitchen. Silently he crept down.

There was Grandmom at the kitchen table, reading. The Easter basket sat on the table and she had a bunny in her hand.

"Grammommmmm!" Quentin yelled.

"Best chocolate I've had in a long time," Grandmom answered in a sassy voice. "Thought you'd have caught me by now."

Quentin said, "So you were the thief?"

"Well, it started out as a little joke. I didn't mean to let it go this far. But you were so funny with your 'catch the thief' scheme." She stood up and walked to the cabinet where they kept the cereal. "Besides, I thought you wouldn't be too mad when I showed you my little surprise." She opened the cabinet and moved the cereal boxes. There were five more chocolate bunnies on the shelf!

"Got these for half price at the after-Easter sale. I can replace yours, give you one more, and still have enough chocolate to last for awhile. Does that help you feel any better?"

Quentin smiled sheepishly. "Yeah, I guess it does. But come Halloween, don't blame me if I put out mouse traps!"

Quentin's grandmother gave back more than she took from him. That's a principle taught in the Bible. As a result of meeting Jesus, Zacchaeus the tax collector made a promise to change his life: "I will give half my wealth to the poor, Lord, and if I have overcharged people on their taxes, I will give them back four times as much!" (Luke 19:8). Even when you willfully do something wrong, you can make it right with God's help.

MYSTERY OF THE
TRAVELING CAT

Sarah stood over the litter of kittens. She knew immediately which one she wanted. "The brown, fluffy one," she said to her mom.

"Are you sure? You'll have her for a long time."

"Yes. I'm sure."

"Would you like to hold her?" Mrs. Lassiter said. Her daughter, Philippa, was a friend of Sarah's from school. When their cat Bobbie had kittens, Philippa offered them to all the kids in the fifth grade. Sarah and several other kids claimed them.

"You can take her in about a week," Mrs. Lassiter said. "She'll be weaned by then."

Sarah set the kitten down. It wandered over to the others where they began batting one another around.

"Be careful, though," Mrs. Lassiter said. "Bobbie is a traveling cat. Sometimes she goes off for a day or two. So her kittens may also like to wander. Keep the kitten in a safe place."

"I will." Sarah glanced at her mother. "What should we name her, Mom?"

"It's your choice."

Sarah thought. "I like the name Angelina, but I want something shorter. So I think . . . Mermaid. After *The Little Mermaid*.

Mom smiled. "So Mermaid it is."

All the way home Sarah smiled, her head full of ideas about what kind of bed, food, and toys she would get for Mermaid.

Bringing a new pet into your house can be an exciting time. They will usually be fun and make you laugh a lot. A Bible verse many people don't know about is Proverbs 12:10: "The godly are concerned for the welfare of their animals, but even the kindness of the wicked is cruel."

Of course, Sarah would never be cruel to her kitten. But pets can be trouble too.

A week later, Sarah brought Mermaid home in a cat carrier box. The kitten immediately took to her new home, though she was shy at first. Soon Mermaid began sleeping on Sarah's bed and they became good friends.

After some time, as the kitten grew into a full-grown cat, she began to appear bored with Sarah's room. She escaped regularly and could be found in the strangest places—behind the toilet, in a closet, and under the sink where Mom kept all the cleaning supplies.

"You think she wants to help with the house?" Sarah asked her mom.

"No, but if she drank some of that stuff, it could be dangerous. We'll have to keep these doors shut."

When Sarah headed off for school one morning, she didn't see Mermaid behind the sofa near the doorway. The moment Sarah opened the door, Mermaid shot out. She disappeared behind the bushes in the garden, and Sarah was frantic.

"Mom, Mom! Mermaid got out the door! What should we do?"

"I'll try to get her back," Mom said. "Meanwhile, you have to go to school. Don't worry. Pray about it. God knows about Mermaid."

Sarah headed up the street toward her middle school. "Please don't let Mermaid get lost," she whispered to God.

Pets, and cats in particular, are amazingly creative and inventive. They'll find ways to get and do what they want, even if you take every precaution. Have you ever lost a pet? Did you get him or her back? Most of the time, animals know where their homes are and after a brief jaunt in the outdoors, they return.

A good verse for Sarah to remember is found in Psalm 34:4: "I prayed to the Lord, and he answered me, freeing me from all my fears." Losing a pet can be a fearful time. But call on the Lord. He will help.

Sarah walked around the neighborhood calling for Mermaid, but she didn't catch a glimpse of her. "Where could she have gone that's better than our house?" Sarah asked herself repeatedly.

When she wearily stepped in the door for dinner, her mother called, "Find her?"

"No," Sarah said sadly and leaned against the wall and sobbed. "What if she got hit by a car? Or what if she can't find her way home? Or what if she just doesn't like it here?"

Mom stepped out the kitchen and hugged her. "Let's not worry yet. Remember, Mrs. Lassiter said Bobbie was a 'traveling cat.' Maybe Mermaid's just taking after her mother. We'll just have to be more careful about her getting out."

"But what if she never comes back?"

Mom patted Sarah's back. "Let's not go crazy yet. Maybe when she's hungry she'll realize she had it pretty good here."

Sarah sighed and wiped her eyes. "I'm going to kill her when she comes back for giving me all this worry."

After dinner, Sarah sat outside with her Bible, praying, reading, and watching. Mermaid, though, was nowhere to be seen.

Finally, at 9:30, her mother called her in to get ready for bed. "I'll leave the door open if Mermaid comes and meows."

Sarah nodded, but her heart was heavy.

Jesus cares about the lost. He cares so much that he told a parable about a lost sheep. He described how frantic the shepherd was to discover the sheep was lost, and how the shepherd left 99 other sheep just to search for the lost one. Jesus compared the shepherd's happiness at finding his lost sheep to God happiness: "In the same way, heaven will be happier over one lost sinner who returns to God than over ninety-nine others who are righteous and haven't strayed away!" (Luke 15:7).

The more Sarah prayed and thought about Mermaid, the more convinced she was that she should visit Mrs. Lassiter and Philippa again. Saturday morning, Sarah rushed to their house.

"Hi, Sarah," Philippa said in greeting. "How's Mermaid?"

"That's why I'm here," Sarah answered. "She's disappeared. She got out yesterday and we can't find her."

Mrs. Lassiter walked out, toweling her hands off from the kitchen. "Be patient," she said. "Mermaid will be back. She'll either go back to you, or come here. Bobbie would sometimes disappear for days at a time."

"Yeah," Philippa said. "She'll be back when she's ready."

Sarah nodded. "That's what my mom says, but our street has a lot of traffic. I'm afraid—"

"Cats are pretty smart," Mrs. Lassiter said. "I really don't think Mermaid would go far. Remember, cats are still animals, and a little wild. They like to roam. When you have her spayed she will be less likely to leave home."

"Definitely," Philippa said. "After she had her litter we got Bobbie spayed, too. Now she's a real homebody. She's not out looking for the boy-cat of her dreams."

They all laughed.

Sometimes you have to think like a cat to outwit a cat. That may sound weird, but Jesus actually compared people's attitudes to animals. He instructed his disciples, "Look, I am sending you out as sheep among wolves. Be as wary as snakes and harmless as doves" (Matthew 10:16).

For a moment, perhaps Sarah needs to give Mermaid some rope and let her travel a little. Patience is always a good way to approach a tough problem.

By Sunday, Sarah was getting frantic. She even asked her Sunday-school class to pray about finding Mermaid. They did so, but when the family returned home, Mermaid was still missing.

"What else can we do, Mom?" she asked her mother with some exasperation in her voice.

"What would you want if you were Mermaid right now?"

Sarah thought about it and then snapped her fingers. "Food."

"Let's put out a dish of her favorite food on the porch, and one in the back on the deck and see if that brings Mermaid back."

"She'll smell it!" Sarah said, and sped for the stack of cat food cans.

She put half of one can on a plate on the back deck. She then did the same in the front. Each time she studied the food to re-member what it looked like so that if Mermaid ate some and then ran off again, she could tell.

All afternoon Sunday, as Sarah studied and did homework at the kitchen table, she listened for Mermaid. But no meows broke the quiet.

As evening drew near, Sarah checked each plate of food to see if any had been eaten. To her surprise, the one in the front of the house was all gone.

"Mom, Mom! The food's gone!"

If you want to bring home a wayward cat, it's a good idea to appeal to her taste buds. Calling her name may not get a response, but hunger will draw even the most disobedient pet.

Dealing with people is different. Jesus said, "Do for others what you would like them to do for you. This is a summary of all that is taught in the law and the prophets" (Matthew 7:12). Treat people the way you want to be treated. How can you do that today?

"She could just stay outside and eat what we put out forever!" Sarah wailed to her mother.

"Then we have to set a trap to capture her."

Sarah stared at her. "Like a mousetrap? Isn't that mean?"

"No, not a trap that would kill her; something that will catch and restrain her until we can bring her inside. Why don't you do a Google search of something like 'humane animal snares or traps' and see what you can find out?"

On the Internet Sarah found pictures of various kinds of traps people used for animals. Sarah studied them and came up with a design using a box. She put cat food in a mesh bag that let out the odor but couldn't be carried off. Then she put the food at the back end of the box, propping it up with the stick from an ice pop. She tied a string to the stick and to the bag of cat food. Now if Mermaid wanted that food, she'd have to pull on the string, the stick would fall, and the box would cover her.

Sarah's mother said, "It's a good idea. But I hope it doesn't frighten Mermaid away."

"I'll risk it," Sarah said. "This time when we get her, she becomes a total house cat for the rest of her life."

Mom laughed, but Sarah frowned as she set out the trap.

Sarah's trap was not designed to punish Mermaid, but to protect her from the dangers she encountered being away from home. People may feel that laws and rules restrict freedom, but they help us to live safely and peacefully. David wrote, "Happy are people of integrity, who follow the law of the Lord. Happy are those who obey his decrees and search for him with all their hearts. They do not compromise with evil, and they walk only in his paths" (Psalm 119:1-3). How has living by God's rules kept you safe and protected?

Sarah prayed long that night. She prayed that the trap would work and that no other animal besides Mermaid would get caught in it. She lay down and closed her eyes, still praying. But in time, she drifted off. In her dreams, she imagined hearing a cat meowing, and it became irritating as she wished Mermaid would come back.

Then suddenly the meows sounded real. Sarah sat up and listened.

Yes, a cat was meowing from outside. She pulled on her robe and rushed down the stairs, threw open the front door and looked out. In the glow from the porch light, she could see that the box lay firmly on the ground. Something was in it. And from the meows, it was definitely a cat.

Not willing to risk lifting the box and having Mermaid dash away, Sarah went back into the house, grabbed her father's fish net, then went upstairs and knocked on her parents' bedroom door. She quickly explained and they pulled on robes and followed her out to the box.

Everyone in place, Sarah gently pulled up the box with the net across the front. Sure enough, Mermaid leaped out and landed in the net. A second later, Sarah had her in the house.

"Mermaid! Mermaid! Do you know how you worried me?" She took the cat up to her room, set out some food, and turned out the lights. Soon Mermaid crawled up onto her bed and fell asleep.

God knows what we need and want, even before we ask. As Jesus said in Matthew 6:8, "Your Father knows exactly what you need even before you ask him!"

God gave Sarah a hearty yes to her prayers. However, sometimes he says no. But even then God is there. He watches. He cares. He wants us always to turn to him when we're afraid or anxious about a situation. He will comfort us, even when he must answer no.

Clint looked up at the rifle hanging on the wall of his father's office at home. "How old is that one?" he asked his dad.

"That's Grandpa's deer rifle. He got it when he was a kid, so that would've been before 1910."

"Is it worth much?" Clint asked.

"They're not rare. Plenty of people have them. You might get a couple hundred dollars."

Clint studied all the guns on the wall. His grandpa had died a year ago, and Dad inherited all these guns from him—several shotguns, deer rifles, and even some pistols. Every one of them, he learned, had a bit of a story, and Clint loved to hear them. He looked up at Grandpa's shotgun, a double-barreled one. "Is that one worth anything?" he asked his dad, pointing to it.

"No, but the pistol under it is worth a lot."

Clint gazed at it. "Why that one?"

His father looked up. "It's a Colt Navy from the Civil War. Grandpa's great-uncle had it."

Why should old things be valuable? Generally, it's not the oldest things that are valuable, but the rarest. The Bible says that there is something rarer and more valuable than gold and rubies. What is it? Read Proverbs 20:15 to find out.

"He was in the Civil War?"

"Yeah," Dad said. "He was a doctor. He had a pair of the revolvers, and he gave one to Grandpa, and one to Grandpa's brother. Somewhere around here is a paper that tells the whole history."

"Can I hold it?"

"Sure." Dad reached up and pulled down the lone revolver. To Clint it was heavy and unwieldy. He wondered how anyone could aim properly with so heavy a weapon.

"Did he ever shoot anyone with it?" Clint asked as his father put the gun back.

"I doubt it. He was a doctor. He probably sawed off a leg or two, though. After all, it was the Civil War."

"Gross!"

Weeks later Clint went back into his father's office, and this time he brought his friend Taylor with him. He had told Taylor about the antique firearms, and Taylor was eager to see them. When they walked into Dad's office, Taylor was wide-eyed. "Wow! Those are cool!"

Clint was wide-eyed too. Below the shotgun, where the Colt revolver should have been, there was an empty space.

An antique gun isn't effective as a weapon. A useless weapon is kept solely as a historical artifact or conversation piece, and can't be used for personal security.

The Bible describes the weapons necessary for the Christian to "stand firm against all strategies and tricks of the Devil. For we are not fighting against people made of flesh and blood, but against the evil rulers and authorities of the unseen world, against those mighty powers of darkness who rule this world, and against wicked spirits in the heavenly realms" (Ephesians 6:11, 12). What gear does the Christian need to do battle with the devil? Read Ephesians 6:13-17 to find out.

"Dad! Dad! The pistol's missing!" Clint called to his dad, who came running to the office. "Did you take it down?"

Dad looked at the space on the wall. "No, I didn't. And I didn't even notice it was missing. Who could have moved it?"

Clint sat and thought. "Well, you have clients through here all the time. And anyone who comes to our house could come back here without our knowing it. That includes neighbors, friends, and all the people in the weekly Bible study—and their kids."

Dad added, "And Mom had some ladies over for some kind of sell-things party. Wait! You didn't take it to school for some kind of show-and-tell thing, did you?"

"Dad, I'm in sixth grade."

Clint compiled a list of everyone who had been in the house. Then he made a list: Borrowed? Stolen? Misplaced?

He looked over the words. Why would someone borrow the gun? It wasn't usable. Besides, if they borrowed it, they'd ask, right? And how could it be just missing?

Then he wrote down something else: Worth thousands of dollars. That was it. The gun was valuable, but only to collectors. Maybe someone stole the gun with the hope of selling it to someone else.

If you saw a rusty old gun, would you think it was valuable? You can't tell an item's worth just by looking. You can't tell a person's worth just by looking, either. While the world values wealth, power, youth, beauty, popularity, and influence, the real value of a person comes from their creator, God. David said to God, "Thank you for making me so wonderfully complex! Your workmanship is marvelous—how well I know it" (Psalm 139:14). Thank God for how much he values you.

"Dad, do you know any gun collectors?" Clint asked.

"You mean besides me?"

"You just have them because of Grandpa," Clint said. "Not because you really collect them."

"True. But with all these guns, I am now a collector. And I might buy another one to add to them."

"From whom?"

Dad shrugged. "There are always gun shows coming to town. There's one this weekend, I think, at the Spring Center."

Clint thought about that. Perhaps someone from a gun show had taken it. "Could we go? Maybe we'll see it there."

So they went. Many dealers had guns just like some of Dad's. But there wasn't a Colt Navy like the one Grandpa passed on. Clint was quite disappointed.

He even saw a friend of the family at the show, Mr. Coleman. But when Clint asked, his dad didn't think Mr. Coleman had ever been at their house.

Do you think guns are too dangerous for people to own? They have served a purpose providing food and protection for people in the past. God allowed his people to possess weapons in the Old Testament. He said through the prophet Isaiah, "I have created the blacksmith who fans the coals beneath the forge and makes the weapons of destruction. And I have created the armies that destroy. But in that coming day, no weapon turned against you will succeed. . . . These benefits are enjoyed by the servants of the Lord; their vindication will come from me. I, the Lord, have spoken!" (Isaiah 54:16, 17). The people's security did not come from their weapons, but from their all-powerful God who protected and provided for them. Is he your God too?

Clint listened to the news on the radio as he and Dad drove home from the gun show. Suddenly, his ears pricked up when he heard the announcer say, "Come to the Civil War reenactment out at Kearney on Sunday. Everyone will be there. And if you've never seen one, you'll be amazed at how real it seems."

Mulling this over in his head, Clint asked his father, "A Civil War reenactment. Is that where they pretend to be fighting a Civil War battle?"

"Right," Dad said. "I have some friends who do that."

Clint zeroed in. "Who?"

"Your Uncle Harry, for one."

"Uncle Harry does that?"

"Well, not so much anymore. But he used to."

"I think we should ask Uncle Harry then."

Dad whistled when Clint mentioned it.

Have you ever heard the term "circumstantial evidence"? That means there are facts that point indirectly toward a person's guilt, but don't prove it directly. It's as though there are a set of clues that point you in a certain direction, but don't add up to a definite conclusion.

You have to be very careful not to judge someone based on circumstantial evidence. A much more reliable predictor of a person's behavior is his character. If he has a past history of honorable behavior and a good reputation, it's wise to give him the benefit of the doubt, even when circumstances seem to indicate otherwise.

This very thing happened to Ruth in the Bible. When there was some question about what she was doing, Boaz said, "And now, my daughter, don't be afraid. I will do for you all you ask. All my fellow townsmen know that you are a woman of noble character" (Ruth 3:11, *NIV*).

How can you develop noble character at your age?

MYSTERY OF THE
ANTIQUE PISTOL

Dad shook his head. "I'd be careful about accusing Uncle Harry of such a thing."

"How come?"

"Well, first of all, he hasn't had much interest in Civil War reenacting since your cousins were born. And second, when we were kids, he got accused of something he didn't do. Uncle Harry still talks about it, and you can really get him going if you ask more than a passing question about it. He's real sensitive sometimes."

They reached the house and went in. Clint kept thinking about it. Finally, he said to his dad, "Why don't we ask Uncle Harry to go see the reenactment with us? Then we can talk to him without accusing."

"It might work," Dad said. "I'll call him."

"Funny you should ask," Uncle Harry told Dad on the phone. "I haven't done much reenacting in the last 15 years, but I agreed to do this one. Some of my old friends are involved, so we're making it a reunion of sorts. That'd be great if you all come!"

Clint and his family went to the reenactment. They spotted Uncle Harry on a horse in full Union uniform. He had a sword, a carbine in his hands, and a revolver in a holster on his hip.

Finally, the battle was over and all the "soldiers" returned to their families. Clint and his dad walked over to where Uncle Harry talked to friends and relatives.

Have you ever suspected someone of something? How did you approach that person? Have you ever been accused of something? How did your accuser approach you? Jesus wisely said, "Others will treat you as you treat them. Whatever measure you use in judging others, it will be used to measure how you are judged" (Matthew 7:2). That's the best advice when in comes to relationships with others.

When Clint and his dad greeted Uncle Harry, he handed Clint the carbine. "How do you like it?"

Clint turned it over in his hands, then sighted down the barrel. "It's great," he said. "What about the one in the holster?"

Uncle Harry pulled it out. Clint looked it over, and his face fell. It wasn't theirs.

"Hey, what's wrong?" Uncle Harry asked. "Don't you like it?"

Clint looked to his dad for help. "I guess Clint's just disappointed thinking about Grandpa's Colt Navy. It's disappeared."

"Oh, man!" Uncle Harry slapped his forehead. "I thought I could get it back before you missed it!"

"What are you talking about?" asked Dad.

"I took the pistol—three days ago. I was having it photographed. I thought that if I kept it just for the weekend you wouldn't be in your office and you wouldn't miss it."

"Having it photographed? What for?" Clint asked.

"I wrote an article about the pair of pistols, and it is being published in a magazine. They wanted photos of the gun, so I took it to a studio yesterday. When the article comes out in the magazine I was going to surprise you with a framed copy to display on the wall with the guns."

"It's a great surprise," Dad said. "It's just early for my birthday—and it caused a little more distress than most surprises. But I can't wait to read your article!"

Before you confront someone, make sure you have all the facts. "There is more hope for a fool than for someone who speaks without thinking" (Proverbs 29:20).

Brandy Wild opened the closet door behind the girls' locker room. She hated the jobs Miss Anson gave her sometimes, but working on the junior high production of *Cats,* just being a part of it, made the crummy jobs worth it. She hit the light, and after she stepped in, the creaky door slowly closed behind her. She bent to put some items in the storage cabinet. She was about to open the door when she heard whispers.

"It's locker 413," one voice said. Whoever the speaker was, it was obvious that she thought no one could overhear.

"You've got the cigarettes."

"Definitely. Marlboros, her brand."

Brandy stiffened and waited. A locker squeaked open. Her heart pounded. What was going on? She turned off the storage closet light, then peered out through the slit in the partially open door. Claire Reims and Hannah Lipscomb stood at one of the lockers opening a purse.

"This'll put her out of the lead for good," Claire said.

Brandy has witnessed a crime; not a federal crime or a state crime, but a crime just the same—two girls trying to destroy the reputation of another. One way a person could respond in similar circumstances is to ignore it. Brandy could say it was none of her business—it was just between Claire, Hannah, and another girl, Janice.

The Bible tells Christians how they are to feel about wrongdoing: "You who love the Lord, hate evil! He protects the lives of his godly people and rescues them from the power of the wicked" (Psalm 97:10). If you say, "It's none of my business," are you hating evil?

Brandy watched with fear and fascination as the two girls put a pack of cigarettes into the pocketbook. It belonged to Janice Larkin, who had the role of Grizabela in "Cats." It was no secret that Claire had wanted the role herself.

Immediately Brandy knew what Claire and Hannah hoped to accomplish. The drama coach, Miss Anson, was absolutely adamant that no smokers would be allowed in the cast. Janice desired a lead role so much that she quit smoking to earn it.

Brandy listened as Claire closed the locker and hurried out with Hannah. Then she made her way to the stage.

When Brandy reached the stage area, everyone had gathered to hear a brief speech. Miss Anson began, "Some of you girls have been smoking. As stated on the contract you signed when you were chosen for the musical, you agreed to unannounced locker inspections. We're going to have one right now."

Janice was obviously surprised and unprepared for what happened. Two other girls were caught with cigarettes, but they were in lesser roles. Miss Anson was furious with Janice. She tried to deny, then explain, but Miss Anson didn't believe her.

"I can't keep you in your role, Janice," she fumed.

Janice stood before the group in tears. "I promise, Miss Anson, I don't know anything about this."

It's amazing what lengths some people will go to in order to get what they want. And sometimes unscrupulous actions result in an advantage. But in the long run, any such advantage fades, because eventually good will overcome evil. The Bible says so. "Evil people get rich for the moment, but the reward of the godly will last" (Proverbs 11:18). When you see injustice, talk to God about how you feel, and be assured that he will do what is right.

MYSTERY OF THE
POWER PLAY

Miss Anson surveyed the group. "Anyone know about this?"

Immediately, Brandy's heart raced. No one looked her way. She was just one of the stage crew.

Miss Anson's voice rang out again. "I repeat: does anyone know how these cigarettes got into Janice's purse?"

Janice glanced hopefully around at the group. No one answered. Brandy noticed Claire and Hannah staring straight ahead blankly.

"Janice, I'm sorry. You'll have to step down."

Janice burst into tears again, but Miss Anson was not easily swayed. Brandy was gripped with fear. Should she speak up? She raised her hand. "Miss Anson?"

The director grimaced and turned toward Brandy. "Yes?"

All the girls turned around to look into her eyes. Brandy froze. Words came into her throat, but her lips wouldn't move. Miss Anson asked, "Do you know anything about this?"

Brandy caught a hard gaze from both Hannah and Claire, and from several others. She searched for something to say, then blurted out, "I just wondered if you want me to get the props."

Miss Anson shook her head. "This isn't a joke, girls. Get back to work and no more of this nonsense. Claire, I'd like to talk to you."

Brandy watched with despair as Claire bounced up to Miss Anson like a happy puppy. *She'll get exactly what she wants now,* Brandy thought miserably.

It takes real courage to speak up about something like this, don't you think? Paul the apostle was known for speaking about Jesus and convincing many people to follow him. But even Paul experienced fear, and Jesus told him, "Don't be afraid! Speak out! Don't be silent! For I am with you, and no one will harm you because many people here in this city belong to me" (Acts 18:9, 10). Ask God for help to be brave and speak out for him.

POWER PLAY

Brandy couldn't sleep that night.

The next day at school Janice didn't appear in English class, the one class Brandy had with her. Miss Anson put Claire in Janice's role, and Claire talked her into giving Hannah a leadership position in the chorus.

Brandy battled guilt and anger. That afternoon, she called Clark Benson, a youth coach from her church. When she asked for his advice about the situation, Clark said, "I'd confront the girls who did it in private. If they wouldn't listen to me, then I'd go with a second party, probably someone whom you know would command some respect from the guilty party. Actually, it's all spelled out in Matthew 18, about the middle of the chapter. Read that, and I think you'll understand."

"But I don't want to do this on my own. I want to take others with me the first time."

Clark went on, "I understand that you'd feel that way. But you need to give them the opportunity to repent before you involve anyone else."

Brandy tried to think of some way of approaching Claire and Hannah privately. But every time she passed or saw them, she tightened up and couldn't muster the courage.

Confronting someone about sin is one of the most difficult things about being a Christian. The Bible, though, is very clear about what steps we should take in such situations. Read Matthew 18:15-17 to find out three steps to take in confronting another's sin.

MYSTERY OF THE
POWER PLAY

On Tuesday Brandy walked over to the group at drama practice. When there was a lull in the talk, she said, "Claire, can I talk to you and Hannah a moment?"

Claire scowled, "Who are you?"

Brandy's heart pounded right into her throat, but she didn't back down. "I'd just like to talk to you privately for a moment."

Claire shrugged. "You can say anything to me and my friends."

Brandy chewed her lip. "It's about Janice Larkin."

Claire's face blanched only slightly. "You want Hannah, too?"

"Yes."

Claire motioned to Hannah. "Let's make this quick. I have to practice my song."

They went to an empty classroom near the auditorium. No one said anything until they stood inside, with Claire lolling in the doorway, as if planning to make a fast exit. Brandy said, "I think we should shut the door."

Claire's closed it. "All right, Wild, what's this about?"

Brandy breathed deeply. "I was in the locker room when you put the cigarettes in Janice's pocketbook."

Hannah swore, but Claire stepped forward menacingly. "Oh, and I suppose you're going to expect a bribe or something?"

Brandy didn't move. "No, I don't want a bribe. I want you to tell Miss Anson the truth."

Why is it important to confront someone? Galatians 6:1 tells why: "Dear brothers and sisters, if another Christian is overcome by some sin, you who are godly should gently and humbly help that person back onto the right path. And be careful not to fall into the same temptation yourself." Confronting sin is not to get the upper hand on someone else; it's to help them do the right thing.

Claire said, "Do you know what we can do to you?"

Brandy nodded. "Yes. But right is right, and what you did was wrong. I want you to go with me to Miss Anson. She'll understand . . ."

"Oh, right! Like she understood Janice. Forget it."

Brandy leaned on a desk. "Then you refuse?"

"Absolutely."

"All right, then I'll have to go to the second step."

Claire said, "What do you mean?"

Brandy took another deep breath. "I'll get two impartial witnesses, all five of us will meet, and we'll discuss the situation."

"And who will the witnesses be?"

"The principal, Mr. Evans, and Mr. James, the assistant director."

Claire's jaw was tight. "Are you threatening me?"

Brandy shook her head. "No, I'm just telling you what I will do if you don't go with me now to talk to Miss Anson."

Claire cursed. "All right. Go outside. Give Hannah and me a minute."

Brandy stood outside the door, while Claire shouted inside. A few minutes later, they both came out, looking shaken and weak. "OK, we'll talk to Miss Anson."

Doing the right thing doesn't mean people will like you. As a matter of fact, it may mean just the opposite. Jesus told his followers, "When the world hates you, remember it hated me before it hated you. The world would love you if you belonged to it, but you don't. I chose you to come out of the world, and so it hates you" (John 15:18, 19). Does anyone hate you because of Jesus?

MYSTERY OF THE
POWER PLAY

Miss Anson was angry and decided to spend several days thinking about what to do. She restored Janice to her old role. In the end, she made Claire and Hannah tell the whole crew what they had done. They felt humiliated and angry, but they came clean. Everyone talked about what their punishment should be, and Janice herself asked that Claire be given her original position. Miss Anson nixed that, and ended up putting both girls back in the chorus. In the end, they decided to drop out of the play altogether.

The school steamed with rumors. A number of kids rejected Brandy or responded with anger, calling her a rat and saying that she shouldn't have made the girls confess. However, a number of others, including Janice, defended her and gave her support.

It turned out to be a rough year. But Brandy and Janice remained close friends. On the Saturday before the last day of school they went to the mall together. They happened to pass a Christian bookstore and Janice found a wooden plaque she liked. It said, "Courage: the decision to do what's right even though all the world stands against you."

She gave it to Brandy and said, "I admire you both as a person and for what you did. I love you." Brandy was grateful for their genuine friendship.

"Remember that some people lead sinful lives, and everyone knows they will be judged. But there are others whose sin will not be revealed until later. In the same way, everyone knows how much good some people do, but there are others whose good deeds won't be known until later" (1 Timothy 5:24, 25). When no other person knows what you're doing, good or bad, God knows, and that's what matters.

Ramon brushed down Quicksilver after their long ride. Mr. Danfield walked into the barn and found him there. "One thing I need to tell you about Quicksilver," he said to Ramon.

"What?" the seventh grader asked.

"Don't go down near the lake with him."

"How come?"

"He likes to swim."

"OK."

Ramon finished up and asked if he could ride the next day.

"Sure," said Mr. Danfield. "I like him getting plenty of exercise. The other horses need it too. You have any friends who like to ride?"

"I can ask around."

"Do it, because I just don't have the time for it anymore. And I don't want to sell them. I wouldn't get enough money for them to be worth the trouble."

"I know a couple of guys."

"Great."

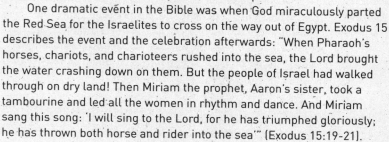

It's fun to ride horses, but today we don't depend on them like people in the past. In Bible times, horses were not only transportation, but they were also weapons.

One dramatic event in the Bible was when God miraculously parted the Red Sea for the Israelites to cross on the way out of Egypt. Exodus 15 describes the event and the celebration afterwards: "When Pharaoh's horses, chariots, and charioteers rushed into the sea, the Lord brought the water crashing down on them. But the people of Israel had walked through on dry land! Then Miriam the prophet, Aaron's sister, took a tambourine and led all the women in rhythm and dance. And Miriam sang this song: 'I will sing to the Lord, for he has triumphed gloriously; he has thrown both horse and rider into the sea'" (Exodus 15:19-21).

Ramon talked to his friends, Sam, Lou, and Crash. None of them had ridden much, but he told them the horses were all pretty gentle.

They rode their bikes to the farm, and Mr. Danfield helped them get saddled up. "Just don't go to the lake," he told them. The boys headed down the road in the opposite direction. They stuck to the road, and Ramon showed them how to lope, canter, and gallop. The boys held on well and no one fell off. It was a lot of fun.

"We should go camping," Lou said when they were unsaddling the horses and cooling them down.

"Where would we go?" Ramon asked.

"There's this site down the road, a campsite. They have a pool and facilities. We could cook out and everything."

"I'll ask Mr. Danfield. I've never done anything like that before."

The boys waited as Ramon knocked on Mr. Danfield's door. Ramon stood explaining and Mr. Danfield nodded. When Ramon turned around to leave, he gave everyone a thumb's up.

"This weekend," he said when he rejoined the group. "He says he even has an old tent we can use."

Horses are beautiful animals. In the book of Job, God himself describes the horse he made. He asks Job, "Have you given the horse its strength or clothed its neck with a flowing mane? Did you give it the ability to leap forward like a locust? Its majestic snorting is something to hear!" (Job 39:19, 20). It sounds as if God is proud of his creation. And you know what? He's proud of you too!

The boys joined up that Friday afternoon at Ramon's house. They hiked to Mr. Danfield's house with all their equipment in backpacks on their shoulders. Mr. Danfield gave them the tent and told them how to set it up. Then they set off on the four horses, with Ramon on Quicksilver.

"How come he's always telling us not to go near the lake?" Crash asked as they loped along down the road.

"The horses like to go swimming."

"How come?"

"He didn't say."

"Maybe we should find out."

"What—you think we should take them down to the lake?"

"No, I just mean, ask Mr. Danfield. It seems kind of weird."

In little more than an hour, they reached the campground. They tied the horses outside the main office, went in and got a site, paying 10 dollars for the night.

"Worse than a motel," Lou said.

"Motels cost 50," Crash said. "And we wouldn't be allowed to take the horses into our room."

"Who would want to?"

Since horses were the tanks or Humvees of armies in Bible times, God used them to help his people in battle against their enemies. But God didn't always use regular horses. Second Kings 6 gives an account of an extraordinary victory that didn't result from a battle. An enemy king surrounded the city with chariots and horses. The prophet Elisha's servant saw the army and was afraid. "Then Elisha prayed, 'O Lord, open his eyes and let him see!' The Lord opened his servant's eyes, and when he looked up, he saw that the hillside around Elisha was filled with horses and chariots of fire" (2 Kings 6:17). To find out what happened next, read 2 Kings 6:18-23.

They reached their site and got everything off the horses, then let them graze in a field the campground offered specifically for people with horses. There were other horses there too, and Ramon said, "I hope we can tell them apart in the morning."

"The brands," Lou said. "Memorize yours."

Each boy studied his own horse till he found the brand, usually on the back haunch.

"Mine's a cross in a circle," said Lou.

Crash said, "Mine's a double Z."

Each boy's horse had a specific brand.

No one slept well that night, but in the morning everyone was ready to roll. They planned to visit a hot spring up the road where steaming water came from the ground. Ramon and Lou cooked a good breakfast of sausage and powdered eggs. No one liked the eggs much, but it was better than nothing, Crash said.

Later, after cleaning up, they saddled the horses and went on their jaunt. They found the hot spring and even took off their shoes and dipped in their feet. The spring was strangely hot.

When they finished, they found out from a guide that the road went back around to the campground the other way. So they decided to try it.

Because horses were so valuable to armies in Bible times, God was explicit in his instructions to his people that they should not accumulate horses or put too much trust in them. In his guidelines for kings, God instructs that "The king must not build up a large stable of horses for himself, and he must never send his people to Egypt to buy horses there, for the Lord has told you, 'You must never return to Egypt'" (Deuteronomy 17:16). God wanted his people to depend on him, not on the weapons and strategies of the world. How are you when it comes to trusting God?

The boys headed off the opposite way. It was a long way around. At one point, all four of the horses started snorting, rearing, and acting a little crazy. It took the boys all they could to maintain control. Finally, at one point, through a break in the trees, they could see the lake.

"Oh, no, it's the lake!" Ramon said, and kicked Quicksilver. "We have to get going the other way."

He tried to steer Quicksilver, and he came around. But Lou couldn't keep his horse from turning every chance it had. And Sam and Crash had equal trouble.

"What's wrong with them?" Lou shouted.

"We're too close to the lake," Ramon said.

At that moment, Lou's horse reared on its hind legs and threw Lou off. The horse bolted off through the trees toward the lake, bridle dragging.

Ramon jumped down to help Lou, but he gripped the reins on Quicksilver.

It wasn't enough. Quicksilver backed up, pulling on the reins and Ramon with him. "Don't do this," Ramon cried.

Suddenly, Sam's horse wheeled and bucked, and Sam came off with a crunch. The same thing happened with Crash.

At that point, Quicksilver jerked the reins out of Ramon's hands.

Horses are smart, strong, and powerful. It's hard to make a horse do something he doesn't want to do. When the prophet Jeremiah complained to God about the evil and injustice he saw in the world, God asked him a question: "If racing against mere men makes you tired, how will you race against horses?" (Jeremiah 12:5). In this way, God was warning Jeremiah of difficult times to come. While you'll probably never have to "race against horses," hard times will come to you, but God will be there for you like he was for Jeremiah.

MYSTERY OF THE
RUNAWAY HORSES

Ramon watched in horror as the horses all bounded through the woods straight for the lake. He helped the others up, and though they were all limping, they followed the horses down to the lake. When they reached it, the other three were out ahead, swimming toward the far shore. Quicksilver was last, but catching up quickly.

"What do we do?" Lou asked. "Mr. Danfield's gonna kill us."

Ramon looked down the lake to a place where it narrowed and they could cross on a little bridge.

"I guess we'd better go over there and get them."

"Let's go," everyone said.

The boys hiked along the edge of the lake toward the bridge. It was rough going, with many large rocks along the shoreline. Houses stood up the hill along the edges and they passed people sitting on docks sunbathing.

One man stood up. "You the guys with the horses?"

Ramon was embarrassed, but he said, "Yeah. They're ours."

"We've seen them do it before. A farm up the road."

"Yeah."

"Hope you catch them."

Have you ever seen galloping horses? It's a powerful sight. God once used the sound of galloping horses to scare away Israel's enemies. According to 2 Kings 7:6, 7, "The Lord had caused the whole army of Aram to hear the clatter of speeding chariots and the galloping of horses and the sounds of a great army approaching. . . . So they panicked and fled into the night, abandoning their tents, horses, donkeys, and everything else, and they fled for their lives."

God still does amazing things. Give him thanks.

They finally reached the bridge, and then the other side. They found the horses' tracks and followed them up to a fenced area where a bunch of horses grazed. Their horses walked along the fence, whinnying and angry they couldn't get in.

A farmer came out toward them. "These your horses?" he asked.

"Yeah. We're sor—" Ramon started to say.

"Mr. Danfield's?"

"Yeah. How did you know?"

"They all come over a couple times a year. Even run over the ice in winter. They're eager. Pent up, I guess, all males in the barn."

"They're after the females?" Sam asked.

"Yeah," the farmer said. He pulled out a cell phone and dialed. "I know Danfield's number by heart now," he said with a laugh.

Mr. Danfield showed up in his truck about a half-hour later. He was laughing when he got out of his truck. "I knew it would happen," he commented.

The truck had a large, four-horse trailer behind it, and Mr. Danfield gave everyone a ride back to the campsite.

"I guess now we know why we shouldn't go close to the lake," Ramon said when they got out.

Many kings in history have ridden horses. But did you know that the King of kings and Lord of lords will one day ride a white horse? In John's vision of Heaven he describes the scene: "Then I saw heaven opened, and a white horse was standing there. And the one sitting on the horse was named Faithful and True. . . . His eyes were bright like flames of fire, and on his head were many crowns. . . . He was clothed with a robe dipped in blood, and his title was the Word of God" (Revelation 19:11-13). Are you looking forward to seeing Jesus some day?

MYSTERY OF THE
ONE-EYED DOG

When Josie stepped off the bus, she noticed the dog again. He stood on the other side of the road in the woods. He seemed to be watching her. Who was he? Why did he come and stand there? He looked like a husky mix—long, thick hair; gray underside, some black and white throughout, a sharp, straight, wolf-like face.

She wasn't sure she should try to make contact, but the dog didn't look mean or vicious. Finally, one afternoon she stepped off the bus and stood there. As the bus roared away and the fumes cleared, she saw the dog. He stood there alone, but suddenly he reared back and barked loudly. What was wrong? Did he mean to get her attention?

She stood there and reached into her backpack. She took out a snack cake she hadn't eaten at lunch.

"Nice doggie," she said and held up the cake. "Would you like something to eat?" The big dog jerked his head twice, then barked again, a deep, mellow woof.

It was a bark of distress, not greeting.

She stood, not sure what to do. Finally, after looking both ways, she stepped out onto the open highway. No one appeared either way, and she reached the white lines in the center of the road.

The dog barked and backed up along the trail. She held out the cake. Finally, she pitched it all the way across the road. The dog just looked at it.

Often, animals have intelligence beyond what we might think possible. God wants us to care for the world he created, including animals. In Psalm 50:10, 11 God tells humans, "For all the animals of the forest are mine, and I own the cattle on a thousand hills. Every bird of the mountains and all the animals of the field belong to me."

ONE-EYED DOG

"What's wrong?" Josie asked.

She sprinted across the road. Before she reached the other side, the dog whipped around and bounded up the trail. She picked up the snack cake and followed.

"What is it?" Josie shouted again as she ran after him. He barked, stopped, waited a moment, then bounded off again before she reached him. It was all uphill and the dog nearly galloped. In a few minutes Josie puffed with exhaustion.

"Doggie, please!" Her side ached and the pack on her back felt heavy. But the dog didn't let up.

He passed Lumpy Rock and the Initials Tree. As they came around a bend, he slowed enough to let Josie catch up.

"Who are you?" she asked. "What's the problem?"

The dog studied her, and waited. But he paced restlessly and whimpered repeatedly.

She bent down and looked into his eyes. "Is someone hurt?"

The dog turned again up the trail. A few yards up he veered off into the woods, barking loudly. He tore ahead through the underbrush, over rocks, around trees. He barked and soon Josie heard a response. She slowed down. Were there other dogs—wild dogs—around? Surely the dog wouldn't lead her into a pack of them.

A moment later, she saw it: a little collie-like dog, maybe a sheltie, by a tree, pulling at something.

A dog in distress can be trouble. They might bite out of fear or by impulse. It's understandable they might act that way. After all, people do it too. When you are sad or angry, do you feel like lashing out at others? The first thing to do is to talk to God. Read why David called out to God in 2 Samuel 22:5-7, and find out what God did. —☺

131

MYSTERY OF THE
ONE-EYED DOG

As she moved closer, cautiously, the big dog stopped. He looked back and forth from the sheltie to her, as if saying, "See, look at this. We need your help."

Josie knelt and looked at the little dog. He was missing one eye, a jagged, painful-looking gash where a deep brown eye should have been. The moment he saw her, he began growling. As she edged closer, the dog jerked his paw back. A trap. He was caught in a trap.

His right foot was cut and bleeding in the teeth of the trap. As she worked to get closer, she held out her hand and spoke softly and calmly. "It's all right. It'll be all right. Just calm down."

The dog growled, then whimpered. The trap was chained to a stake. She knew trappers came to these woods to bag foxes, rabbits, and squirrels. But it was a larger trap. Was someone trying to trap wild dogs?

She spoke low and kindly, trying to calm the little sheltie. But as she reached out to touch the trap, the dog bared his short, spiky fangs, revealing black angry lips tinged with froth. She knew if she got too close he might bite her. The big dog barked. Obviously he couldn't help her with this.

How could she do this? And what would she do with the dog if she did set him free? He needed medical attention.

She needed someone else to help. "Dave," she whispered.

The dog stopped growling, but when she stood he bared his teeth again.

This is a dangerous situation. Would you ask God for wisdom about solving such a problem? Read James 1:5-8 to find out how God will respond when you ask. Is there something you need wisdom to face today?

"OK," Josie said. "You stay here. Protect him. I'll get Dave." The dog seemed to understand, because he didn't follow Josie when she turned and went back down the trail.

Dave lived at a cabin in the woods with his wife, Merrilee. Josie found them both at home and explained what she'd found. They brought an old blanket from the shed and some rolls from lunch. All three hurried through the woods to where the dogs were.

The smaller dog remained just as terrified and vicious as before. Josie spelled out her plan. Dave volunteered to throw the blanket, while Merrilee and Josie would pull apart the trap.

Josie crept closer to the dog while Dave went around behind him with the blanket. She dropped a roll in front of the dog. He remained wary of Dave, but after he sniffed the food, he bent down to take a bite. Josie smiled to herself, thinking, *Even when they're in pain they still like to eat.*

Dave moved closer. He threw the blanket. It sailed down over the dog's back and head. Dave jumped quickly. He pulled the bottom of the blanket over the dog's head and clamped it down. The dog squirmed and growled, but the blanket protected Dave from his teeth.

"Do it!" Dave yelled.

What a smart way to take care of this problem! Look at Proverbs 14:12: "There is a path before each person that seems right, but it ends in death." Why does God tell us this? Because every decision has only two possibilities—right or wrong. Some decisions you make are trivial, but others will set the course for your entire life. What decision do you need to make this week?

MYSTERY OF THE
ONE-EYED DOG

Josie grabbed the jaws of the trap in her hands and Merrilee pushed down the latch. The jaws came apart and the dog jerked his leg up. Dave picked him up in the blanket, then set him down easily. Everyone stood back, as the dog squirmed and squealed.

Dave let him go.

Instantly, the dog worked his way out of the blanket, then scorched a three-legged gallop through the trees. The big dog exploded after him and caught up in a few bounds. Both dogs stopped in the woods about 40 feet from Josie and the couple. The big dog's tail wagged and the little sheltie held up his paw, panting. The big dog bent down and licked it. Then he turned his head toward Josie, Dave, and Merrilee, and shook it up and down, barking.

"He's saying thank you," Josie whispered, her eyes filling with tears at the thought of the poor little dog. Would his leg ever be good again? What could she do now that the dog was free?

The sheltie held its bloody paw up gingerly. He stared at them with his one eye.

"Not exactly a show winner, I'd say," Dave commented.

"Well, at least he's out of that wretched trap," Merrilee said. She put her arm around Josie's shoulders. "We're going to call you Florence Nightingale."

Josie smiled. "I couldn't just leave him there."

"Of course not. But he can't just roam around in the woods either," Dave said, wiping his forehead.

"But we can't make him come with us," Merrilee replied.

Have you ever tried to make someone do something? If a person, or an animal, doesn't want to do something, it's often impossible to make him. What you can't do by force, however, you may be able to do by persuasion. An example of this is in Philemon 8-11, 14. Read it to find out how Paul persuaded his friend Philemon.

They waited. The big dog walked back and forth between them and the sheltie several times. But the little dog wouldn't come closer.

Merrilee said, "Well, what are you going to name them?"

"I don't know," Josie said. "I'm afraid to get close. Daddy will never let me bring them home. I don't want to be disappointed."

Dave laughed. "Aw, go ahead. It can't hurt."

"OK," Josie said. "The big one, Corky, the little one, Bunkie. How's that?"

"Don't look like a Corky and a Bunkie, but whatever," Dave said.

"I'll bring them both something each time I come into the woods," Josie said. "Maybe we will become friends. That would be really cool if both of them were like my 'woods dogs.'"

Merrilee turned. Dave put his arm over her shoulder and they began walking back toward the trail. Josie watched Bunkie as Corky gave him another lick on the foot. The huge husky and the sheltie looked like a real pair of ruffians, she thought with a smile. She called to them, "Stay out of the traps, you guys. We don't want to find your bones one of these days rotted away."

Sitting on his haunches, Corky threw his head back, dribbling out his tongue and woofing happily. Bunkie gazed up at him, looking like a toddler who didn't understand the joke.

Josie laughed. "I'll be back," she said.

Why do you think Josie and her friends helped the dogs? How do you decide whether or not to help someone?

Jesus told a parable about someone who helped a wounded stranger. Why did the Good Samaritan help someone he didn't even know? Find out by reading Luke 10:30-37. Pay special attention to Jesus' instructions in verse 37. How can you "go and do the same" today?

MYSTERY OF THE
ONE-EYED DOG

As she hurried down the path toward home, Josie worried about the two dogs. But she was sure they'd be all right now. "Just don't let them get into any more traps," she prayed out loud as she passed the Big Rock.

"I wish I could tell Daddy about all this," she murmured as she reached the other side. But somehow that seemed impossible. He had already referred to the feral dogs in the woods as "dump dogs" and mongrels. He'd never let her have one of them as a pet.

Over the next few weeks, Josie brought tidbits of hot dogs, pretzels, and even some dog food she bought with her own money. Soon both dogs met her each day as she returned from school. Though Bunkie stayed aloof, Corky allowed her to pet and groom him.

One day as Josie stooped next to Corky, feeding him, Bunkie wove back and forth, trying to make the decision to come closer. Josie coaxed him, held out the food, but didn't pitch it to him directly like she usually did. Finally, he edged within arm distance. Josie held out the bit of food, and he took it, then retreated a few feet away, crunching it. But after a few more bites, he sat down and let her pet him.

When she went home that night, a joy filled her. Because she helped them, the dogs grew to trust her. Who would've thought that two "dump dogs" would become her friends?

What can you do to make peace with wounded people? Romans 12:18 tells us: "Do your part to live in peace with everyone, as much as possible." Think about people you know, and pray about how you can patiently reach out to people who are hurting.

Barb saw it on the news that night. A valuable painting had been purchased by a local museum. The problem was no one knew who the girl in the painting was, and they were having a contest to see who could find out.

The painting, a portrait of a little girl with a sand bucket on a beach, was done by Thomas Hart Benton, a famous Missouri artist who painted landscapes and scenes of average people. He was one of the first artists who concentrated on "common folk," since most artists only painted famous people or portraits for those who could afford them.

At the library, Barb found information about Benton and his paintings, but found no reference to the one that had been bought. Barb thought little of it. She was curious but not really serious about the contest. Then she found out that first prize was $100, and her attitude changed.

"One hundred dollars!" Barb exclaimed when she heard it on the news.

"You can buy a lot of chocolate cones for that kind of money," her mom said.

"Chocolate cones? I'm thinking more like my own horse!" Barb promptly went to the computer to find out what she could on the Internet.

For Solomon, learning was a privilege. God gave him wisdom, and Solomon set out to learn everything he could about the world. Solomon wrote, "It is the glory of God to conceal a matter; to search out a matter is the glory of kings" (Proverbs 25:2, *NIV*). To Solomon, to "search out" knowledge was glory. Do you agree with Solomon? Do you like to learn, or find it a chore?

137

Barb found mounds of information on the Internet about Benton and his paintings. One site listed numerous paintings, and even identified the people in the paintings. It was interesting reading. Benton's subjects were mostly poor. Many were painted during the Great Depression. Amazingly, he was one of the first painters to show such scenes.

Barb studied the paintings. "He was really good, Mom," she said.

"He's a Missouri treasure," she said. "I learned about him in college."

"How can I see the painting that they're having the contest about?"

"You might try the museum's Web site. According to the newspaper, the painting's not on display at the museum yet. You're really interested in this, aren't you?"

Barb smiled. "Yeah, I guess so. I like figuring things like this out. Maybe when I grow up, I could be an investigator."

"So have you come up with any ideas about who the little girl might be?"

Barb shrugged. "I'm working on it. So far, I just know that she was a young girl in the 1930s, so she'd be nearly 80 now."

At first, Barb wasn't too motivated to research the girl in the painting. But as she learned more, her motivation grew stronger. That's similar to people who become Christians. Their motivation changes. Paul described it like this: "Therefore, if anyone is in Christ, he is a new creation; the old has gone, the new has come!" (2 Corinthians 5:17, *NIV*). New life in Christ means new motivation, new priorities, new hope—new everything! How has knowing Jesus changed you?

Barb plugged away at the details of the painting. Most of the Web sites had the same information, but she kept on searching, and every now and then she'd find a useful nugget that she could use to search some more.

One site said that the little girl in the painting was a neighbor of Benton's when he lived in Kansas City, and that some of his personal notes referred to her as Catherine. Barb dug further to see if she could unearth a last name, but nothing turned up.

She went in to talk about it with her mom again. "The girl's name was Catherine."

"A very common name."

"I wish I could find out her last name."

"You'd probably have to discover her married name, too. But there are ways."

"How?"

"Genealogy Web sites. They might tell you something."

"What's genealogy?"

"Who your ancestors are—family trees, things like that."

"But I'd have to find out a last name first?"

"Probably."

Barb went off determined to find out this bit of data. Finally, she thought of the most obvious place: the museum itself.

When you have a question about your math homework, whom do you ask—a teacher, or your little brother? If you want to find out the time that a movie is showing in the local theater, do you ask a nurse, or call the theater? When it comes to getting your questions answered, you must carefully choose where to get your information. The Bible says, "Get all the advice and instruction you can, and be wise the rest of your life" (Proverbs 19:20). Who are the people from whom you learn the most?

MYSTERY OF THE
GIRL IN THE
PAINTING

"I'll tell you what I know from the documentation we received with the painting," Paige Lincoln from the museum of art told Barb. "But that's not much. That's why we're having the contest—to see if anyone can help fill in the information we don't have."

"Great," Barb said.

"Benton didn't always leave a lot of details about his paintings. But you might try the Thomas Hart Benton house in Kansas City. They might have something."

Another clue. Barb looked up the phone number and called the house. A man named Davis answered. "I know we have some of Benton's personal papers," he said. "But it will take a while to go through them. Can you call back in a few days?"

"Thanks." Like tiny pieces of a huge puzzle, Barb got information one bit at a time. It required Internet searching, phone calls, and trips to the library. Soon she was quite well known around town as the "sleuth" on the trail of the girl in the painting. People were always nice, and they were willing to help her solve the mystery. Whenever she seemed to hit a snag, someone would encourage her not to give up and send her in a different direction.

People are often willing to help, and many times a group can do what a single person cannot by bouncing ideas off each other and cooperating. Solomon wrote, "Plans go wrong for lack of advice; many counselors bring success" (Proverbs 15:22). When was the last time you benefited from the wisdom of a group?

When Barb called Mr. Davis at the Thomas Hart Benton house back, he was excited to talk to her. "I found something! A reference to Catherine Sawyer," he told Barb. "She may be the girl in the painting. Mr. Benton's notes refer to her as an eight-year-old, which seems about right for the girl with the pail. The notes are dated 1936, which is also consistent with the painting. He mentions Catherine in connection to two other paintings, but we're not sure whether it's the same Catherine or a different one. We'd have to see the other two paintings to know."

"Those paintings are lost?" Barb asked.

"Well, they were owned by a Samuel Teuse. He died, though, and we have no records."

Barb thanked him. "The only thing that links them together is the name Catherine. Wouldn't it be amazing if she's still alive? She could help solve the mystery."

"Your genealogy will help there," Mr. Davis said. "Let us know what you find out."

Barb went back to her computer, ready to dig deeper. She started on some genealogy Web sites, but then someone told her that the courthouse might have records of a marriage.

The Bible is full of records—genealogies of God's people in the Old Testament, records of armies, lands allocated to different groups, and census counts. Records are important in Scripture.

However, in one sense, the Bible says records are not important, and people should not keep them: "Love is patient, love is kind. It does not envy, it does not boast, it is not proud. It is not rude, it is not self-seeking, it is not easily angered, it keeps no record of wrongs" (1 Corinthians 13:4, 5, *NIV*). When you are wronged, are you tempted to keep a record? Ask God to help you to let go of past hurts.

MYSTERY OF THE
GIRL IN THE
PAINTING

On a genealogy Web site, Barb hit pay dirt. She found out that Catherine Sawyer married Luke Hempstead after World War II.

Her jaw dropped. Catherine Hempstead? She knew a Catherine Hempstead—could it—no! It couldn't be! "Mom, Mom!" she shouted. "Come quick!"

Mom raced up to Barb's room in an instant. "What is it? What's wrong?" she asked in a panicky voice. "Are you hurt?"

"No—not hurt, Mom, but shocked! I can't believe it. The little girl in the painting—her name is Catherine Sawyer Hempstead. Catherine Hempstead."

Mom's eyes widened. "Catherine Hempstead? You mean like Miss Katie? Our Miss Katie?"

Miss Katie had been the teacher of the third grade Sunday school class at their church for over 40 years. Every child who grew up in the congregation knew Miss Katie as a wonderful, friendly, loving, and soft-spoken elderly lady. But the girl in the painting?

"Maybe," Barb said. "What was Miss Katie's husband's name?"

"Well . . . I don't know," Mom said. "She's been a widow for so long, I don't remember. And nobody's ever called her Mrs. Hempstead—she's been Miss Katie for as long as we've been at the church."

If you were the subject of a famous painting, would you tell people about it? If you accomplished something important, would you want to be recognized? It's natural to want the recognition you deserve. But there's a fine line between being proud of some accomplishment, and being arrogant in general. Remember this verse from the book of James: "Humble yourselves before the Lord, and he will lift you up" (James 4:10, *NIV*).

Barb called the church office. "This is Barb Newcomb. Could you please tell me Miss Katie's husband's name?"

"Miss Katie Hempstead? Well, I'm not sure. Let me look that up. Can you hold on a minute?"

Barb smiled at her mom. If it were true, what a fantastic story.

"I've got it," the voice came back on the phone. "It's Luke. Luke J. Hempstead."

Barb took a deep breath. "Thanks, thanks so much," and she hung up. "It's her," Barb told her mom breathlessly. "Miss Katie is the girl in the painting! What should I do next?"

"Why don't you call her?" Mom asked.

Later that day, Barb and her mother sat with Miss Katie in her living room. "I always knew the day would come when someone would connect me to that painting," she said. "But I never thought it would be someone I knew—and a young person at that!"

"How did this happen?" Barb's mother asked Miss Katie. "How come you never told anyone your story?"

"Well, I never thought it was all that important. Somebody painted my picture. He got the fame he deserved. I always thought the artist was the important one—not the subject."

"Well, do you mind if I tell the museum?" Barb asked. "I'll share the contest prize with you."

"Nonsense!" Miss Katie said. "You did all the research. You deserve the prize. And it's fine with me if you tell the museum. It's been my secret for years, but I guess it's time to share it."

"There is a time for everything, a season for every activity under heaven. . . . A time to be quiet and a time to speak up" (Ecclesiastes 3:1, 7b). How do you decide when to keep quiet, and when to speak up?

20
Day 1

MYSTERY OF THE
SWIPED CDS

Laura met Shyla at the door and they both headed up the stairs to Laura's room. "Whazzup?" Laura said to her best friend.

"Nothing much. We're going on a trip next week."

"To where?"

"Hawaii."

"Wow, really? Hawaii. That is so cool. I wish I could go."

"Yeah."

Laura opened the door. Her room looked like a picture from a decorating magazine, with posters on the walls and everything in its place. Laura kept everything neat. Shyla was just the opposite. Often when Shyla came for a visit, Laura had to spend 20 minutes just cleaning up after she left.

"Want to play a game?" Shyla asked.

"No. I want to play you my new CD." Laura went to the stereo and took out the CD. "Listen to this. You'll go nuts."

A rock band began playing with a clear female voice in the lead. Laura told about how they were new and getting popular. The girls listened and talked, and had some cookies. Laura went to put on another CD after the first one was over, but when she opened the case, it was empty.

"What happened to my CD?" she asked Shyla. "I always put them back in their cases. Could someone have stolen it?"

Laura might have been mistaken, but since she was so neat, her fear about a theft was realistic.

Unfortunately, our world is full of people who steal things from others. What does the Bible say about stealing? The eighth of the Ten Commandments is this: "Do not steal" (Exodus 20:15). But people steal, and many times they never get caught. What do you think you would do if you were Laura?

Laura quickly looked through some of her other favorite CDs. They were all gone, the cases empty. "What is going on?" Laura said, a tone of panic in her voice.

Shyla tried to help. "Maybe your mom took them. You're always saying that she doesn't like some of your music. Besides, why would someone else take them?"

"I'm going to ask my mom." Laura marched out the door and Shyla followed. They found Laura's mom in the kitchen preparing dinner.

"Mom, did you take some of my CDs?"

Mom looked up and squinted slightly. "Why would I do that? I like Barry Manilow, not your music."

"Yes, but a whole bunch of them are gone."

"You didn't put them somewhere else?"

"No, I always keep them in their cases. I don't like to get them scratched."

"OK," Mom said. "Go upstairs and list every CD that's missing. Maybe we can figure it out by what was taken and what was left."

Laura sighed. "I can't believe it. I can't."

When something bad happens in your life, you must remember to keep a cool head. It would be easy for Laura to start considering every person who might be the culprit and thinking hateful thoughts about them before she knew they were guilty. The Bible tells us to "Love your neighbor as yourself" (Matthew 22:39). That means not accusing people unnecessarily, or assuming nasty things about someone when you don't really know all the facts. You love them as you would like to be loved—thinking good, kind thoughts about each other.

Laura quickly discovered that of her 22 CDs, 13 were missing. Strangely enough, the ones that weren't taken were all Christian music, or children's CDs she'd listened to when she was younger.

"They took all the good ones!" Laura wailed.

"Let's write them down like your mom said," Shyla offered, picking up a pen.

With Shyla's help Laura quickly completed the list, and then remembered two other CDs that were missing. Apparently the thief had taken those too, along with the cases.

"I can't believe it. Why would someone do this to me?" Laura asked.

Shyla shook her head sadly. "Some people can't be trusted."

"When could they have done it?" Laura thought back. "I know! Mom's party!" she cried.

"Right," Shyla said. "That would have been easy."

The previous week Laura's parents had thrown a party for people in the neighborhood. Lots of people came, and wandered in and out of the house as they enjoyed a cookout.

"Someone might have done it during the party," Laura said. "I haven't played anything but this new CD since then."

She rushed out of the room with the list.

"Where are you going?"

"To get a list of all the guests from my mom."

Laura really is getting somewhere now. She has narrowed down the list of suspects to the ones most likely to have taken the CDs. A Scripture verse in the book of James tells us what to do when we have a problem: "If you need wisdom—if your want to know that God wants you to do—ask him, and he will gladly tell you. He will not resent your asking" (James 1:5).

Laura, Shyla, and Mom sat down at the kitchen table. Mom began reeling off the names of the people who came to the party. They eliminated the adults, and then children who were too young to have ventured into Laura's room alone. Soon Laura had a list of four boys and three girls who might have wanted to take the CDs.

"What now?" Laura asked.

Mom glanced at Shyla, then said, "What do you think?"

"Maybe we should pray about it," Laura answered. "I don't want to hurt anyone's feelings."

"You know, you could just go and buy replacements for all the CDs," Shyla suddenly said.

Laura shook her head. "They were all more than 10 dollars each! I don't have that much money."

"Let's keep our focus," Mom said. "Go ahead and pray, Laura."

They bowed their heads and Laura prayed, "Jesus, please help me to do this wisely. I don't want to hurt people who aren't involved. But I do want to get my CDs back. Amen."

She looked up. "Should I start calling these people now?"

Mom looked thoughtful. "Let's think about it awhile first. We don't want to accuse people without a reason."

"OK. But I'm already missing those CDs."

Mom touched her hand. "God will help us, honey. Just be patient."

Psalm 37:7 says, "Be still in the presence of the Lord, and wait patiently for him to act." Sometimes you have to give God time. He won't do some things immediately because other events and situations have to fall into place. How can you use your time waiting? Pray. Tell the Lord how you feel. Let him speak to your heart. God will help.

MYSTERY OF THE
SWIPED CDS

Shyla seemed a little uncomfortable and quickly got ready to leave. She said goodbye and wished Laura well with the CD problem.

After she left, Laura helped Mom finish fixing dinner. "Shyla sure left in a hurry," she said. "Do you think she felt strange when we prayed with her? It's something we've never done with her before. Should I have asked her if it was OK?"

"Maybe," Mom said, "but we've never hidden the fact that we're Christians. Maybe she'll feel like talking about it the next time you see her."

At dinner, everyone discussed the missing CDs. Dad thought Laura might just have to let them go. Laura didn't much like that answer. Her older brother Greg said that the music was all lame anyway, and she should listen to some decent stuff. Laura *really* didn't like that answer, but before she could think of a cutting remark about her brother's favorite music, Mom spoke: "I've thought about it and I think you should call each of the people on the list. Be very gentle about it. Do not accuse or get angry. Ask each person if they happened to 'borrow' some CDs from you that they intended to return. That would give them an easy answer without admitting to being a thief."

"That sounds good," Laura said, and she went to the phone.

It's always wise to be gentle with people when you have to ask a tough question, especially one as sensitive as Laura's situation. The question has to be asked, but couching it in kind, understanding terms will help the other person to be less hostile or defensive.

In his Sermon on the Mount, Jesus said, "God blesses those who are gentle and lowly, for the whole earth will belong to them" (Matthew 5:5).

Laura started with Cassie, who seemed chipper and friendly. She was in the sixth grade like Laura, but not in her class.

"What's up?" Cassie asked.

"I have a problem, Cassie. I'm missing a bunch of CDs that I kept in my room. My mom thought someone at the party might have borrowed them. Did you see anyone going up to my room alone at the party last Friday?"

Cassie paused to think. "I was mostly outside with all the other people," she answered. "I only came in once to use the bathroom on the first floor. Sorry, I'm afraid I don't know."

Laura checked Cassie off her list and called Briley. Briley told Laura she hadn't seen anything or gone upstairs. "My mom doesn't let me snoop," she said with a laugh. "I like to look around, but my mom always makes me ask for permission."

"Good thought," Laura said, checking off Briley.

The next call was to Beth: "Yeah, Laura, I went in the house with Shyla and she asked me if I wanted to see your bedroom. Shyla showed me around and even showed me a couple of your CDs. But I heard someone outside call me and I had to go. Shyla stayed behind and said she wanted to write you a note."

Laura drew in breath. There had been no note from Shyla after the party. She decided to hurry upstairs and look around again. But she found nothing.

She went downstairs with a heavy heart and a sick feeling in her stomach. She found Mom in the family room.

Could Shyla have taken the CDs? How deceitful she had been, acting as if she was just as interested in solving the mystery as anyone. The Bible tells us the source of dishonesty: "The human heart is most deceitful and desperately wicked. Who really knows how bad it is?" (Jeremiah 17:9).

MYSTERY OF THE
SWIPED CDS

After Laura spilled out the story, Mom looked concerned and upset. "Has Shyla ever done anything like this before?" she asked.

"I don't think so. But we've just been friends this year. I guess this officially ends our friendship. I never want to speak to her again."

"Don't write her off so fast," Mom warned. "You don't have all the facts. I think you should see if you can save the friendship. Just remember how you feel knowing Jesus forgives you when you sin. Ask him to help you say the right things to Shyla."

At Shyla's house, her mother said, "Go on up to her room, Laura. She's working on something."

Laura was amazed at how easy it was. She went up, knocked on the door, and Shyla called, "Come in."

The moment she saw Laura, she jumped up and stood in front of her stereo, as if she knew what Laura was there for.

"I talked to Beth," Laura said.

For a second, Shyla looked stricken and broken. Then she burst into tears. "I'm sorry. I'm so sorry. It was so stupid—"

Laura felt a bunch of emotions—sadness, and some anger at Shyla's betrayal, but also sympathy, and forgiveness. Shyla seemed genuinely sorry, and Laura's heart went out to her.

Shyla stammered, "Can—can you ever forgive me?"

Lord, Laura prayed silently, *Is this how you feel when I ask for your forgiveness?* She gave Shyla a hug. "I do forgive you. And our friendship is worth more than some CDs. But next time, just ask me, and I'll let you borrow them, OK?"

In a very difficult situation, Laura followed Scripture: "You must make allowance for each other's faults and forgive the person who offends you. Remember, the Lord forgave you, so you must forgive others" (Colossians 3:13).

Sin destroys relationships. Forgiveness restores them.

Sandi saw the man that afternoon as she and her mother drove home from getting a haircut. "Look at that guy," Sandi said.

"What about him?"

"He has tattoos all over his arms."

"Lots of people do."

"But why's he digging there?"

"Maybe he's from a road crew."

Sandi turned to watch him all the way to the next street, which was where their house stood. When she got out, she thought she might walk over and get a better look.

Mom watched her. "I don't think so," she said.

"What's wrong with just looking?"

Mom put her hands on her hips. "What do you think?"

"He's a stranger. He's big and strong. He has tattoos. And he might be a serial killer," Sandi said with a bored tone in her voice.

It's natural to be curious about people, especially people who are different from you. However, you must be cautious when it comes to strangers. The Bible gives instructions for how to live in a world full of sinful people: "So be careful how you live, not as fools, but as those who are wise. Make the most of every opportunity for doing good in these evil days. Don't act thoughtlessly, but try to understand what the Lord wants you to do" (Ephesians 5:15-17).

"Can I just walk by like I'm on my way somewhere?"

Mom cocked her head. "Why don't you call Sherrie and see if she'll go with you? I'd feel better about that."

They went inside and Sandi went right to the phone. "Sherrie there?" she said in Mom's hearing.

When Sherrie answered, Sandi said, "Hey, there's this strange guy over by the farmer's field. He's digging a hole. Wanna come with me and see him up close? He's full of tattoos."

Sandi hung up. "She's always ready for a mystery."

"I know," Mom said. "That's what I worry about with you two."

Fifteen minutes later Sherrie stood in their foyer. Their house was on the edge of a suburban area, and there was a large farmer's field where the tattooed man had been digging. The street that went by him wasn't used much.

Before the girls left, Sandi's mother gave them a warning: "Please be discreet, girls. The man's not a sideshow attraction. Don't bother him while he works, and don't call attention to yourselves."

"We'll be careful," Sandi agreed, and she and Sherrie headed down the driveway.

"What do you think he could be doing?" Sandi asked when they were out of earshot.

"Oo-eeee-ooooo!" Sherrie imitated scary music. "Maybe he's digging up a dead body," she said, raising her eyebrows suspiciously.

Have you ever heard the old expression, "There's safety in numbers"? When you're away from home it's always wise to take a friend.

Solomon, the world's wisest man, described the advantages of companionship. Read Ecclesiastes 4:9-12 and discover four specific benefits of doing things with a friend.

As the girls neared the place where the man was working, Sherrie said, "How will we work this? Should we just walk by?"

"Yeah. I don't really want to talk to him yet."

"OK. Don't go too close."

"Close enough to see what the tattoos are all about."

They shuffled along. Sandi's heart beat a little harder with each step. Soon they were less than 25 feet away.

"Talk about something," Sandi whispered, "so he doesn't think we're snooping."

Sherrie said, "Have you seen that new movie yet about the teenagers with—"

She stopped there and Sandi waited. "Yeah, I liked her braces."

"Braces?"

"You know. The heroine, what was her name?"

"Sally. Yeah, Sally."

Sandi couldn't help it. She giggled. Now they were less than 10 feet away, walking on the macadam road. She hadn't thought about it, but now she realized they should have crossed to the other side. Too late now.

The man stopped digging when they reached him, leaned on his shovel and looked at them.

The only place in the Bible where tattoos are mentioned is Leviticus 19:28: "Never cut your bodies in mourning for the dead or mark your skin with tattoos, for I am the Lord." Some Christians believe that they should not get tattoos, even now, because of this Scripture.

Other Christians read this Scripture as a specific instruction to Israel in the Old Testament. God wanted his people to be different. He didn't want Israel to pick up certain pagan habits and customs, so he forbade them. Ask your parent or another adult how they feel about tattoos today in light of this Scripture.

21
Day 4

MYSTERY OF THE
TATTOOED MAN

The man smiled. His front teeth were silver and several others were missing.

"Hi, ladies," he said, grinning at them.

"Um, hello," said Sandi, as she elbowed Sherrie.

"Right. Hello," Sherrie said awkwardly.

Sandi stopped and watched as the man resumed his digging. Both of his arms, up to the torn-off sleeves of his shirt, were full of tattoos. She could see a cross, a skull, one that said "Mother," and a naked woman leaning back on his bicep. On his other arm was a picture of someone stabbing another person with red blood gushing all over.

The man looked up. "You need somethin'?" he asked.

"N-no, I was just—"

Sandi looked at Sherrie. She added, "We were just walking along. We live around the corner."

Uh-oh. Should she have told him that? What if he came to her house when no one was home but her?

"Far down from the corner," she added, and ducked her head.

The man threw another shovelful of dirt over his shoulder.

To *discern* is to recognize or figure out. You can discern some things about a person's character by observing and talking to them, as the girls in this story are doing. Job 34:3, 4 says, "Just as the mouth tastes good food, the ear tests the words it hears.' So let us discern for ourselves what is right; let us learn together what is good."

The man didn't look up, so Sandi thought she'd ask him something. "You have a lot of tattoos," she said. "Do they—"

She stopped. What should she say? Then it came to her. "Do they hurt when you get them done?"

He looked up and grinned. "Some."

Sandi felt a little bolder. "Do they mean anything?"

"You want to see all of 'em?"

What would that mean? Surely he wouldn't just strip in front of them. Before she could answer, he pulled off his shirt. His whole chest was covered with tattoos. He held up his arms and turned around. "See?" he said.

They were all crazy tattoos: people's faces, some looking monsterish; some monsters too; a vampire and a werewolf. One looked like a map of the state of Missouri. There were words, too, like a list.

"Very interesting," Sandi said, not knowing what else to say. She looked at Sherrie.

Sherrie just looked back at her blankly.

"Is that a map of Missouri?" Sandi blurted suddenly.

The man looked down at his chest and grinned slyly.

Why do you think people get tattoos? For some, it's for the same reasons that they choose their clothing or hairstyle. They use their bodies to express themselves.

The Bible tells us that our bodies are special, and that they don't belong to us. Who does your body belong to? Read 1 Corinthians 6:19, 20 to find out.

MYSTERY OF THE
TATTOOED MAN

"Yeah," he said.

Sandi just stared. "And that list? Is that a list of people or something?"

"I wish," he said. "It's directions."

"Directions?" Sandi stared at him, astonished. She took a couple of steps toward him to look closer. She couldn't make out a single word.

"Can't read 'em, right?" he commented.

"No."

He stepped closer to them. Sandi steeled herself. Would he try to grab her?

No, he just pointed to the directions. "Look at 'em close," he said.

She studied them. "They're backwards," she said. "The letters are reversed."

"Right," he said. "So I can read 'em by lookin' in the mirror."

Sandi nodded. That made sense. How could he read them on his chest like that? He couldn't bend his head that much.

"So what are they directions to?"

When you meet someone different from you—strange, even— you may find them hard to like. But God sees all people as precious, and his Word gives this instruction: "So accept each other just as Christ has accepted you; then God will be glorified" (Romans 15:7).

"Tells me where the treasure is buried." He looked down at the hole. "Right here." Then he laughed a big, booming, scary laugh. Sherrie stepped back and Sandi forced herself not to move.

"Buried treasure?" Sandi asked. "Here?"

"Guy I met in prison. He did tattoos. Tattooed the directions right here to my chest, in case I ever got out and could go and find it."

He pushed the shovel deep into the dirt in the bottom of the hole. A blunt, hollow noise sounded. "That's it," he said.

The girls watched as he dug quickly. They said nothing as he unearthed a big steel box from the dirt.

He had it out on top of the ground, but it was locked with a padlock. He grabbed a hammer lying on the ground, hit the padlock a couple of times, and it broke. He pulled back the side latch and then lifted the top.

Both girls leaned closer. Soon they saw what was inside: a big teddy bear. The girls stared.

He threw the box back into the hole and started covering it.

"That's it," he said.

"What do you mean, 'that's it?'" Sandi asked boldly. "That's just a stuffed bear! What kind of treasure is a bear?"

The tattooed man finished filling the hole without comment. Then he picked up his tools and the bear and turned to leave. He smiled and held up the bear's arm. On it was a gold watch.

"Rolex," he said, and walked off.

A teddy bear treasure? The tattooed man certainly went to a lot of effort to obtain what he considered a treasure.

What do you consider a treasure? Jesus said that what you value determines how you think and act. Read his teaching about treasure in Matthew 6:19-21.

157

MYSTERY OF THE
LIGHTS IN THE
PARK

I saw it the first night I got to Gram's house: lights, reddish-purple, a ring of them. They were right over the park Gram told me not to go near while I was visiting. I stared at them, trying to figure out what they were: a new building project? kids with a tree house? UFOs?

I mean, I don't really believe in UFOs, but who knows? Maybe they are out there. Maybe they really exist. If the people who see them and talk about being abducted would just calm down, some of us would believe them.

The cats meowed like crazy, and Jester barked it up like he was being attacked by the cats. Naturally, I couldn't sleep. That was when I saw the lights hovering out there.

Every summer I spent a couple weeks visiting Gram at her old house. Now I'll admit, that house always gives me the spooks. There's just something about that old dark house late at night when I should be sleeping, but I'm awake thinking about what I want to do tomorrow. Her attic is at the top, and I can just imagine some weirdos from outer space camping up there. And the cellar is just dug out of dirt. Go down there and you're sure to catch a flea or two.

I watch a lot of spooky movies too at Gram's, all about UFOs and aliens and supernatural creatures, so it's easy to scare me. She has a great collection of videos, unlike my mom and dad.

Are there beings from another dimension in the world? The Bible identifies two categories. Read Hebrews 1:14 and Mark 1:34 to find out what they are.

Gram's farmhouse is a big old white clapboard place with a horde of rooms and a giant cellar. Gram has everything down there she ever bought, found, or received as a gift, I suppose, and I don't like going down there all alone to feed the cats. It's quiet and there are dark shadows. I can always see somebody with fangs behind one of those piles of junk, staring right at me, and slobbering for a neck bite.

Then there were those lights in the park that really had me spooked. What were they? Could it really be a UFO?

Then I noticed something else: the next morning when I came down to breakfast, Gram's scrambled eggs weren't laced with cheese the way she usually makes them. I said to her, "How come no cheese?"

She squinted at me with these big catlike eyes, and it made me shiver. "Oh, honey," she answered after too long a pause, "I—I ran out. Uh, you're staying out of the park, aren't you?"

"Yes, Gram."

"I don't want you going down there."

I should have asked her why, I guess, but I kept quiet. The way she stared at me was all squinty, like that witch from Hansel and Gretel measuring to see whether they were fat enough to eat.

The Bible describes the activity of angels and demons. Luke 4:41 says, "Some were possessed by demons; and the demons came out at his command, shouting, 'You are the Son of God.' But because they knew he was the Messiah, he stopped them and told them to be silent."

We see here that a demon can "possess" a person—live inside of them and hold them hostage—and that they know who Jesus is. But Jesus is more powerful than any demon, and they cannot remain if he sends them out.

I also noticed Gram hadn't been making cookies like she always did. I asked her about that too.

"Oh, I'm just too tired, dear. I'll make you some tomorrow."

But she forgot. And Gram never forgets anything! What was happening to her? Was she under the influence of aliens?

That next afternoon I took Jester for a long walk. He kept growling for no reason. No cars went by, and we didn't see any cats. He was growling and barking for all he was worth, and he turned in the direction of the park. What was going on? Did even Jester sense something?

I couldn't put my finger on any specific thing, but things didn't feel right. It seemed everywhere I looked, something was amiss. I decided now I had to do a real investigation and find out what was going on.

Two nights later, I decided to video the lights with the digital camera my dad gave me. He's always trying to make up for not seeing me much by giving me these big gifts.

The way of wisdom is always to seek the truth. Listening, observing, reading, and searching are tools for discovery. What kind of seeker of truth are you?

The Bible compares being wise with being rich. Which is better, and why? Read Ecclesiastes 7:11, 12 to find out.

I started the camera rolling, and I got everything. Purplish-red lights spinning and twirling and then hovering. It had to be something weird. I planned to show it to the police.

That was when I walked downstairs. I passed Gram's bedroom and the door was cracked. There stood Gram in the shadows, and from her left hand dangled something strange. I nudged the door a little, and suddenly I saw it: a long, clawed hand with huge, snaky, shiny fingernails. I gulped.

I caught a glimpse of Gram's face in the mirror. She was blue! The whites of her eyes stood out against the blue like two golf balls on her face.

Now I knew the horrible truth: Gram had been taken over by an alien, like in *Invasion of the Body Snatchers* or one of those old movies you see on cable. The aliens landed in the woods and sneaked up to the house, and now they'd gotten Gram! And next in line to be taken over was you know who.

I ran for my room and looked around for weapons. But all I had was my Swiss Army knife. I stuck it in my pocket and said, "Let's see what you got, aliens!"

Can you believe your eyes? If you saw your grandmother with huge shiny fingernails and a blue face, what would you think? Would you think of an alien abduction first, or would you think of another explanation?

An appropriate warning comes from 1 Timothy 4:7: "Do not waste time arguing over godless ideas and old wives' tales. Spend your time and energy in training yourself for spiritual fitness." Have you ever been fooled into believing something absurd? Ask God to help you think clearly and discriminate between wisdom and foolishness.

MYSTERY OF THE
LIGHTS IN THE PARK

My heart was pounding. I had to get to the police. But first I needed to check out the video.

I switched the camera to view mode. Nothing happened. When I hit MENU, it said, "Image unavailable." And then it hit me: the aliens had taken over my digital camera!

Now I was really scared.

I hurried out of the house. I found Jester in the back still tied up, but I checked him out. No blue snout. No long claws. He was still OK. As I retrieved the flashlight from the garage, I prayed that God would protect me. But I wasn't sure what he would do. He'd allowed the aliens to land in the first place and take over Gram. Would he protect me?

All right, I told myself. *You have to go to the park. Get one last piece of proof.*

You can always talk to God, no matter what. You don't have to worry about whether you're right, making sense, or worthy of his time. He loves you, no matter what. Remember Psalm 55:22: "Give your burdens to the Lord, and he will take care of you. He will not permit the godly to slip and fall." Do you trust in God's unconditional love?

Jester and I hurried off toward the park. Soon we found the trail I used to explore there. I shined the light on the ground, looking around for tracks.

We walked for what seemed an hour, but when I looked at my watch, only a few minutes had passed.

Then I saw the open area of the park. The lights were coming right down on top of me! I looked up. I gestured. I shouted, "Go away!" But they kept right on coming, hovering over me.

Were aliens going to let down a ladder and come and grab me? Or would they "beam me up" like they do on *Star Trek*?

I was about to scream. Jester was barking, and all these lights went on right in my face. They had nailed me!

"What are you doing here?" someone in a baseball cap and an undershirt yelled.

I could barely stammer, "Please don't hurt me."

"You were almost hit by the whirlaround."

I gasped. "What's going on?"

"We're setting up for a carnival."

I gulped. "I'm sorry," I stuttered. "I didn't know."

When you're afraid, it doesn't matter whether it's for a good reason or a bad reason. All you know is that you're afraid. But there are ways to avoid unnecessary fear: talking to a trusted adult, getting more information, asking questions. What do you do when you find you're in a bad situation?

The psalmist spoke of the comfort he knew because of God: "I wait quietly before God, for my hope is in him. He alone is my rock and my salvation, my fortress where I will not be shaken. My salvation and my honor come from God alone. He is my refuge, a rock where no enemy can reach me" (Psalm 62:5-7).

MYSTERY OF THE
LIGHTS IN THE PARK

Jester and I watched for the next half hour as they worked on the whirlaround. It was covered in lights, and they flashed in different patterns as the ride moved faster and slower. Then we went home.

When I stepped into the house Gram called to me: "That you, Jimmy?"

"Yeah, Gram."

She came downstairs. Her face was still blue! And the long clawed hand was dangling from her robe.

I almost screamed.

"What's the matter with your face?" I asked, leaning closer.

"Oh, this?" Gram touched her cheek. "This is cream to smooth out my wrinkles. I guess it looks a little strange. It doesn't bother you, does it?"

"And what happened to your—your hand?" I pointed to the snaky fingernails.

"Just my backscratcher. Isn't it funny? Do you want to use it?"

I wiped the sweat off my face. "Uh, no—thank you. A backscratcher." I smiled and started up the stairs. There was one last thing I had to check out: my camera. Yup, I had left it in "preview mode" instead of "video mode" so it never recorded while I was shooting. So everything was OK again. Summer vacation at Gram's would be fine after all.

Now if I would just stop imagining things, life would be great!

"Dear brothers and sisters, don't be childish in your understanding of these things. Be innocent as babies when it comes to evil, but be mature and wise in understanding matters of this kind" (1 Corinthians 14:20). Mature thinking will keep your imagination from running away with you. Are you being mature?

Erica was watching her favorite after-school TV show when the phone rang. She decided to let the answering machine get it. She was home by herself. Mom was out shopping or something, and had left her a note about starting dinner, but there was plenty of time for that.

The lady's voice was low, and she sounded scared. It was Nathan's mother, Mrs. Tombley. "Erica? . . . I was just calling to see if you've seen Nathan around. . . . He should be home by now, and we're pretty worried . . ."

Erica jumped up from the couch and grabbed the phone. "Mrs. Tombley? It's Erica. I'm here."

"Did Nathan come from school with all of you?"

"No, I haven't seen him."

"We're worried. I've called the police, and I'm concerned. Do you know where he might have gone?"

Erica thought about the benches near the fountain outside the big white church. Sometimes their friends would stop there when they were skating or riding their bikes. Since it was still light out, she said, "I'll go and take a look. Give me about a half hour."

Erica took off toward the white church. As she went, she thought of a couple other places that Nathan may have gone after school: the computer hub at the library with free Wi-Fi, or the game room at the community center where the gamers hung out.

It's always serious when a child is missing. Parents can be frantic. Did you know that Jesus was once missing when he was 12 years old? Read the account in Luke 2:41-52. How did Jesus get lost? Where did his parents find him? Since Jesus is God, he could take care of himself. He didn't need his parents' protection. Yet notice that the Bible says he obeyed them and submitted to their authority. Why do you think he did? What does that mean to you?

23
Day 2

"Nathan! Nathan! You there?" Erica called out as she approached the fountain. Nobody was there. She walked down to the library and looked through the windows of the computer hub. A bunch of kids were there, but not Nathan. Same with the community center. There were only two guys in the game room, and neither one was Nathan.

She took the path that came out above the farm where the kids sometimes played. Mr. Creston had a barn with some horses, and often he let the kids ride them. Erica walked up to the house. Mr. Creston answered the door.

"Have you seen Nathan?" Erica smiled, trying not to show how worried she was.

"No, not today. Sometimes he'll come and ride Jasper, or just spend some time taking care of him. Let's go out to the barn."

They both hurried to the barn. There they found Jasper in his stall with the reins and saddle hanging up in their usual place. "If I see him, I'll let you know," Mr. Creston told her.

Erica thanked him and hurried out again. This time she walked down the street where Nathan's friend, Johnny Waters, lived. She headed for Johnny's house.

"No, I haven't seen him since school," Johnny said. "I don't know where he could be. Do you want me to help look for him?"

"No," Erica answered. "I can do it."

Erica is acting out of concern for Nathan. The New Testament epistles have some instructions for Christians that apply in this case. Some people call them the "one another" commands, because they instruct Christians how to treat each other. One of them is Ephesians 4:2: "Be humble and gentle. Be patient with each other, making allowance for each other's faults because of your love."

Erica sat down on the curb to think. Had Nathan said anything about doing something that might be a little crazy? Had he mentioned any plans? She couldn't remember a thing.

Then she thought of the park. He might have gotten involved in a ball game. The park was always filled with people.

She started to jog down to the park. When she got there 15 minutes later, she was so out of breath she had to stop and lean against a post. She looked across the park. Several baseball games were going on. There were people cooking on grills. Little kids played on the playground equipment. She studied the ball field, but none of the players was Nathan. She headed for the batting team's dugout.

"Is Nathan Tombley in there?" she asked, stooping down at one end.

"Who?" someone said.

"Nathan Tombley?"

"Never heard of him."

Erica has spent a fair amount of time and energy searching for her friend Nathan. She must know Romans 12:9, 10: "Don't just pretend that you love others. Really love them. Hate what is wrong. Stand on the side of the good. Love each other with genuine affection, and take delight in honoring each other."

Who are friends in whom you take delight? How has God blessed you through friends?

MYSTERY OF THE
FRANTIC SEARCH

Erica walked all around all the ball fields looking for Nathan, but she came up with nothing. As she went, she came across different groups of people, and she asked, "Have any of you seen a kid walking around in a blue Royals shirt?"

"Lots of those," one man said. "What does he look like?"

"He'd be wearing a green John Deere hat, pudgy face, smiles a lot."

"I don't know. I haven't noticed anyone. But you can ask around."

Erica did just that, but no one had seen Nathan.

Walking to the edge of the park, Erica took one more scan around. Where on earth could he be? Why hadn't Nathan called by now? Why hadn't he told someone where he was going before he went?

She trudged along the street toward the Tombleys' house. Maybe he'd come home while she'd been searching. When she reached the house and knocked on the door, Mrs. Tombley answered. A police officer stood there with her.

"I'm beside myself," she said. "Have you seen him?"

Even though Erica couldn't care for Nathan as much as his family members, she has showed true love for him in the spirit of 1 John 4:9-12: "God showed how much he loved us by sending his only Son into the world so that we might have eternal life through him. This is real love. It is not that we loved God, but that he loved us and sent his Son as a sacrifice to take away our sins. Dear friends, since God loved us that much, we surely ought to love each other. No one has ever seen God. But if we love each other, God lives in us, and his love has been bought to full expression through us."

Erica went inside and listened as Mrs. Tombley explained what she knew. Erica thought over the school day. Did anything unusual happen? Just that fight in sixth grade, but Nathan wasn't involved in that. And then, Mrs. Wise had done that science experiment that exploded.

Wait! Didn't Nathan say something about staying after school to try it again? Yesssss!

"Mrs. Tombley, call the school. Nathan told me he might stay after with Mrs. Wise to try to redo an experiment."

Mrs. Tombley found the number in the phone book. She dialed and listened.

"It's just an answering machine. School is closed. He couldn't be there, could he?"

"A teacher could stay late; I know that."

"Maybe we'd better try there."

The police officer nodded. "I'll drive over. Do you want to come with me and show me where the room is?" he asked Erica.

"Sure."

The three of them went out to the cruiser and climbed in. Soon they were speeding to the school with the lights on and the siren blaring.

In a few minutes they stood at the school door.

In times of crisis, it's essential to help those who need it. Paul wrote to the Galatians, "For you have been called to live in freedom—not freedom to satisfy your sinful nature, but freedom to serve one another in love. For the whole law can be summed up in this one command: 'Love your neighbor as yourself'" (Galatians 5:13, 14). How can you serve God by serving your neighbor?

In spite of a thorough search of the school building, Nathan was still missing. Erica and Mrs. Tombley returned with the officer to the cruiser. He took Erica home first.

"You can just let me out at the corner," Erica offered. "My house is just two doors down."

"Thank you for all your searching," Mrs. Tombley said, her voice weak and shaky. "Please pray that Nathan will be safe, and that we will find him."

"I will. I promise." The officer opened the door so Erica could get out, and then he drove away with Mrs. Tombley.

As she walked along, someone came down the sidewalk toward Erica. It was Nathan! He was wet, and hair stood up in spikes all over his head. "Where have you been?" he shouted from a distance, before Erica could say anything.

"Huh?"

"I just stopped at your house. Your mom's really worried about you. She said she might call the police!"

Erica was stunned. "I was out looking for you!" she half-spoke, half-shouted at him. "Like everyone else!"

"What do you mean?" Nathan said.

"*You're* the one who's missing! You need to get home. Your mom is scared out of her mind!"

"Why?"

Sometimes people get lost—not physically, but spiritually. They may not know they're drifting in their walk with God. That's why "You must warn each other every day, as long as it is called 'today,' so that none of you will be deceived by sin and hardened against God" (Hebrews 3:13).

"Didn't you call her?" Nathan asked, a tremble in his voice.

"Why would I call her?" Erica responded.

His eyes went wide. "Didn't you read the note I put in your backpack?"

She stared at him. "What note?"

"Oh, no!" The color drained from his face, and Nathan took off running toward his house.

Erica ran inside her house and pounded up the stairs to her room. She found her backpack and rummaged through it. She could hear her mom's voice. "Erica? . . . Erica, come down here! Where have you been?"

Quickly, Erica found a note. She unfolded the paper and read it: *Erica—I have to babysit the Simpson kids after school. They have a pool. You should come over. We can swim and stuff.*

Call my mom to tell her. I forgot my cell, and Mrs. Simpson doesn't let me use her phone.

Erica sighed and put down the note. "Be right there, Mom!" she called. "I can explain!"

It was just like Nathan to do something like this. She texted him so he'd get her message on his cell phone:

U R A TOTAL GOOFBALL.

What a terrible mixup! Even though they meant no harm, both Nathan and Erica caused a lot of distress for others. The Bible calls Christians to "Think of ways to encourage one another to outbursts of love and good deeds" (Hebrews 10:24). How can you put this Scripture into practice this week?

MYSTERY OF THE
STRIP MALL
BULLIES

Youngie and Westurn walked up to the strip mall to buy some fishing worms. "This time I'm catching a 12-incher," Youngie said to his friend.

Westurn was equally boastful. "I'll beat you."

They came around the corner to the little sidewalk going the back way to the mall. They took this walk several times a week, so they never thought much about it being dangerous.

But when they walked across the back lot macadam, two boys they knew from school stepped out to meet them. O'Donnell, the sixth grade bully, stepped out in front of them, holding up his fist. Morgan, his little mascot, was smaller, although known to be a fighter.

"What're you guys doing here?" O'Donnell asked with contempt, flicking his half-spent cigarette onto the blacktop.

"What's it to you?" Youngie said nervously. "It's a free country."

"Stay outta here," O'Donnell said. "Go around the long way, or your face meets my fist."

It's never a good idea to look for trouble, but there are people who seem to make it a pastime. The book of Proverbs speaks of such people: "Anyone who loves to quarrel loves sin; anyone who speaks boastfully invites disaster" (Proverbs 17:19). If you can possibly avoid it, don't hang out with people who invite disaster. Try to be a peacemaker whenever you can.

"What is with O'Donnell?" asked Westurn as the two stepped into the sports and fishing store.

"He's always looking for a fight," Youngie answered. "We better not go home that way."

"Why shouldn't we?" Westurn said.

"I don't want to get into a fight with him. You saw what happened with Collins, didn't you? He had two black eyes."

"All we have to do is walk away."

"He might come after us."

The night crawlers were in the live bait aisle, and they bought a little dirt-filled cup of them. They paid $2.88 and walked out.

"Let's just go the long way," Youngie said. "I don't need this."

"But it'll look like we're cowards."

Youngie sighed. "OK, but I am not taking on O'Donnell or his little mascot."

They shuffled along slowly until they reached the corner that led to the back lot area. Sure enough, O'Donnell stepped out. "I thought I told you not to come back here."

"We're just going home," Westurn said. "We have the right."

O'Donnell advanced on them.

"Let's go," Westurn said, and both boys tore away to the path between the trees.

There's no shame in running from a fight, especially when the person against you is bigger and more experienced. David knew what it was like to be chased by enemies, and he always talked to God about it. Psalm 59:3, 4 records one of his prayers: "They have set an ambush for me. Fierce enemies are out there waiting, though I have done them no wrong, O Lord. Despite my innocence, they prepare to kill me. Rise up and help me! Look on my plight!" David knew he could depend on God for help. Do you?

MYSTERY OF THE
STRIP MALL
BULLIES

When they reached the street, both boys stopped to look back, panting. O'Donnell had disappeared.

"Guess we showed him," Westurn said with a laugh.

"Yeah, we're really tough guys."

They walked home, laughing and joking about the whole thing. But as they reached Youngie's house, he turned and said, "Why was O'Donnell so mad? Why should he care about two kids walking down a path by the shopping center?"

"Maybe we should find out," Westurn said.

"Let's dump this stuff and go back. We can sneak in behind the trees and see what's going on. O'Donnell has been in trouble before."

The boys went inside and Westurn saw it was past five o'clock. His mom would have dinner ready soon, but there was enough time to run back and check things out.

Then they hurried back to the shopping center and hid among the trees and shrubs that shielded the back lot from the houses. Both boys watched for about 30 minutes.

O'Donnell sat on one of the loading docks talking to his little friend and laughing. Just as Youngie was about to say it was time to go, three more boys walked up to them.

"One bad apple spoils the whole bunch." Have you ever heard that expression? It's true of fruit, and unfortunately, it's true of people as well. When one apple rots, the apples next to it begin to rot too. And when one person makes a bad decision, he can negatively influence a whole group. While we wish it were so, good apples don't prevent bad apples from going bad, and good people often can't prevent others from getting into trouble. The Bible puts it this way: "Do not be misled: 'Bad company corrupts good character'" (1 Corinthians 15:33, *NIV*). Ask God to help you choose friends who will help you do good.

STRIP MALL BULLIES

"Who are those guys?" Westurn asked.

"I know the tall one's O'Donnell's big brother," Youngie said. "The other two are high school guys. I think they dropped out."

"Something tells me they're up to no good. I mean, why would they meet here instead of at home or in the park?"

Youngie sucked his lip, watching. "What do crooks say when they're looking around a place, planning something?"

"Casing the joint?"

"Yeah. Maybe they're doing that."

"Let's watch them for a few more minutes."

The five toughs walked around the back lot, looking into places, stopping and talking. The boys couldn't hear what they were saying.

"What do they use this area for?" Westurn asked.

"I think trucks come in here, to unload stuff, or maybe even pick it up."

Westurn studied the area. "Do you think they could be planning to steal something?"

"When do the trucks come in?"

Westurn looked at his watch. "I think at night."

People hide in the dark when they're doing wrong so they won't be seen. The Bible compares good with light and evil with darkness. "For you are all children of the light and of the day; we don't belong to darkness and night. . . . Night is the time for sleep and the time when people get drunk" (1 Thessalonians 5:5, 7). What are characteristics of "children of the light"?

"You want to sneak back here tonight and see if they're doing anything?" Youngie said.

"I thought you were the one who wanted to avoid O'Donnell."

"Yeah, but maybe we could catch them. Report them to the police. Maybe there'll even be a reward." Youngie looked at his friend and raised his eyebrows up and down in enticement.

"OK. But I have to be in by 10."

"Let's do it."

They crawled back to the edge of the trees, then jumped up and ran two whole blocks before they stopped. When they got home, they talked about what they could bring. Westurn brought his flashlight, his Bowie knife, and a camera. Youngie thought the most important thing was binoculars and his mom's cell phone.

"What should I tell her about what we're doing?"

"Just say you're on a mission of mercy with me."

"OK, but I'm not lying about it."

"Fine with me."

When other people around you are making bad choices, you may be tempted to follow them. Making good decisions can be hard work. David confessed to God: "I will be careful to live a blameless life—when will you come to my aid? I will lead a life of integrity in my own home. I will refuse to look at anything vile and vulgar. I hate all crooked dealings; I will have nothing to do with them. I will reject perverse ideas and stay away from every evil" (Psalm 101:2-4). Ask God to help you avoid temptation and to reject evil when you see it.

The boys hiked up the street to the shopping center, and took their old position under the trees. Both looked through the binoculars, but there was no sign of any of the teenagers they'd seen before.

"Maybe they gave up. Or maybe it's not tonight," Westurn said.

"Let's give it till 9:30. Then we really do have to go."

The boys settled down, munching on chips and bananas as they kept their eyes on the back lot from the far right to the left. Then about 8:00 a truck pulled in. It backed up to the dock at the electronics store. The boys watched as the driver let down the front legs of the trailer, then detached the cab from it. He pulled away, leaving the trailer parked in place, but unopened.

"If it's electronics stuff, that would certainly be the stuff to steal," Youngie said.

"But no one's here."

"Just sit tight. That's what private investigators have to do."

"Oh, is that what we are now?" Westurn asked with a grin.

Night was falling. Nothing moved. Only an occasional bird call or dog's bark broke the quiet. Both boys fidgeted, obviously bored.

Then there was the sound of subdued voices.

Avoiding evil and doing the right thing is important. The apostle Paul gave this reason: "Another reason for right living is that you know how late it is; time is running out. Wake up, for the coming of our salvation is nearer now than when we first believed. The night is almost gone; the day of salvation will soon be here. So don't live in darkness. Get rid of your evil deeds. Shed them like dirty clothes. Clothe yourselves with the armor of right living, as those who live in the light" (Romans 13:11, 12).

Sure enough, it was O'Donnell and his friends. They whispered among themselves and paced along the edge of the trees, walking right in front of Youngie and Westurn. They had a crowbar, a sledgehammer, and some other tools.

"Quick, guys, quick." Big O'Donnell talked into a cell phone. "It's now. Hurry."

A pickup truck appeared, running slowly and quietly and backed up to the end of the trailer. Two guys with tools jumped into the bed of the pickup and started pounding on the latch of the trailer. There was a loud snap when they broke it, and soon they were pulling boxes out of the trailer and stacking them in the pickup.

"Come on," whispered Youngie. "We've seen enough."

They crept back out of the trees and hurried to the road. Youngie pulled out the cell phone and dialed 911.

Moments later, two police cars with lights flashing pulled up. The teenagers tried to run, but four officers jumped out, guns drawn. Soon they had them all in handcuffs.

Youngie said, "I think we fade into the sunset. I don't like the idea of O'Donnell knowing we sprung the trap."

Westurn nodded. "Right. Let's go home."

Sometimes when you do the right thing, nobody but you and God will ever know. You won't be recognized or rewarded. In times like those, you may say with the psalmist, "God has spoken plainly, and I have heard it many times: Power, O God, belongs to you; unfailing love, O Lord, is yours. Surely you judge all people according to what they have done" (Psalm 62:11, 12). God will reward you for doing good, but you may have to wait to receive it. Can you be patient and trust him?

Lonetta and her family had looked forward to this camping trip for months. Now they headed out for Yellowstone. They'd all heard and read so much about it, but had never been there. Lonetta looked forward to seeing Old Faithful and the bears, as well as going fishing for cutthroat trout, one of the most flavorful fish of the trout family.

The family traveled the eight hours from their home to Wyoming and soon passed through one of the main gates into the park. They located a campsite and began pitching their tent. While Dad, Lonetta, and her little brother Azrael got everything situated, Mom started a fire and began frying hamburgers, baking sweet potatoes, and heating up a pot of beans for dinner.

Everyone sat down to a great meal. Even with the mosquitoes buzzing about and the warnings about feeding bears posted everywhere, it looked to be a good time.

Lonetta read one of her mysteries before bed, then turned in. Mom and Dad sat out by the fire talking. Azrael had hiked down a short trail near their campsite. She sat down on her sleeping bag and reached for her comb.

It was gone.

Vacations with your family can be special, even if you don't travel far away. God created the family, and gives instructions in the Bible as to how families are to treat each other. Which of the Ten Commandments deals with family relationships? If you don't know, read Exodus 20:1-17 to find out.

MYSTERY OF THE
COMB AND SPATULA

Lonetta searched everywhere: under her sleeping bag, on the other bags, in the cooler, even. Finally she stepped out of the tent in her pajamas. "Mom, did you use my comb?"

Mom looked around at her. Their Coleman lamp lit up the campsite, and Lonetta had another in the tent.

"No, but I saw it there on your sleeping bag with your other things when I was in the tent a while ago."

"I know. I put it right there."

"Look in my toiletries bag," Mom said. "I might have thought it was mine and absently put it in there."

Lonetta walked back into the tent and checked her mom's bag. Then her father's. Finally, she took the lamp and walked around outside the tent. She found nothing.

"It was a big red comb, Mom. Yours is blue."

"I know. That's why I thought—well, go ahead and use mine. If we have to, we'll go to the trading post and get a new one tomorrow."

"OK." Lonetta combed her hair while looking in her little compact mirror. Then she turned off the lamp and lay down on the sleeping bag and closed her eyes.

She had a fitful sleep, dreaming of all kinds of monsters and animals traipsing through the tent during the night.

When have you had fun times with your parents? Do they ever tell you that they're proud of you? Most parents and grandparents take pride in their children. But children can be proud of parents too, according to Proverbs 17:6: "Grandchildren are the crowning glory of the aged; parents are the pride of their children." For what reasons can you be proud of your parents?

The next morning, Lonetta thought no more about her lost comb. They all went out to one of the lakes and fished most of the day, catching six cutthroat trout. That night, they dined on the filets, then took a long walk down the road by the campsites. Lonetta stopped at one and made friends with a girl named Janette, and they promised to link up the next morning for a walk around the lake.

Everyone settled down for a nice evening of reading and talking. Mom had left the dishes out earlier and began cleaning them up. Suddenly she asked, "Did anyone see our spatula?"

Everyone looked up.

"Not me," said Azrael.

"Me, neither," Dad answered.

"I'll help you look," Lonetta volunteered. "First my comb, now the spatula. What's going on?"

"Methinks there's a thief in the neighborhood," Mom said.

"Who could it be?"

"Really, now. Why would anyone want a used comb and a dirty spatula?"

Do you have good memories of times spent with your parents? Have your parents made you happy? Have you made them happy? Proverbs 23:24, 25 describes family happiness: "The father of godly children has cause for joy. What a pleasure it is to have wise children. So give your parents joy! May she who gave you birth be happy."

MYSTERY OF THE
COMB AND
SPATULA

The family visited Old Faithful the next morning, and then went shopping for souvenirs. Dad and Azrael went down to the lake to fish again and came back with one 17-incher that Azrael had hauled in. They all dined on fresh fish again.

Lonetta, though, had searched the campsite and the nearby woods. She stayed on the lookout for an errant bear, fox, or other animal that might like to collect shiny things. She found nothing, although she did pick up a rusty fish knife in the woods that she gave to Azrael. He soon had it cleaned up and in working condition.

That evening, Lonetta stretched fishing line in three lengths around the tent. She tied a little bell she'd found at the trading post to each section. If anything came around, it would jingle the bell and alert her to its presence.

She settled down on her sleeping bag in the early evening and listened. She felt on edge, but heard no bell.

By the time her mom came into the tent, Lonetta was frustrated. "I set a trap, Mom! Why couldn't I catch the thief in the act?"

"Animals are pretty smart, and they have to be sneaky to survive," Mom answered. "It may have caught your scent from the tent and run away," she said.

"I'm not gonna quit," Lonetta said solemnly. "I'm going to solve this mystery."

It seems as though Lonetta has a good relationship with her family. What does God want for families? He wants them to love and respect each other, learn and work together, have fun together, and love and serve him together. Read Ephesians 6:1-4 to discover what God expects of children, and what he expects of parents.

The following night Lonetta asked if she could stay behind at the campsite while her parents and Azrael went up to the lodge for a nighttime nature program.

"Surely you don't want to waste your time over a comb and a spatula?" Dad asked. "They're not important. Just come with us."

"It's a mystery, and I want to solve it. Please?" Lonetta begged.

"Suit yourself," said Dad. "But stay within sight of the tent. Don't go off by yourself into the woods."

Lonetta took a flashlight, and walked up a little hill overlooking their tent. She sat down next to a tree. As the sky grew darker and darker, her eyes adjusted, and she could see the whole campsite. But no intruder came.

The sky was clear, the air was cool, and Lonetta was tired. Soon she dozed off with her head against the tree.

She awoke with a start when she heard the bell. She jumped to her feet and ran to the tent. She checked each of the fishing lines carefully. It was the third one that had been tripped. She knew because the bell was missing.

Lonetta stood staring into the darkness. What could it be? Was it an animal? And if so, was it the thief? Even if she found it, would that explain what happened to the comb and spatula? Maybe this trap-setting wasn't such a good idea after all.

Suddenly, she heard the bell tinkle again, and from not far away.

She hurried off in the direction she thought she heard it.

Lonetta's parents could trust her to be alone. Have you earned your parents' trust? Listening and obeying is essential. "My child, listen and be wise. Keep your heart on the right course" (Proverbs 23:19).

MYSTERY OF THE
COMB AND
SPATULA

Lonetta looked all around. She stopped about a hundred feet from their tent, listening.

Nothing.

She took a few steps, then stopped, looked, listened. "Come on, bell, ring again," she whispered.

Tingle. Tingle.

She whipped around. There. She saw a glint of something in the beam of her flashlight. She walked slowly toward it. If there was an animal there, she didn't want to approach too quickly.

There it lay on the ground: the bell, half buried in a pile of leaves.

Lonetta stooped and picked up the bell, then held it up in the light. "Hey," she called into the darkness. "You want this? Come and get it."

She stood holding the bell.

"See it? Isn't it beautiful? Wouldn't you like to have it again for your little stash?"

Nothing happened. Then she had another idea. She stooped and put down the bell. "There. I'm leaving it for now. You want it? Come and get it. I won't disturb it. Just show yourself. I'll move away from it so you don't have to be afraid."

Lonetta's having quite an adventure on her family's vacation. They'll have many stories to tell when they get home.

God's desire is that families get along with each other. That doesn't happen all the time, though. Families can go through difficult times when nobody's happy. However, God still cares and wants all families to thrive. Even in bad times, it pleases him if children are obedient: "You children must always obey your parents, for this is what pleases the Lord" (Colossians 3:20).

Lonetta drew back into the woods, stopping next to a tree. She slipped behind it, turned off the flashlight, and waited.

"Come on," she whispered. "Don't be afraid. I'm not going to hurt you."

There was a rustling of leaves. *Rustle. Crunch. Rustle.*

She waited and watched. Something moved out there.

Tinkle. Tinkle.

It had the bell. She flicked on the flashlight. There it was, a hunched, hairy figure. What was it? A raccoon? A large squirrel?

She charged out after it. It scurried through the woods, the bell tinkling all the way in its mouth. Then suddenly, it disappeared. She lost it, until she saw the log—a large, hollowed-out log.

She stepped closer. "Easy. Easy now," she said out loud. "I'm not going to hurt you."

She reached the log and shined the light inside. Two large golden eyes stared back. A fox. It was a fox, up close, like she'd never seen. And there, scattered in and around the log, were the comb, the spatula, the bell, and a hundred other things.

Lonetta laughed. "Keep them," she said. "You deserve them. You've worked hard." She walked off for her tent, giggling all the way. She could hardly wait to tell her family!

The Bible says that when you respect your parents, you are showing love for God. "The Lord also said to Moses, 'Say this to the entire community of Israel: You must be holy because I, the Lord your God, am holy. Each of you must show respect for your mother and father, and you must always observe my Sabbath days of rest, for I, the Lord, am your God'" (Leviticus 19:1-3).

All of us—T.M., Jerry, Corrinne, Alan, and I—were walking up the road with nothing in sight but trees and the muddy trail of the parallel truck ruts. We had come back into these woods for adventure, but none of us had ever gone this far.

Coming around a bend, we suddenly spotted a lone, ramshackle house. It looked like it might collapse any second, with all the windows broken out, paint peeling, and shingles hanging off it at odd angles.

"And what have we here?" T.M. asked and stopped, striking the ground with his walking stick.

We gaped at the house and I got a better look at it. It stood off the road about a hundred feet, overgrown with weeds. The front screen door hung out, about to fall off its hinges. T.M. took a small pair of binoculars out of his backpack. He studied the house through them; then handed them around to everyone.

"All right. It's quite obvious," T.M. said, crouching down and drawing on the ground with his stick. "We approach straight in. Like this." He drew an arrow in the dirt. "If anyone's there, they'll know we mean no harm because we're not approaching it like we mean to cause trouble."

Corrinne stared at T.M. "You're going inside?"

In a parable Jesus told, he compared those who ignore his words to the builder of a house that collapses. "Anyone who hears my teaching and ignores it is foolish, like a person who builds a house on sand. When the rains and floods come and the winds beat against that house, it will fall with a mighty crash" (Matthew 7:26, 27). The wise builder builds on a foundation of solid rock. On what foundation are you building your life?

"Maybe," T.M. answered, standing up and rubbing out his diagram with his shoe. "The main thing is that this house could be a thieves' hideout. If not that, it could be haunted and we may have to do some ghostbusting before the morning is through. We have to find out what's there, don't you think?"

"Are you sure no one lives there?" Corrinne said, a tremble in her voice.

"Of course not," T.M. said. "That's what we have to find out. What lives there? Animal, vegetable, or mineral? Wolfman, Mummy, or that Phantom of the Opera dude?"

I knew T.M. was in one of his goofy moods, so I grinned and walked after him as he swaggered jauntily toward the house.

In a few seconds we stood at the front door of the house. We all stared at it, and I noticed my heart was pounding. Up close, it looked even worse than from a distance. Strange scratches were cut into the front door under the door handle as if some animal had tried to get in, and a troll was painted on the upper half of the door.

"What should we do?" Corrinne said.

T.M. answered, "Allow me to show you." He walked to the door and rapped with his walking stick. He yelled, "Oh ho! Anyone home? Looking for some kids to eat? I have several out here."

Corrinne cried, "T.M.!"

In the Bible, knocking on a door is a word picture for praying. "Keep on asking, and you will be given what you ask for. Keep on looking, and you will find. Keep on knocking, and the door will be opened. For everyone who asks, receives. Everyone who seeks, finds. And the door is opened to everyone who knocks" (Matthew 7:7, 8). In what way do you continue to "keep on knocking" in prayer, waiting for the door to be opened?

"Just making it enticing is all," T.M. explained. "This way they will be sure to answer."

We waited, each of us listening intently. Jerry said, "I have to go to the bathroom."

"Be quiet," I told him, although I suddenly had the same problem.

"Guess no one's here," T.M. said. "So we may as well look in the windows."

I stepped over to the window and looked in. Cigarette butts and beer cans lay all over the floor, and what looked like punch-marks were on the sheet rock. Someone had definitely been smoking and drinking and pounding on the walls.

When Jerry, Corrinne, and Alan looked in too, T.M. said, "Guess we'll just have to go in and check it out."

"Go in?" all of us said at the same time.

"Of course," T.M. said, as if this were something he did every day. "There could be a damsel tied upstairs and a vampire who wishes to drink her blood after dark. There could be—"

"You are not going in there!" Corrinne almost shouted.

T.M.'s theory that there's a vampire in the house is absurd. But think about it for a moment: what dangers could there be in a seemingly vacant ramshackle house? Here are some possibilities: the floors or steps could be rotted, and the kids could fall through and get hurt. There could be an animal making a home in the house, or even a swarm of bees or wasps. There could be dangerous mold, chemicals, or asbestos in the house that the kids could be exposed to. Can you think of more?

In Psalm 119:125, the psalmist asks for God to give him discernment. If you ask God for discernment, he will help you to evaluate whether something is dangerous or safe.

HAUNTED HOUSE

T.M. walked over to the door and pushed it in with his walking stick. "Watch me," he said.

We all stared at him. I couldn't believe he was doing this, but staying outside seemed even scarier at the moment.

While we waited, T.M. disappeared inside, then suddenly stuck his head around the door. He had some fake vampire teeth. "Velcome to my castle. So pleased if you let me suck your blood."

"Stop it, T.M.! Get serious!" Corrinne cried out, and Jerry threw an air punch at him.

T.M. ducked and said, "Oh, come on. There's nothing here but the dead bodies."

"Well, I'm not going to stand here," I said, as if that sounded perfectly logical. "Let's go in."

Jerry followed me inside, and reluctantly Alan and Corrinne followed. We stood in a small foyer with rooms on either side, empty as caverns. Except for the cigarette butts and empty beer cans all around, the house looked deserted. T.M. leaned down to pick a butt up.

"It smokes Marlboros," he said confidently.

Corrinne squealed, "It?"

Do you think that if Jerry or Corrinne had been at the house by themselves, they would have gone in? Sometimes when you're in a group you do things you wouldn't do alone.

There are several Scriptures that warn against being swayed by peer pressure: "Do not join a crowd that intends to do evil" (Exodus 23:2a); "My son, if sinners entice you, turn your back on them!" (Proverbs 1:10); and "Don't copy the behavior and customs of this world, but let God transform you into a new person by changing the way you think. Then you will know what God wants you to do, and you will know how good and pleasing and perfect his will really is" (Romans 12:2).

T.M. regarded us all with dark, solemn eyes. "It," he said soberly.

He led us through the foyer into the hallway by a staircase in the middle of the house. The back hallway opened into a kitchen. Nothing much lay around except more of the Marlboro butts and beer cans. The sink and cabinets had been taken out of it, leaving gaping holes like lost teeth in their place. The kitchen led out to a small porch with the screens all torn to pieces and hanging down from the window tops. Outside they could see a driveway, though it didn't look like anything had been parked there for a while.

To the right of the porch in the kitchen, we all turned to face what must have been a basement door. It had a padlock on it.

For a second, we all stood staring at the shiny silver combination lock, looking like it had been bought the day before.

T.M. stepped over and gave it a pull. "It's locked. Can vampires work lock combinations?"

T.M. grinned and twitched his eyebrows, then looked at us solemnly. "It could be a diversion. They want us to go down there where they will impale us on spikes. But we aren't stupid, are we? We know the real evidence is upstairs."

When the kids found a combination lock on the basement door, that should have been an important sign to them. It was proof that the property was owned by someone. An owner has the right to restrict others' access to his property.

The Bible teaches respect for private property: "Do not steal. Do not cheat one another. . . . Do not cheat or rob anyone" (Leviticus 19:11, 13). Respecting private property is a way to show respect for God and the people he created. If you have a doubt, ask an adult to help you identify private property so you can respect the owner's rights.

I gulped, gave everyone a look, and then all of us followed T.M. No one wanted to be left alone.

As we hurried along behind T.M. Corrinne whispered, "He's going up there?"

"What can I say? He's eaten too many of those little chocolate doughnuts. His brains are like scrambled eggs."

Corrinne gave me a shove. "Some help you are."

The stairs creaked and grumbled as we mounted them together in a little group behind T.M. The boards on them were chipped, cracked, and even had chunks gouged out of them, and I wondered if they could support our weight. Fortunately for us they did.

At the top of the stairs were two more rooms on either side of the foyer with a bathroom in the back between them. I looked in the bathroom, but all the fixtures were gone.

T.M. picked up an old newspaper lying on the floor. "Ah, Babe Ruth hits his 60th home run!" he said, like it happened yesterday. "Here," he said, gesturing to me, "Keep it for posterity."

Jerry, Corrinne, and Alan crowded around me to look at it. It was the employment ads.

"Hey, just keeping it interesting, folks," T.M. said with his eyebrow twitch.

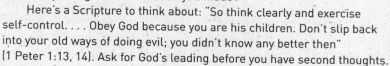

Do you think the kids in the story are having second thoughts about going into the empty house? When was the last time you regretted a decision you made?

Here's a Scripture to think about: "So think clearly and exercise self-control. . . . Obey God because you are his children. Don't slip back into your old ways of doing evil; you didn't know any better then" (1 Peter 1:13, 14). Ask for God's leading before you have second thoughts.

26
Day 7

MYSTERY OF THE
HAUNTED HOUSE

We looked through the rooms, but there was nothing else there. T.M. suddenly looked up. A small rectangular covered hole that must have led to an attic was in the ceiling.

"Ah, the observatory for studying the stars," T.M. said.

"You're not going up there!" Corrinne exclaimed.

"No, our time is finished here. Let us go in peace."

I was glad to go back downstairs. We were about to head out of the house when we heard a truck pull into the yard. We all froze. T.M. whispered, "We look to see which way they're coming in, and go the opposite."

We heard voices as they came around the front, and T.M. pointed to the back door. We all dashed out the back and ran for the trees on the side so they wouldn't see us. T.M. pulled out his binoculars and watched the people. There were two of them and they sat out on the front stoop smoking for a while.

T.M. said, "Well, this case is solved. A vampire and a werewolf live here. And they smoke Marlboros. We should go tell Stephen King so he can research his next novel."

We walked off through the woods, laughing.

Why did the kids run when they heard someone coming into the house? Do you think their consciences were bothering them? The conscience is a gift from God to give people a sense of right and wrong, and to help them make decisions accordingly. It's always good to listen to your conscience.

Job said, "I will maintain my innocence without wavering. My conscience is clear for as long as I live" (Job 27:6). How do you feel when your conscience is clear? How has your conscience helped you to decide to do the right thing?

Lance and his sister Luvey groomed the two horses they would ride in the Fourth of July parade. Lance swished the brush over Thunder's haunch, while Luvey threw a blanket over Sadie's back. "Has Daddy got the float ready yet?" she asked. The smaller horse shivered, then stamped her front foot.

"Not yet, but I'm sure it will be ready in time. He just has to get out all the stuff and arrange it on the trailer." Every year Lance and Luvey's dad prepared the float for the high school homecoming queen and her court. This year was special, because the homecoming queen was their friend and former babysitter, Jennie Sowers. Lance had had a crush on Jennie since he was six.

"You gonna talk to her?" Luvey asked slyly.

"Who?"

"You know who," Jennie said, shaping her lips into a kiss.

"She's five years older than me."

"Doesn't mean you can't love her from afar." Luvey grinned and threw the western saddle over Sadie. Lance saddled up Thunder.

Their dad walked into the stable. "Have either of you seen Mickey Mouse?"

Have you ever seen a parade? Have you ever been in one?

Parades took place in the Bible. The book of Nehemiah describes an elaborate parade and celebration after the rebuilding of the walls of Jerusalem. Nehemiah 12 gives details describing who was in the parade and where it went. And what a celebration it was! "Many sacrifices were offered on that joyous day, for God had given the people cause for great joy. The women and children also participated in the celebration, and the joy of the people of Jerusalem could be heard far away" (Nehemiah 12:43).

MYSTERY OF THE
MISSING MOUSE

"Mickey's missing?" Luvey asked as she bridled Sadie. The horse was ready.

"He's not in the loft," Dad said. "Everything for the float was there, except the Mickey Mouse figure."

Lance looked up toward the loft. "Too bad Mom's not here. She might know where it is." Their mom was out of town helping a sick relative. It was the first parade she'd ever missed.

Dad rolled his eyes. "We've always had Mickey on the float. Besides the girls, he's the main feature."

"Glad you said that, Dad," Luvey said.

"What?"

"That the girls are more important than Mickey." She giggled.

"Watch out, Dad," Lance said. "Luvey's in a weird mood."

"Just because I said you were in love with Jennie Sowers."

"What?" Dad asked. "You're in love with Jennie Sowers?"

"Shut up, Luvey. You're in love with Hank Distman."

Dad looked from Lance to Luvey. "How come I never heard this?"

"You never hear anything, Dad," Luvey said. "You're too concerned about Mickey Mouse."

Everyone laughed. "Speaking of which," Dad said, "help me look around. Mickey couldn't have walked off on his own."

When kids accuse each other of being "in love," what do they mean? Have you ever been in love?

Attraction to a boy or girl is natural, and can be fun when you're young. Ultimately, the attraction between a man and woman is a God-given basis for the family. In God's plan, a man and woman commit to only each other for a lifetime. "This explains why a man leaves his father and mother and is joined to his wife, and the two are united into one" (Genesis 2:24).

"We only get Mickey out once a year," Dad said. "It's not like we'd have any reason to move him out of the loft." He walked to the back of the barn and began looking through the bales of hay.

Luvey and Lance helped, scouring the whole stable for any sign of anything. In time, several of the other men who helped with the float arrived and began to put the float together. Dad worked on that while Luvey looked in their farmhouse. Lance made a trip around the whole yard area.

In an hour, they had searched everywhere. "Nothin'," Lance said.

"I guess it wasn't misplaced," Dad said.

"Do you think someone would steal it?" Lance asked.

"Let's go in the kitchen, have a soda, and write down some ideas," Luvey said, always the most organized of the two. They walked inside. Lance pulled a couple of drinks out of the fridge and Luvey found a yellow pad and pen.

They sat down and started to exchange ideas. "Well, someone might steal it if they wanted to ruin the float," Luvey said.

"But why ruin the float? It's just a bunch of high school girls—not the Dallas Cowboy cheerleaders."

"You're such a nice guy, you know," Luvey said.

If someone wanted to ruin the float, he or she would likely be acting out of jealousy. Jealousy can be destructive, causing broken relationships and hurt feelings. The writer of Proverbs compares jealousy to anger and wrath: "Anger is cruel, and wrath is like a flood, but who can survive the destructiveness of jealousy?" (Proverbs 27:4).

Do you ever struggle with jealousy? Ask for God's help to adjust your attitude.

"What about Sam Stevenson?" Lance asked. "Remember last year how he mocked the Fourth of July and said it was stupid and someone should blow up all the floats?"

"Do you think he'd really do something?"

Lance shrugged. "I don't know. I guess he's a big blowhard mostly." Luvey wrote down Sam's name, and then two other names of high school toughs who got into trouble.

"I would think they would have taken the Queen's throne," Lance said. "Not the Mickey Mouse. It's just a big, plastic ornament, like the Frosty we put up at Christmas."

"You never know what people will do when they get some weird idea."

Lance shook his head. "It has to be something else."

"OK, remember last year when those people came around and told Dad what a wonderful float he had? What if it was one of them—someone who liked it?"

"Let's ask Dad."

They got up and went back out to the barn. The float was almost ready. The men stood around studying it.

People have all sorts of reasons for taking things. One of the most dramatic stories in the Bible is about Achan, a man who took items after the walls of Jericho fell. You can read the story in Joshua 6 and 7. God commanded the Israelites to take nothing from the city, but Achan said, "I saw a beautiful robe imported from Babylon, two hundred silver coins, and a bar of gold weighing more than a pound. I wanted them so much that I took them. They are hidden in the ground beneath my tent, with the silver buried deeper than the rest" (Joshua 7:20, 21). God's punishment for Achan's stealing was quick and dramatic. To find out what happened to him, read Joshua 7:24-26.

Dad walked around talking to the kids. "I received a lot of compliments last year, from a lot of people. It's a pretty popular float, you know."

"Right, Dad," Luvey said with a grin. "Next stop—Macy's Thanksgiving Day Parade!"

Dad gave her a clip on the back of the head. "You wait. Me and Mickey just might make it that far! Now, seriously. Let me see. There was that woman who offered me 50 dollars for the Elvis statue, but we couldn't junk the King for a mere 50. And then there was the man who said he could sell me a statue of Babe Ruth, but I said—"

He seemed lost in thought.

Lance spoke up. "Was there anyone who offered you something for the Mickey Mouse?"

Dad shook his head. "No, no money. But—hey, wait a second—" He strode over to the trailer and looked down at the place where Mickey usually stood. "There was one lady who said she collected Mickey Mouse memorabilia."

"Who was she?" Luvey asked.

"She gave me a card with her name and address."

Do you collect anything—stamps, coins, baseball cards, unicorns? Collecting can be an interesting hobby, and for some people, a profession. Some things you collect aren't valuable, but to you they may be a treasure.

The Bible tells us what things in life are valuable. The book of Proverbs says that wisdom is a treasure. "Follow my advice, my son; always treasure my commands. Obey them and live! Guard my teachings as your most precious possession. Tie them on your fingers as a reminder. Write them deep within your heart" (Proverbs 7:1-3).

"Right under here." He lifted the base that Mickey stood on. Lance and Luvey immediately saw the card.

Dad picked it up. "Charlotte Amenson," he read off the card. "5135 Oakmill Road."

"Do you really think she could have stolen it, Dad?" Luvey asked.

"I don't know. But she was pretty interested. She measured Mickey, like she had a place already picked out for him. Kept clucking her tongue."

"Should we just go to her house?" Lance asked.

"What have we got to lose?" Dad said. "Mickey's already gone. And maybe she's got some other Mickey Mouse statue we can use."

They got in their truck, and it didn't take long for Lance, Luvey, and their dad to arrive at 5135 Oakmill Road. It was easy to recognize the house; there was a Mickey Mouse mailbox, a Mickey Mouse flag on a flagpole, and a chair shaped like Mickey Mouse, so you looked like you were sitting in his lap when you sat on it. And there—standing on the front porch with his familiar wave—was their Mickey Mouse figure!

If someone has something that belongs to you, is it stolen? Think about it. Could there be some reason besides theft that a person has something of yours without your permission?

"Don't make accusations against someone who hasn't wronged you" (Proverbs 3:30). Before you take any action to retaliate against someone you feel has wronged you, make sure you know the facts. Ask God to help you be wise and not jump to conclusions.

Dad's jaw dropped. "What in the world?"

Mrs. Amenson met them at the door. "I've been expecting you," she said in a friendly voice—too friendly for someone who had stolen their Mickey and boldly displayed him on the porch.

"Expecting us? Why?" Dad asked. "We just came to find out if you knew anything about—"

Mrs. Amenson interrupted. "Well, your wife told me that you'd need Mickey for the Fourth of July parade, since you use him every year. It was part of our agreement."

Luvey and Lance looked at each other, and then at Dad. "Agreement?" asked Lance.

"Why, yes!" Mrs. Amenson said. "You knew about it, didn't you? I asked your wife if I could display your Mickey on my porch. She said I could 'borrow' Mickey since you only use him on the Fourth of July."

Dad shook his head, and motioned Lance toward Mickey. Together they picked him up and took him to the car.

When they got home, there was a message on the answering machine. It was Mom: "I'm so sorry! I forgot to tell you that I let Mrs. Amenson display our Mickey Mouse on her porch. She knows you'll need it for the parade, though, so you just need to go to her house to pick it up. I hope I didn't cause you any trouble!"

Have you ever been accused of something you didn't do? How did it feel? Was there anything you could do to prove your innocence?

If you've been falsely accused, you may be more patient to get all the facts before you accuse someone else. If so, you're showing the same kind of mercy God does. According to David, "The Lord is merciful and gracious; he is slow to get angry and full of unfailing love. He will not constantly accuse us, nor remain angry forever" (Psalm 103:8, 9).

J.J. yelled as he ran toward us on the street. "Have you checked out those new houses going up across from yours? I think we need to make sure we want the new owners to be part of our community."

As James and I caught up to him, I said, "What do you mean?"

"I think if anyone wants to be part of our community, they should have one of several things," J.J. offered. "I'd say a pool table is number one, or a tennis court, swimming pool, fishing boat, or season tickets to the Phillies' games. And they should be willing to share with their neighbors." J.J. twitched his eyebrows and grinned his toothy grin. We stopped in the middle of the street, looking down toward the new houses.

"These people are rich, I bet," James said as he pointed to one of the houses. "They'd better have kids our age!"

Do you ever choose friends on the basis of what great toys they have, or how rich they are? You're missing a lot if you do; and worse, you are not pleasing God. James wrote to Christians, "My dear brothers and sisters, how can you claim that you have faith in our glorious Lord Jesus Christ if you favor some people more than others? For instance, suppose someone comes into your meeting dressed in fancy clothes and expensive jewelry, and another comes in who is poor and dressed in shabby clothes. If you give special attention and a good seat to the rich person, but you say to the poor one, 'You can stand over there, or else sit on the floor'—well, doesn't this discrimination show that you are guided by wrong motives?" (James 2:1-4). God does not judge on the basis of worldly wealth, and neither should his children.

We sauntered up to the side of the house and looked around it. Sheetrock lay in some places on the ground, along with shingles and two-by-fours. The house was mostly filled in, but it needed painting and a front door. Someone had written "Keep out" in big red letters on the side of the building that still required painting.

There were concrete blocks arranged in a temporary stairway in the front. We climbed up and peered in. Nails lay about in piles and boxes. No one was around, so we walked through the rooms like we owned them. Sheetrock walled the rooms in, and spackling adorned their faces in large off-yellow blotches. Big five-gallon cans of paint, unopened, sat in the middle of the rooms.

We climbed the stairs to the second floor and found four large bedrooms with a bathroom in the middle. Nothing out of the ordinary. It all needed painting, or paneling, whatever was the plan of the soon-to-be resident.

We stepped down the stairs from the second floor and spotted a back door out to the yard. We opened it and looked out. To our pleasant surprise, a large rectangular pool with a white bottom had been dug. It was empty, but I could almost feel the cool water around my body while swimming. Turquoise tiles lined the apron. It looked magnificent.

Have you ever watched a house being built? It's interesting, and particularly thrilling if it's your house. There's a lot to learn about design and construction.

"Unless the Lord builds a house, the work of the builders is useless". (Psalm 127:1). This verse reminds us that we are to involve God in all the plans of our lives—education, career, friends, and activities. How can you include God in your plans for today?

MYSTERY OF THE
POOL INTRUDER

J.J. cried, "Whoa! These are the kind of people we want in our community."

We stepped through the doorway and onto the back concrete stairs, then ran down to the apron around the pool. The yard stretched down to the small creek at the end. On the other side stood the vast woods I occasionally explored with my friends.

J.J. stood looking down into the pool. It was empty, but in the main well murky water lay in a smaller pool about eight feet across. The water smelled rancid and was tinged green with algae.

"Guess we won't be swimming in that," J.J. said.

"Not unless we want to test for nuclear radioactivity," I said. J.J. laughed.

We stared into the water when something splashed.

James cried, "A frog! That was a frog!"

J.J. scurried down along the apron to the shallow end and jumped onto the concrete at the bottom. "Let's get him!"

We followed him down into the pool depression that sloped down another five feet. We paused at the edge of the disgusting water. J.J. yelled, "Get a stick! Or get something to swish with!"

I spotted a piece of two-by-four at the end of the pool.

For some kids, there's nothing like a big frog to stir up fun. But did you know that God used a plague of frogs to convince Pharaoh in Egypt to release the Hebrew slaves? God told Moses to tell Pharaoh: "I will send vast hordes of frogs across your entire land . . . into your houses, even into your bedrooms and onto your beds! Every home in Egypt will be filled with them. They will fill even your ovens and your kneading bowls. You and your people will be overwhelmed by frogs!" (Exodus 8:2-4). Imagine the scene! If you were Pharaoh, what would you have thought of God?

From the edge of the water, I hit the surface with the two-by-four, making waves. A large bullfrog the size of my hand peeped out on the surface of the water in the middle of the pool.

"Drive him to me and James, Ken," J.J. said, hurrying around to the other side of the pool. "Swing the wood and drive him!"

I plunged the stick in deeper and pulled it back and forth to scare the frog. The bullfrog dove, then surfaced a second later nearer to James and J.J.

"He's going!"

J.J. cried, "Keep doing it. Slap a little."

I slapped the water with the stick. The frog jumped out of the pool between James and J.J. They both dove for it and came up with the frog in their hands.

"We got him! We got him!" James cried.

I ran around to them. J.J. grasped the frog firmly in his fingers.

"What do we do with him?" I asked, almost out of breath.

J.J. said, "We have to give him a good bullfroggy name."

"Greenie?" James suggested.

"Nah, something majestic. Something kingly. He looks like a king," J.J. commented, holding the frog so tight its eyes bulged even larger.

When God sent a plague of frogs to Egypt, it must have been awful. But things actually got worse. Pharaoh's magicians tried to show their power, but they only made more!

Only God could get rid of all those frogs. Moses said to Pharaoh, "'You will know that no one is as powerful as the Lord our God. All the frogs will be destroyed, except those in the river.' . . . The frogs in the houses, the courtyards, and the fields all died. They were piled into great heaps, and a terrible stench filled the land" (Exodus 8:10, 13). Yuck! What a horrible way to learn a lesson. What is God teaching you, and how is he doing it?

MYSTERY OF THE
POOL INTRUDER

I said, "How about Solomon? He was a king."

"Yeah," J.J. said. "King Solomon, the wisest frog of the east. Of course, he can't be too smart if we caught him that easily." J.J. twitched his eyebrows and we all laughed. "He feels so weird," he said, holding the frog out for James. "Try it."

James took the frog gingerly. "Yuck!" He handed it to me.

"So slimy," I said. The frog wiggled and stretched, his long, muscular legs stretching out. I squeezed a little, and he simply bulged out here and there.

I gave him back to J.J. "I wonder if we can get him to say something," he said.

"Like what?"

"Like, let me go, you idiot!"

We laughed as the frog twisted and squirmed in J.J.'s hand. Seconds later, he wriggled free and jumped back into the dirty water. We watched as he disappeared back under the surface.

"Guess we'll have to do it again," J.J. said.

A frog named Solomon? Funny, maybe, but Solomon was certainly a famous person. The Bible describes him like this: "So King Solomon became richer and wiser than any other king in all the earth. People from every nation came to visit him and to hear the wisdom God had given him" (1 Kings 10:23, 24). What special gifts and abilities has God given you? Ask God to help you use your gifts wisely for him.

We started doing the same thing as before, except J.J. suddenly stopped us.

"Look!" he yelled.

A flat, black head of something appeared in the water of the pool with the frog—Solomon!—in its mouth. Everyone jumped back.

"It's a snake!" I said.

The snake slithered out onto the dry area. It began to swallow Solomon the frog. We all stared in fascination and horror. "It's a black snake," J.J. said.

"What should we do?" I asked.

"Catch it," he said.

"Yeah, right."

J.J. laughed. "It's not dangerous. Black snakes are good snakes. They eat rats and mice and things like that, including frogs, apparently." The snake had almost swallowed Solomon completely. A big lump appeared in its neck.

"He'll dine on that frog for a week."

First a frog, and now a snake! Are you afraid of snakes? If so, you're not alone. Many people are repulsed by snakes. Some people believe that attitude was ordained by God in the Garden of Eden. After Adam and Eve sinned, God cursed the serpent: "You are singled out from all the domestic and wild animals of the whole earth to be cursed. You will grovel in the dust as long as you live, crawling along on your belly. From now on, you and the woman will be enemies, and your offspring and her offspring will be enemies" (Genesis 3:14, 15). As a part of God's creation, snakes are good and play their role in the balance of nature. But when you see a snake, remember the influence of sin in the world.

MYSTERY OF THE
POOL INTRUDER

"Surround him," J.J. said.

We all moved in, but J.J. went right after the snake. "He won't feel like moving much with that big meal in him," he said.

He went around behind the snake and crept up on it. It lay still, its eyes watching us, but not trying to escape.

Suddenly, J.J. pounced. He grabbed the snake just behind the head and held it. He motioned to James and me. "See where that big lump is? Start pushing on it."

"Are you kidding?" I asked him. "Why?"

"I saw this on The Discovery Channel. To discover what snakes eat, they make them throw up."

"That's gross!" James said.

"Gross, maybe, but we might be able to save Solomon. Now push!"

James made a face, and he and I started pushing the lump in the snake up toward its mouth. Remarkably, in just a few seconds, its jaws separated, and out came Solomon! He leaped like he'd been shot out of a gun, and sprang away.

James looked at me and shook his head. "That's the most disgusting, most incredible thing I've ever seen."

"What'll we do with the snake?" I asked.

"Why not let him go?" J.J. said. "He'll be fine."

"Yeah," I laughed. "And maybe he's lost his appetite for frogs."

While the snake was cursed by God in the Garden of Eden, later God used an image of a snake as a tool of healing. How? Read Numbers 21:6-9 to find out.

Today, an image of a snake on a pole is often used to symbolize the medical profession. Thank God for his practice of changing bad into good. When has he done that in your life?

Emma looked through the books in her father's library. He had such old ones, she was amazed. There was *Robinson Crusoe,* by Daniel Defoe, and one by Charles Dickens: *David Copperfield*. She wanted to read them all. Then she came upon one she'd never heard about: A *Connecticut Yankee in King Arthur's Court* by Mark Twain.

She pulled it out. "Hey, Mom, look at this one." She showed her mother.

"Dad loves that one. It's his favorite Mark Twain book."

Emma opened it at the flyleaf and paged on. She came to the title page and looked down. There in ancient ink were the words, "My best to you. Mark Twain." Emma stared at the signature.

"Mom, is this for real?" She showed her the signed page.

"Hmmm. I didn't know about that. Dad never said anything—" She took the book and sniffed the page. "Surely it isn't real."

"Why not?"

"Well, Mark Twain—I mean, really."

"Is there a way to find out?"

"I suppose. It's probably quite valuable if it's real."

Finding an old book like this could be a real blessing to Emma and her family. Signed books are big business. But there are also fakes.

The Bible tells about some famous fakes. The book of Acts tells about a false prophet named Bar-Jesus, also called Elymas. He pretended to share spiritual truth with the governor, but he did not. When Paul discovered Elymas's deception, he declared God's judgment on him: "You son of the Devil, full of every sort of trickery and villainy, enemy of all that is good, will you never stop perverting the true ways of the Lord? And now the Lord has laid his hand of punishment upon you, and you will be stricken awhile with blindness" (Acts 13:10, 11). Do you know any fake Christians? Have you ever been one?

MYSTERY OF THE
AUTHOR'S
AUTOGRAPH

"Who would know how to determine if the signature is real?" Emma asked her mom.

"You might call a used books store. They might know something. You could also try eBay."

Emma went on eBay first and tried different combinations of searches. Finally, she found some listings for "rare signed books." There was one by Mark Twain: *The Adventures of Tom Sawyer.* The listing said the signature had been authenticated, and there was a picture of it. Emma grabbed her book and compared the signature on hers to the one pictured. Amazing. They looked the same.

Then she looked at the price on the book: $10,000. She gasped and ran to her mom again.

"Mom, Mom! Guess what? A signed copy of *Tom Sawyer* is on eBay, and it's selling for ten thousand dollars!"

"You're kidding."

"That's not all. The signatures are similar. The one on eBay was signed by Mark Twain. And it looked just like the one in Dad's book."

"We'd better check this out. Find out where Dad got it."

Emma picked up the book again and put it back in its slot on the shelf. "We've got to protect this one," she said with a smile, and walked away thinking of all the things they could buy with ten thousand dollars.

The problem with fakes is that they often look like the real thing. The Bible tells of seven brothers who were all fakes. They didn't believe in Jesus, but used his name to cast out demons. They may have faked out some people, but they couldn't fake out the demons, and they were publicly embarrassed. How did it happen? Read Acts 19:13-15 to find out. —☉ Ask God to help you tell real faith from fake.

Emma looked up the names of sellers of rare books in the Yellow Pages. She called the first one on the list and talked to Mr. Abscrow. She explained about the book and what she'd done.

"There are lots of forgeries out there these days," he said. "People can pretty much mimic anyone's signature, and even use old materials so it seems authentic. I'd be very careful."

"Is there an expert who might know?"

"Not around here," Mr. Abscrow said. "But you'll find several in New York City. You might want to talk to an appraiser."

Emma hung up and dialed another dealer. The third one she talked to, Mr. Burns, said he might be able to help: "I've seen Mark Twain's signature before, and I even sold a signed book of his, but that was almost 30 years ago. You have to be very careful about things like this."

"Do you know any experts?" Emma asked.

"Yes," the man said, and gave her a phone number. "I've never found him to be wrong. But he's old now, and his eyesight isn't so good. In fact, I think he might be living in a nursing home."

When Dad came home for dinner, Emma showed him the book.

Have you ever owned a knockoff—an inexpensive imitation of some expensive product, like clothing or electronics? Sometimes an imitation is just about as good as the real thing, and you're satisfied.

But sometimes substitutes are unacceptable. Paul warned the early church against "false apostles. They have fooled you by disguising themselves as apostles of Christ. But I am not surprised! Even Satan can disguise himself as an angel of light" (2 Corinthians 11:13, 14). Satan deceives and fools people into sin. Ask God to help you to resist temptation.

MYSTERY OF THE
AUTHOR'S
AUTOGRAPH

Dad gazed at the book. "Yes, I remember this one. I found it in an old used books store. But I don't remember there being a signature. Surely I would have noticed it. When I was young some kids collected stamps or baseball cards, but I collected books."

"Do you think it could be real?" Emma asked.

"I guess it's worth finding out."

That Saturday, Emma and her father traveled to see Mr. Burns at the rare books store he owned. When they got there, he put on some high-powered special glasses and studied the signature. He kept shaking his head. "It's a very effective forgery, if that's what it is. I can't be sure."

He turned to an old catalog he had on famous artists' and authors' signatures. When he turned to Mark Twain, the book had pictures of five different signatures. They were all about the same. All the signatures showed Mark Twain's name with sharp tops on the M and a long crossbar over the T.

"It looks real," Mr. Burns said. "But I'm not enough of an expert to tell you what you need to know to sell it."

Emma looked at her dad. "Where to now?"

In the history of humankind, people have often chosen and made for themselves fake gods—idols. Jeremiah wrote, "Can people make their own god? The gods they make are not real gods at all!" (Jeremiah 16:20). At other times and in other places, the idols were statues of gold, wood, or stone. But today many people make idols of inanimate things: fame, wealth, power, influence, knowledge, or talent. Is there anything in your life that takes your attention away from God? Make sure it's not an idol to you.

Emma showed the book to several people. Two "experts" said it might be real. Three others weren't sure, but thought it was probably a forgery because the ink looked more contemporary than that available to Twain in his lifetime.

"You'd have to have it scientifically tested," one of the experts said, "and that would be expensive. Sometimes the best thing to do is to take it to a rare books convention. There's one in St. Louis coming up in a few weeks."

Emma and her dad made plans to attend. They also looked through his books and found two other famous signatures: Charles Dickens, valued on eBay at $6,000, and Ernest Hemingway on *The Sun Also Rises,* which was valued at $3,000.

"How could I have missed these when I bought them?" Dad asked.

"When did you buy them?"

"Mostly in high school and college. And I found them in all sorts of places—garage sales and secondhand shops. One I found in a box that someone put out with their trash. They were just old books. I didn't really think of them as valuable."

"Wait till we get to the convention," Emma said. "Then we'll see what's really valuable."

You can't tell by looking when something is valuable. Valuable antiques may be ugly and broken, but they are valuable because they are rare. You can't always tell by looking whether a person is good or bad, either. Jesus warned, "Beware of false prophets who come disguised as harmless sheep, but are really wolves that will tear you apart" (Matthew 7:15). Ask God to help you think clearly when you're listening to someone who may be a "wolf in sheep's clothing."

MYSTERY OF THE
AUTHOR'S
AUTOGRAPH

"How could we tell if it's a forgery?" Emma asked.

At the convention, Emma and her dad talked to many experts. As usual, everyone had an opinion, and they were all different.

"You look for little differences that a forger might not have noticed," one said. "You look at not only the style of the handwriting, but also the words that the writer uses. Like yours says, 'My best to you.' You could find out if that was an expression Twain used at times. I don't know the answer to that. But Twain was quite the curmudgeon and was inclined to sign with a joke instead of a nice sentiment like that."

Emma came away from the convention quite discouraged. She kept worrying that the books might be forgeries and worthless.

"What are we going to do, Dad?" she asked one night.

"There is one possibility, and I'm a little reluctant to consider it."

"What's that?"

"A prank. Maybe someone's trying to trick me. It would have to be someone who knows about my collection of old books."

"Who would do that?"

"That's what you have to find out."

Sometimes pranks are funny. Other times they result in hurt feelings. You have to be careful that the "victim" of the prank will take it in good humor and not be angry.

Worse than a prank is deceiving someone on purpose. That happened in the life of Jacob, who deceived his father Isaac in order to get his brother Esau's inheritance. He wore a disguise to fool his father. What was it? Read Genesis 27:15-23 to find out what the disguise was, and what happened as a result. ➔ Think about how you may be deceiving someone—a parent, friend, or teacher—and ask God to help you be true to him.

Emma sat down with her dad and talked about the people he thought might do something like this.

"There are really only two people I'd think capable of it. Uncle Peter might have done it. He was enough of an artist, even as a teenager, to do a pretty good job copying the signatures. But after all these years, wouldn't he have gotten tired of waiting for me to discover them? He's not patient enough."

"Yeah, you're right," Emma said. "He can't keep a secret, even as simple as a surprise birthday party. Who's the other?"

"Julie, my cousin," Dad said. "She's an antiques dealer. She knows a lot about valuable old items and how to market them."

Emma called Julie the next day. "No, it's not me," Julie said. "If I had rare signed copies of those books, I would have sold them long ago and moved to Hawaii."

Her hand trembling, Emma dialed her uncle's number. "Uncle Peter, Dad and I have these books, one by Hemingway, one by Dickens, and a third by Mark Twain. They're all signed, and we can't figure out whether the signatures are real."

Uncle Peter started laughing. "What have you done to find out?"

She told him everything. He laughed so hard he could hardly speak. Finally, he said, "I'm good, aren't I?"

"What do you mean?"

"You'd better put your dad on the phone," Uncle Peter said, still laughing. "I've got a lot of explaining to do!"

"But this is what you must do: Tell the truth to each other" (Zechariah 8:16a). Remember this verse when it comes to playing pranks, and when it comes to life in general.

MYSTERY OF THE
BLUE FLASH

Darby O'Malley and her best friend Peter Chang walked along the street kicking at stones.

"Oh boy, here comes trouble," Peter said suddenly.

Darby looked up. He was right. It was Conk Fielding. Conk had the slingshot in his hand that he had been bragging about in school for a week now. When he saw them, he held the sling back and silently aimed it at them.

Immediately, Darby yelled, "Don't point that slingshot at me, Conk Fielding! That's not right."

Conk fired it. A brass BB soared over Darby's head in an arc and bounced on the street a hundred feet down from them.

"You know slingshots are dangerous!" Peter shouted. "Put it away."

Conk swaggered onto the sidewalk and stared Darby and Peter down. Then he shrugged. "I don't have time for this," he said, and went off up the street, leaving them standing there.

Bad guys come in all forms, even kids. Why do you think some kids enjoy destroying and hurting things, including people? Have you ever been such a kid?

Look at what God says about reverence for his creation in Genesis 2:15: "The Lord God placed the man in the Garden of Eden to tend and care for it." The job of all humans ever since has been to appreciate God's world and to use it carefully. How do you treat God's creation?

"He's going to end up in jail one day for sure," Darby said. She felt angry. The idea that Conk would purposely aim his slingshot at them was infuriating.

Peter touched Darby on the shoulder. "Don't let him bug you."

Darby wasn't listening. She was staring up at the sky. "Did you see that?" she asked Peter.

"What?" he asked, looking up.

"That blue flash. It just went past my—look! There it is again!"

Peter looked skyward. He shielded his eyes from the late morning sun. "What is it?"

"A parakeet!" Darby said. "Look!"

The blue, white, and black-spotted bird landed on one of the wires close to the pole. It looked perfectly content, and its fluffy chest puffed out as it chirped a moment.

"He's beautiful!" Darby said. "He must have escaped from a cage around here."

The bird suddenly leaped off the wire and flew down the street.

"Let's follow him! Maybe there's a reward," Darby cried as she started running down the street. Peter was right behind her. Both kids sprinted to where the parakeet had settled again. When they reached it, they saw another blue flash as the bird took off toward the creek and the woods behind the houses.

God was generous to give us birds that we can keep as pets. Parakeets are gentle and friendly, and can be taught to imitate voices and sounds.

God cares for both wild and domestic birds and animals. In Psalm 104:16-18, the psalmist lists several kinds of animals and the homes God provides for them. Read those verses to find out what they are. Thank God for other ways he sustains living things on earth.

MYSTERY OF THE
BLUE FLASH

As Darby and Peter ran, the parakeet headed straight for the creek. They stumbled down the steep bank. There on one side hung a rope that the kids often used to swing across.

The blue parakeet landed on a tree on the other side of the creek. It eyed them with a friendly stare, and bobbed his head up and down.

Peter handed Darby the rope. "You go first," Peter said. Darby sailed across the creek on the rope swing. She jumped off on the other side and swung the rope back to Peter. She wasn't sure how smart birds were, but this one definitely seemed to be leading them.

Peter dropped down next to Darby and looked up at the bird. At that very moment the parakeet took flight one more time.

Keeping her eye half on the bird and half on the trees around her, Darby followed. Peter was close behind.

They had explored some of the woods near the creek, but not much. They hadn't gone any farther than the old stone wall, but as the parakeet flew past it they scrambled over and kept running. Darby's heart was beating hard.

"Where do you think it's going?" Peter asked, panting as he ran.

Soon, they hit a steeper part of the woods. As they wound around the rocks, keeping to a foot trail, they both suddenly spotted a cabin up ahead. The bird seemed to be heading for it.

"Who lives there?" Darby asked between deep breaths.

The God who cares for the birds also cares for you. Jesus said, "So I tell you, don't worry about everyday life—whether you have enough food to eat or clothes to wear. For life consists of far more than food and clothing. Look at the ravens. They don't need to plant or harvest or put food in barns because God feeds them. And you are far more valuable to him than any birds!" (Luke 12:22-24). How does it feel to be valuable to God? How do you know you are valuable to him?

MYSTERY OF THE
BLUE FLASH

30

Day 4

"Let's be careful," Darby said. "Sometimes woods people don't like visitors."

"Yeah, but the parakeet invited us," Peter said with a smile.

They tramped up the little hill and reached the back of the cabin. They didn't hear anyone, so they walked around front. There in the front yard was a large cage—and about 10 parakeets on it, inside it, and hovering around it!

Darby's jaw dropped. "Wow! Look at them all. Green. Yellow. Blue. They're beautiful." She stepped forward, and then fell. Something had caught her shin. Immediately, some cans rattled.

Peter helped her up.

"It's a trip wire," Peter said. "Booby trap."

"Warning signal," a sweet woman's voice said from the doorway. For the first time, Darby noticed a plump woman standing just inside the door. Her face was hidden by shadows. Darby noticed she had something in her hand. It was a long stick.

"We don't mean any harm!" Peter immediately cried.

The woman put down the stick. "I can see you're just kids," she said. "Are there any more of you?"

"Just us," Darby said, rubbing her shin where the wire had dug into it. She now saw that the whole area around the house had a wire rigged with cans. This person didn't want strangers coming around without announcing their presence.

Jesus once compared people to birds. "Not even a sparrow, worth only half a penny, can fall to the ground without your Father knowing it. And the very hairs on your head are all numbered. So don't be afraid; you are more valuable to him than a whole flock of sparrows" (Matthew 10:29, 30). Isn't it remarkable that the God who sees every single bird and cares about all of them knows you even better? What will you say when you talk to him today?

"We don't get many visitors here," the woman said, stepping out into the sunlight. She had long gray hair tied up in a bun. Her double chin wobbled as she spoke, but she didn't look funny.

Peter stepped forward. "We saw your parakeet up by our houses. We followed him here."

"That'd be Junior. He's a traveler."

Two of the birds flew over, and with a great fluttering of wings settled down on the woman's shoulders. "We didn't know there was a house back here. Have you lived here long?" Darby asked.

"Many years," the woman answered. "And your name is—"

"Darby O'Malley. And this is my friend Peter Chang." Peter stepped forward and shook the woman's hand.

"I'm Bessie Lannock," the lady said. "My husband Hank is working down at the mill right now. He has the truck." The woman took out a pipe and lit it. "I hope you don't mind if I smoke."

Darby had never seen a woman smoke a pipe before. Mrs. Lannock struck a match on the bottom of her boot. It flamed up. Then she sucked on the pipe. "Come to the picnic table. Have a sit."

Darby gave Peter a wondering look. Peter just nodded and they walked shyly across the yard. Mrs. Lannock went inside the house as the kids sat down. Soon she returned with a pitcher full of iced tea and some glasses.

Some bird mothers protect their young by gathering them under their wings. This is a word picture used in the Bible. David said to God, "Let me live forever in your sanctuary, safe beneath the shelter of your wings" (Psalm 61:4). And Jesus said, "O Jerusalem, Jerusalem, the city that kills the prophets and stones God's messengers! How often I have wanted to gather your children together as a hen protects her chicks beneath her wings, but you wouldn't let me" (Matthew 23:37). When do you want to be protected by God's "wings"?

Soon they were all talking and laughing. Mrs. Lannock was a delightful person who seemed glad to have Darby and Peter there. She told them how she'd had parakeets as a little girl and had always loved them. "I let them roam about during the summer," she explained. "They need the wing time, if you know what I mean. Most of them stay real close. But a couple travel far and wide."

"We were wondering about that," Darby said. "Junior seemed to be leading us."

"I've never seen him do that," Mrs. Lannock said between puffs on her pipe. Three birds were now perched on her shoulders. She let one climb onto her hand and she held it out to Darby. "Go ahead, let him grip you. He won't hurt. They're all real gentle."

Darby held out her hand and the bird hopped onto it. The little feet and nails gripped her finger. Mrs. Lannock gave Peter one too.

"I don't know what I'd do without these birdies," she said.

As it drew past noon, Darby said they'd have to go.

"Come back anytime," Mrs. Lannock told them as she escorted them to the edge of the property. "I like having visitors."

On the way home, Darby said, "That is so cool, having all those parakeets."

"Yeah, they're—uh-oh." Peter pointed. There was Conk with his slingshot aimed at a flying bird. As they watched, he released the slingshot, feathers flew, and a bird fell to the ground.

Without thinking Darby started running.

Have you ever watched a bird and wished you too could fly? David did, when troubles overwhelmed him. "Oh, how I wish I had wings like a dove; then I would fly away and rest! I would fly far away to the quiet of the wilderness" (Psalm 55:6, 7). When problems get tough, you don't have to fly away. You can talk to God, no matter where you are.

Darby ran up to Conk and didn't even stop. She knocked right into him, bowling him over. His slingshot fell to the ground. Darby was up right away and grabbed it. "I'm giving this to the police as evidence."

"There's nothing wrong with a slingshot."

"Not if you're using it to kill birds."

Suddenly two of Conk's friends appeared behind him, glaring at Darby. "Give it to me, or else," he said.

"Oh yeah," Darby said sarcastically. She turned to Peter. "Dial 911." She leaned down, picked up a stone, and loaded the slingshot. Then she pulled back the patch and aimed it at Conk's head. "How does it feel, Conk? You want one of these in your head?"

Conk pursed his lips and stepped back. They stood frozen in place until a police car pulled to the curb up by the bridge over the creek.

"Let's go," Conk cried, and he and his friends ran off.

The police officer found Darby and Peter and got a full report. "I'll confiscate this," he said about the slingshot. "Shooting birds with slingshots is illegal in this township. With the information you've given me, I'll follow up with Conrad Fielding and his parents. I'm sure he won't be using it again."

As he got back into his squad car, a flash of blue went over their heads.

Peter smiled. "Hey, look! It's Junior!"

When David described going to God's house to worship, he wrote this: "Even the sparrow finds a home there, and the swallow builds her nest and raises her young—at a place near your altar. O Lord Almighty, my King and my God! How happy are those who can live in your house, always singing your praises" (Psalm 84:3, 4). For what can you praise God today?

"Cool!" S.T. cried as the two boats floated along under an overpass. This was a wide one, like a tunnel, and the kids' voices echoed eerily off the walls. Cummings Creek was big enough for their little boats, but not much bigger.

"Look, a culvert!" S.T. said again. "We should go in and see if anything's there."

"Like what?" Everett asked.

"A home for snakes," Louisa answered. "I'm not going in there."

"It'll be cool," S.T. answered. "Come on. It's a mystery to solve." He paddled over to the concrete apron and he and Linc stepped out. Everett and Louisa followed. A moment later, they stood at the mouth of the tunnel. It was higher than any of them standing up, and looked cold and dreary inside. S.T. waved around a flashlight, letting the beam shine on the walls. He stopped on a large gray packing on the roof.

"Wasp's nest," he said. He picked up a rock lying in the water and threw it up at the nest. It struck right in the middle, but no wasps appeared.

"Deserted," he said. "Come on, let's go inside."

Cool, stinky air hung around the entrance. S.T. stepped in, straddling the little stream of orangey clear water. Stains—gray, orange, brown—lay in strips on different levels inside the tunnel.

When you go into a dark place like this, there's a great verse to remember from 1 Kings 8:57: "May the Lord our God be with us as he was with our ancestors; may he never forsake us." You can depend on God wherever, whenever. How does this fact encourage you?

MYSTERY OF THE
DARK PASSAGE

S.T. pointed the flashlight at the stains. "It shows how high the water rose in a flood. Look at that one," he said, pointing at the highest one up, at about hip level. "That must have been a real flood when that one happened."

Moving inside, they could see that the tunnel didn't narrow. S.T. waved the flashlight around at things and they all proceeded.

They didn't get but 20 feet when there was a fluttering above them. Suddenly, the cavern was filled with an echoing screeching sound and the whir of wings.

"Get down! Bats!" S.T. yelled.

Everett hit the ground and Louisa crouched beside him. Linc lay flat out next to the stream of water. The bats fluttered all around them, their high-pitched squeaks sounding terrible and deadly in their ears. The bats flew deeper inside the tomblike cavern and soon their cries and wing-rushes diminished. S.T. rose hesitantly.

They walked along single file, keeping to the right side of the stream of water. They could hear dripping, and they could smell mold and decay.

Everett didn't like this place, but he didn't want to chicken out from going inside with the others. As they moved in farther, the light from the opening completely disappeared. Without the flash-light, they would have stood in pitch darkness.

Going into dark places can be either scary or exciting, some-times both. Read these verses from Psalms: "I could ask the darkness to hide me and the light around me to become night—but even in darkness I cannot hide from you. To you the night shines as bright as day. Darkness and light are both alike to you" (139:11, 12). How do you know God is with you wherever you go?

Everett felt sure S.T. would turn around, but suddenly he stopped. Everyone had been talking, but he whispered, "Quiet!"

Everyone froze.

"What is it?" Louisa asked, low and raspy.

"Listen!"

Everett strained his ears. He heard a little rumble, a growly, throaty noise.

"What is it?" Louisa said again.

"It's a dog!" S.T. suddenly said out loud. He shined the light and two golden brown eyes glowed in the dark. It was a brown female with a face like a collie. She didn't look vicious, but Everett could see she had several tiny puppies.

"Be careful," S.T. said, waving everyone back. "She might attack us if she thinks we're threatening her puppies."

S.T. and Everett knelt down about 10 feet from the dog. S.T. pulled off his backpack and rummaged through it. A moment later he drew out a pack of butterscotch snack cakes. S.T. held the cake flat on the palm of his hand. "You shouldn't give chocolate to dogs so it's a good thing it's butterscotch."

Feeding a hungry dog is an act of compassion. Compassion comes from God, and is part of his character. Psalm 145:9 says, "The Lord is good to everyone. He showers compassion on all his creation." When have you experienced God's compassion? When have you shown compassion to someone else?

The dog looked away, and S.T. turned the flashlight off her face. He handed it to Everett, who shone it in a circle of light in front of them. S.T. waved the butterscotch cake around. "Here, doggie," he said. "We won't hurt you. You must be hungry. Come here."

The dog moved her head back and forth as if she couldn't make a decision. Then she slowly stood and walked over, wagging her tail uncertainly. She had been lying on several pieces of boxboard, leaves, and other things she must have dragged into the tunnel to keep her puppies dry. She took the cake gently off S.T.'s hand, chewed it a few times then swallowed. S.T. quickly produced a second one, and she scarfed it down, this time with speed and relish. In another second, a third cake was gone.

Everett reached out and patted the dog's head. Soon all four of the kids petted the dog happily. A moment later, Louisa picked up one of the puppies. There were three others, and each of the kids picked up one. The mother dog's tail lashed with friendliness as the kids nuzzled and stroked the furry little ones.

"I wonder why she's in here," Louisa said.

"A lot of dogs go off somewhere to have their puppies," S.T. said right away. "They want to be private, I guess. We had one that disappeared for three weeks. Then she brought her puppies home. We have no idea where she was."

One Bible verse that gives us a glimpse of how much God cares for the animals he created is Jonah 4:11: "But Nineveh has more than 120,000 people living in spiritual darkness, not to mention all the animals, Shouldn't I feel sorry for such a great city?" God expressed his care not only for the people, but also for the animals of Nineveh. What evidence do you see that God cares for animals today?

"I wonder what her name is," Linc said as he knelt by the dog and hugged her. "She's real friendly. Maybe she's a stray."

"Looks like a mutt," Everett said. He was thinking about how nice it would be to have his own dog. But he knew he couldn't take this one home today. "She's got some collie in her, and lab."

"German shepherd, too," S.T. said. "Not a purebred."

The mother dog soon went back to her nest and the kids released the puppies. She lay down and they began to nurse.

"Well, I guess we've seen enough," S.T. said. He started to turn around when he suddenly crouched and whispered, "Hush!" He turned off his flashlight, and everything was pitch black.

"What is it?" Everett whispered in the darkness.

"Someone's coming."

Straining to hear, Everett heard scraping noises in the tunnel and saw the beam of a flashlight.

"Queenie!" a voice said—a male voice, but definitely a kid. "Hey, Queenie, girl? You there?"

Everett felt the dog brush past him, and with a sudden charge of energy, it barked.

"There she is!" the same voice said.

"She looks OK," another voice answered. This one was a girl, probably younger, Everett thought.

"How ya doin', girl? Everything OK?"

The kids thought nobody else knew about the dog in the culvert, but they were wrong. What they thought was a secret was not. While you can keep secrets from other people, you can never keep a secret from God. He knows everything. Psalm 44:21 says, "God . . . knows the secrets of every heart." You can share your secrets with God, because he knows your secrets already, and he loves you more than anyone.

The dog turned around padded back toward the kids. Everett could see it clearly in the light. Then it stopped, looking at the foursome. The kid with the flashlight walked jauntily toward them. "What is it, girl?" He raised the beam of the flashlight and leveled it right in Everett's eyes.

"Who are you?" S.T. said immediately.

The dog jumped back and scurried over to the boy again. Obviously, she was his dog. He let his hand rest on her head; then he eyed the foursome with hard eyes. "What are you doing here? We saw your boats. You're not going to take my dog, are you?"

S.T. stepped forward, holding out his hand. "Put down the flashlight. It's right in my eyes."

"I'll put it down when I'm good and ready. You have any weapons?"

"No!" S.T. said. "We were just exploring. What's your name?"

"That's none of your business."

"Well, I'm S.T. Frankl. This is Everett Abels, and Linc and Louisa Watterson. We were just looking around. We didn't expect to find a dog and a passel of puppies in here."

The boy lowered the flashlight slowly till it shone in a circle on the concrete floor of the culvert.

Dogs have a way of bringing people together. Just take a walk with one, and people will notice your dog and speak to you. When you show friendliness to others, you show God's love to them. "And this is love: that we walk in obedience to his commands. As you have heard from the beginning, his command is that you walk in love" (2 John 6, *NIV*). Ask God to help you show his love, even to people who aren't yet your friends.

The boy turned back to the foursome. "My name's Jesse Hawkins. I'm 11. This is Boop. But her real name is Deanna. She's only 8."

Everyone stood still, saying no more. Then S.T. said, "What's the dog's name?"

"Queenie," Jesse answered. "Haven't named the pups." For the first time he smiled.

"She's a nice dog," Everett said, when everyone lapsed into silence.

"Best dog ever," Jesse said abruptly.

Louisa walked over and stooped down in front of the little girl. She smiled, and Louisa saw that her two front teeth were missing.

"Boop and me came to give Queenie some food," Jesse said. He walked over to the little bed on the ground and the dog followed him. He put down a bowl and poured some dry dog food into it. The dog immediately started eating.

Deanna grinned happily and stepped into the circle of light. "Jesse's gonna give one of the pups to me," she said, her eyes glittering with enthusiasm. "I want the littlest one. I call him Michael."

In less than three minutes they stepped out of the stinky air of the culvert onto the flat concrete under the overpass.

"Dear friend, do not imitate what is evil but what is good. Anyone who does what is good is from God. Anyone who does what is evil has not seen God" (3 John 11, *NIV*). Caring for animals and being kind to people is a good thing. But loving God is the most important thing of all. Express your love to God today.

Nikki stood at the fence staring at the four horses. A new foal kicked up its heels and leaped. "They're so beautiful!" she said.

Mr. Beamer waved to her from the barn. He didn't mind Nikki watching his horses. His farm was just across the road from Nikki's house.

Nate, her twin brother, walked up behind her. He had on his backpack full of cupcakes, baseballs, tools, and pilot goggles. At 10 years old, Nate liked to be ready for anything. "Want a cupcake?" he asked Nikki.

Frowning, Nikki said, "No, I want a horse."

"Let's see," Nate said, looking through his backpack. "Nope. No horse."

Nikki didn't laugh. She said, "Does God answer your prayers, Nate?"

"Of course," Nate said. "He always answers. Sometimes he says no, but I know he always answers."

"God always says no to me," Nikki said sadly.

Nate's eyebrows went up. "Always?"

"Always."

Do you feel as if God always says no to your prayers? Some Christians feel that way. They look at good things that happen to others who pray, and yet feel as though God is ignoring them.

Generally, God's answers to prayer can range from, "Yes, here it is," to "No, never." But in between are other answers like, "Maybe later," "Wait until you grow some," or "When you show me you're ready." In his book of the Bible, James gives one clear reason God answers no to prayers. Read James 4:2, 3 to find out what it is. Then think about whether any of your prayers fall into the category James mentions.

Nate took out his slingshot and loaded a pebble. He aimed at his foot. "Pow! The dinosaur dies in a drooly dump of dirt!"

Nikki reached out and grabbed his arm. "Nate, I want God to say yes for a change."

Nate nodded. "I prayed for a bike for my birthday."

Nikki said, "Daddy got it for you."

Nate wrinkled his nose. Then he said, "I prayed for wind when I flew my kite. And wind came."

"Did it always come?"

"No," Nate admitted.

"See," Nikki said. "God says no to you sometimes. But he says no to me ALL the time."

"If it's any help, I'll pray for you," Nate said. "I'll ask God to help you trust that he loves you, even when he says no."

Nikki shook her head. "Just ask him to say yes next time."

Nate frowned. "Nothing I say is going to get you out of this mood. I'm going for a swim. This is between you and God."

Nikki sighed. "I guess you're right."

Nate trudged across the road, dragging his backpack. Nikki stayed for a few minutes, still gazing at the horses, especially the little golden foal. Then she followed Nate home. She got some juice out of the fridge and sat out by the pool.

If you're sometimes confused by prayer, you're in good company. Jesus' disciples had some trouble with prayer too, and asked Jesus to help them. Jesus said, "your Father knows exactly what you need even before you ask him!" Read Matthew 6:7, 8.

If God knows what you need, can you trust him to answer your prayers in the way that's best?

MYSTERY OF THE
GOLDEN HORSE

Nate sat down by the pool. He dipped his squirt gun into the water. Then he squirted some on Nikki. She yelled. He laughed. He loved spraying water on Nikki. She was such a wimp.

He asked her, "What if we pray a secret prayer?"

"A secret prayer?" Nikki asked.

"No one will know about it. Not Mom. Not Dad. No one but God."

"Sounds different," she said. "How do you do it?"

Nate ran into the house and came out with a notebook. "What should we pray for?" he asked.

"Someone to throw water on you!" Nikki said, kicking at the water.

"No, be serious," Nate said.

"That Mom won't lose her mind over her son!" Nikki said.

"No, that's too hard. She loses it every day."

Nikki laughed. "OK," she said. "A horse. That's what I wanted for my birthday. That's what I wanted for Christmas."

Nate wrote. "Yeah! A horse! What kind of horse?"

"A horse with a flowing mane. A long beautiful tail. Golden colored. A palomino. Like Mr. Beamer's new foal."

Nate wrote everything down. "Anything else?"

"By tomorrow," Nikki said.

"Wow!" Nate said. "That's fast. Can God grow one that quick?"

"God can do anything," Nikki said.

Can God really do anything? If you mean whether he's all-powerful enough to create a horse as big as the earth, or a world full of talking horses, yes, he could do that. But would he? And why?

God works within the laws and principles of our world, but he's not limited by anything. In Ephesians 3:20, Paul says this about God: "By his mighty power at work within us, he is able to accomplish infinitely more than we would ever dare to ask or hope."

"OK," Nate answered. He finished writing it down. Then he folded the paper. He said, "Come with me."

They walked to the edge of the swimming pool. Nate found a flat rock and lifted it up.

"Yuck! A slug!" Nikki cried.

"He'll protect our prayer," Nate said. He hid the paper under the rock. "God, now it's up to you."

Nate dove into the pool. Nikki sunned on the side. Nate splashed Nikki six times. She screamed all six. Whenever Nate came up for air, he yelled, "It's up to you, God."

Nikki just laughed. She thought, *If God answers that prayer, He can do anything.*

That night, Nate and Nikki's parents took them out to dinner.

"Do you think God will answer tonight?" Nikki asked.

Nate said, "We'll see."

Nate had a hamburger. Nikki had chicken tenders. Afterwards, they stepped outside. Behind the restaurant was a fenced-in paddock with a horse. It was big and black, with a long black mane.

"It's not the answer," said Nikki.

"I know," said Nate. "But I'd take him."

"So would I," Nikki said. Her heart pounded with hope. They walked over to the fence and both petted the horse. It snorted right in Nate's face.

"'My thoughts are completely different from yours,' says the Lord. 'And my ways are far beyond anything you could imagine. For just as the heavens are higher than the earth, so are my ways higher than your ways and my thoughts higher than your thoughts'" (Isaiah 55:8, 9).

While we might expect God to answer our prayer one way, he could choose to do something else. Have you ever had a prayer answered that was even better than what you had in mind when you asked?

MYSTERY OF THE
GOLDEN HORSE

In the morning, Nikki and Nate woke up to shouts.

"They're fox hunting!" cried Nikki's mother.

Everyone ran to the window. There across the way ran 10 horses with riders. The horses were brown, black, spotted, and white. One rider blew a trumpet. Dozens of hunting dogs barked and howled.

"It's not the answer," said Nikki.

"I know," Nate said.

Nikki looked at her Super-Duper Underwater Perfect-Time-All-the-Time Watch. "God still has 16 hours."

All day they expected a horse to come. God would answer. It might drop out of the sky. It might run up the road.

But nothing happened. Nate threw a ball against the little barn. Nikki shot baskets. Nate went for a swim. Nikki weeded in the garden. Nate ate cupcakes. Nikki prayed.

Late that afternoon, Nikki and Nate took a walk. They went to Mr. Beamer's fence. The horses rolled and ran. The little foal whinnied. It was beautiful. Nikki turned around. "I can't look anymore. It makes me wish too hard."

Habakkuk prayed that God would rid the land of Israel of sin and evil. God answered by telling him that he would send the Babylonians to conquer them. Habakkuk was aghast. He cried out, "O Lord my God, my Holy One, you who are eternal—is your plan in all of this to wipe us out? Surely not! O Lord our Rock, you have decreed the rise of these Babylonians to punish and correct us for our terrible sins" (Habakkuk 1:12).

God answered Habakkuk's prayer, but not in the way Habakkuk wanted or expected. Do you know people who have had that happen?

Nate sighed. "Come on, God!"

"That's not how you do it," Nikki said.

"Then how?"

"You say, 'Father in Heaven, please, please, please, please.'"

Nate chuckled.

Soon it was late afternoon. Mom and Dad were working in the garden.

Nate and Nikki went down to watch. They picked up the stone by the pool and opened their paper. The slug crawled away. They read the note again.

"I guess God said no again," Nikki said sadly.

Mom looked at them. "God said no to what?"

"Our prayer," said Nikki.

"What prayer?"

"It's a secret. . . . Oh, I guess it doesn't matter now. We prayed for a horse. Actually, it was my prayer, but Nate joined me. We wrote it down so God would know exactly what we wanted."

Mom shook her head. "Did you ask God for a place to keep a horse? And for money to buy food and pay veterinarian bills? If God gave you a horse, how would you take care of it?"

Nikki wanted to cry.

Mom is turning Nikki's prayer on end with things she didn't think of. Where would she put a real horse? How would she feed it and take care of it?

Many times when God says no it's because we're not ready yet. But does that mean he won't answer at all?

John wrote about one very important element to getting a yes answer for our prayers. Find out what it is by reading 1 John 5:14.

233

Her mother said, "Honey, sometimes God answers yes. Sometimes He answers no. And sometimes he says, 'Wait.'"

"I know," Nikki said. "It's just that I always get a no."

Nikki was about to walk away, when suddenly Mr. Beamer rode up on a golden horse, the foal's mother.

Mr. Beamer smiled. "Nikki, I want to ask you something. I need someone to take care of my little foal. I see you out on the fence all the time, so I know you love horses. Would you like a job?"

"To take care of the golden foal?" Nikki asked.

"Right," Mr. Beamer said. "He'd be yours until he grows up."

Everyone dropped their jaw. Nikki was too amazed to speak.

Mr. Beamer said, "Will you?"

Nikki cried, "Yes, sir!"

Nate shouted, "God does answer prayer!"

Nikki smiled as she walked up the road with Mr. Beamer on his horse. When she saw the foal leaping and running, she said, "Thank you, God, for saying yes!"

Amazing, isn't it? God knew what was needed, and how to answer so that Nikki really could have a horse in a place where she could take care of it and meet its basic needs. It wasn't quite what she expected, but it was what she wanted. God came through in a way she never could have predicted. The psalmist wrote, "Taste and see that the Lord is good. Oh, the joys of those who trust in him!" (Psalm 34:8). How do you taste and see that the Lord is good? What prayers do you have today that you can take to the Lord? Will you wait and watch for his answer?

Lily and Tomas rode their horses along the main road. Up ahead, it appeared there had been a traffic accident, so both sixth graders slowed their horses to a walk.

"What is it?" Lily asked.

"Looks like some kind of truck turned over," Tomas answered.

There were police cruisers with lights flashing, and several colorful pickups. "It's a circus!" Tomas added.

They were about a hundred feet away when a police officer ran across the road waving his arm. Lily pulled up her horse and Tomas followed.

"You'll have to wait for a couple of minutes," the officer said. "We have a situation here."

Lily nodded and sat petting her horse's neck to keep it calm. But the horse reared and backed up as if frightened by something.

"What's wrong?" asked Lily.

"There's a bear out of control," the officer said.

"Bear?" Tomas asked.

As if called, a bear lumbered across the road. It dragged a chain, and a man ran after it, shouting. "Stop, Wooly, stop!"

A bear? On a public street? That's not something you see every day. Even when you see them in the wild, you should avoid bears. They can be dangerous, even if they look friendly.

When David faced the giant Goliath, he recalled his experience with bears. He told King Saul, "When a lion or a bear comes to steal a lamb from the flock, I go after it with a club and take the lamb from its mouth. . . . I have done this to both lions and bears, and I'll do it to this pagan Philistine. . . . The Lord who saved me from the claws of the lion and the bear will save me from this Philistine!" (1 Samuel 17:34-37). The God who saved David from bears will save you from harm. Do you trust him?

The bear came right at them and stood up on hind legs, roaring. Lily's horse reared and spun around.

The man running after the bear grabbed the chain, hauling back on it. The bear fell back.

"Sorry, sorry," the man said. "Wooly has—"

The bear whipped around and swatted the man on the shoulder, knocking him over. Then it tore off the chain, turned, and ran into the woods behind the trucks.

In a split second, everything went crazy. Lily kicked her horse and it headed down the road at full tilt, Tomas and his horse right behind.

A hundred yards from the wreck, Lily pulled up and looked back. Tomas turned with her. "Wow, that was close," he said. "I thought that bear was going to rip that man to pieces."

"It saw its chance at an escape. Now it's free," Lily said.

"Let's put the horses away and walk back up, see what's happening," Tomas suggested.

They trotted down to the small barn and tied the horses up.

Lily and Tomas walked back to the scene of the accident, and found a group getting ready to track the bear. There were three men with big rifles, and another man with two bloodhounds. "They're not going to shoot the bear, are they?" asked Lily.

Lily and Tomas were smart to get away from the attacking bear. People have been seriously hurt and even killed by bears. The Bible records a time when bears mauled 42 boys—as punishment for something they did. What had the boys done? Find out by reading 2 Kings 2:23-25).

The man who originally chased after the bear walked over to them. "I'm Harry Shultz." He held out his hand. "If you want, you can help us."

"What can we do?" Tomas asked, shaking Mr. Shultz's hand.

"Watch the road. Wooly probably won't go far away, and he may cross back onto the side with the houses in search of food."

"I guess we could do that, for a while," Lily said. "But we'll have to go home for dinner."

"We'll probably have him by then, if he doesn't cross," the man said. "Thanks."

Lily and Tomas stationed themselves a couple hundred yards down from the trucks. There was no sign of Wooly.

"What should we do if we see him?" asked Lily. "What if he comes after us?"

"I'm not sure, but hopefully if he does, all those men will be following him," Tomas answered.

After a while it was time for supper. "We'd better get home," Tomas said. "Mom will be watching for us." He looked at Lily and winked. "And I'm hungry as a bear!"

Lily groaned.

What happens when a captive animal suddenly goes free? Sometimes the animal panics. Sometimes freed animals starve or put themselves in danger because they don't have skills learned in the wild. Whenever an animal is stressed, it's best to stay out of the way.

The Bible uses the image of a mother bear who has lost her cubs as particularly fierce and dangerous. Yet, according to Proverbs 17:12 the bear is safer than a foolish person: "It is safer to meet a bear robbed of her cubs than to confront a fool caught in folly." What people do you know of who are more dangerous than bears?

237

At dinner, Lily and Tomas's dad listened to the story. "I saw all those trucks when I drove home from work. Wondered what it was."

"Do you think they'll shoot Wooly?" Tomas asked.

"I'd think it would be an easy capture," Dad said. "But you might talk to Mr. Jameson down the street. He used to hunt bear in Alaska. Still does, I think."

Lily looked at Tomas. "Could we go ask him tonight?" she asked her dad.

"All right with me. Don't tangle with that bear, though."

Lily and Tomas traipsed down to Mr. Jameson's house. When they told him the story, he said he'd seen it on the news that evening.

"What will they do to track him?" Lily asked.

"They sound like a bunch of amateurs," Mr. Jameson said. "Dogs aren't always good with wild animals—big ones, anyway. They're too scared, and they often don't track right. If they don't catch him by tomorrow morning, come on over. I'll take you out looking for him."

The next morning, Lily and Tomas awoke with the sun, and the 5:30 news. There was a short segment about the circus and the bear. It was still missing at the time of the broadcast.

The kids dressed and quickly hiked over to Mr. Jameson's. He was already standing by his truck.

If you think about bad things that could happen to you, encountering a wild bear is not likely. You're far more likely to be hurt by a car than a bear. Yet the Bible describes the worst possible thing that can happen to any person—God's judgment—in this way: "In that day you will be like a man who runs from a lion—only to meet a bear. After escaping the bear, he leans his hand against a wall in his house—and is bitten by a snake" (Amos 5:19).

Mr. Jameson drove his truck along slowly, but they saw no signs of the bear until he suddenly stopped in the middle of the road. There in front of them was a pile of animal droppings.

"See that flop there," he said to Lily and Tomas. "The bear's been here. We have to make him feel a little more at home."

They all got out and Mr. Jameson grabbed a shovel in the back of his truck. He picked up the flop and put it on the hood of the truck.

"What will that do?" Lily asked.

"It has his scent. He'll either think it's safe cause he's already been here, or he'll think it's another bear. Were there other bears at the accident?"

Lily shook her head. "I didn't see any."

But Tomas said, "The truck that had turned over said, 'Shultz's three dancing bears.' Maybe there were two others they'd already trucked off."

"Good, good," said Mr. Jameson. "Let's just hope none of those hunters are trigger happy."

Animal trackers often use animal waste as evidence of where the animals have been. They also use footprints, scratches and marks made by horns or antlers, and hair that the animals have shed to identify their location and habits.

The Bible says that God knows where all animals are all the time. Since he created them and is in control, no animal is out of his sight or out of his care. Read Job 39:1-8 to find out what God says about the animals he created and how much he knows about them.

When they got back into the truck, Mr. Jameson handed Tomas a large package of hot dogs, probably two dozen of them. "Throw one out onto the road every hundred feet. That bear will be real hungry by now. He probably doesn't know how to feed himself in the wild."

They drove along up the mountain. Finally, with all the hot dogs gone, Mr. Jameson turned the truck around. Every few hundred feet, he stopped and Tomas put some of the bear droppings on the roadbed.

Lily saw the undisturbed hot dogs as they went back down the mountain. Mr. Jameson said, "He's probably sleeping. About seven o'clock this evening, he'll awake to his stomach growling. We'll come back then. I'll drop you off at your house now, and come back to pick you up around seven."

"Great."

That evening, Mr. Jameson was right on time. As the kids climbed into the truck, he said, "I have a flashlight, in case it gets dark. Also my cell phone. If we find the bear, we can call Mr. Shultz."

If you're looking for a bear, you wouldn't look in the sky, would you? Yet there are two bears in the nighttime sky—constellations Ursa Major, the Big Bear, and Ursa Minor, the Little Bear. They're easy to find. Ursa Minor is also called the Little Dipper. And the Big Dipper is part of the body and tail of Ursa Major.

The bear constellations are mentioned in the Bible, along with a couple of others. What are they? Read Job 9: 9 to find out.

They hadn't driven very far up the road when they saw where they'd left the first hot dogs. They were gone.

"There's a fresh flop," Tomas pointed out.

"I think he's out and about."

As they drove up the road, every hot dog was gone. Then, up ahead, they saw the bear, bent down and eating another hot dog.

Mr. Jameson left his headlamps on and they watched the bear. He didn't seem afraid.

"He's really beautiful," Lily said.

"Kodiak, I'd say," Mr. Jameson commented. "Biggest bear there is. He's a young one. They probably had him from a cub." They watched for a few minutes as Mr. Jameson took out his phone. "You want to do the honors?" he asked Tomas as he handed him the phone.

Fifteen minutes later, three pickups pulled up behind their truck. One had a big cage in the back. Mr. Shultz stopped at Mr. Jameson's window. But Lily was watching through the windshield. "Look," she said. "Look at Wooly."

Everyone turned. There in the beams of the headlights, as though spotlighted on a circus stage, the bear stood, dancing.

Bears won't always be fearsome creatures, and neither will lions or wolves. How do we know? Because the Bible says so. In describing the kingdom of God, painting a word picture of what Heaven will be like, the prophet Isaiah wrote, "In that day the wolf and the lamb will live together; the leopard and the goat will be at peace. Calves and yearlings will be safe among lions, and a little child will lead them all. The cattle will graze among bears. Cubs and calves will lie down together. And lions will eat grass as the livestock do" (Isaiah 11:6, 7). Isn't that a wonderful future to look forward to?

MYSTERY OF THE
THING UNDER
MY BED

Every night the thing under my bed twitches and coughs and growls. I don't know what to do anymore. I'm afraid to stick my hand under there because he might bite it off. And I'm afraid to crawl under there with a flashlight and shine it in his eyes because he might look so horrible, I'll wet my pajamas right there.

My dad says I should get the broom and sweep around and swish it out of there. But what if he grabs the broom in his teeth and pulls me right under? He could bite out an eyeball, or chomp off my nose.

The worst was tonight. I heard him hacking and snuffling, and then scratching on the mattress from the bottom. I'm worried he'll dig through the mattress and come right through to me. He's scratching right now. I can hear him—*scritch, scritch, scritch.* What should I do? What if he really does claw through everything and bite me right in the behind? Or gnaw off one of my toes?

When you're afraid, you can't think clearly. You imagine the worst, and that feeds your fear. What can you do when you're afraid? David the psalmist wrote this: "When I am afraid, I put my trust in you. O God, I praise your word. I trust in God, so why should I be afraid? What can mere mortals do to me?" (Psalm 56:3, 4).

At the first pang of fear, go to God in prayer. He is more powerful than anything in the world. He can calm your fears.

I'd like to call my dad to come in, but he's a marine. He says it's all my imagination.

I can't tell Mom because she'll say, "Oh, don't be such a wimp. Tell it to go away and then go to sleep."

Scritch. Scritch. Scritch. Cough. Cough.

I can hear him. I've got to do something.

"Hey, you! You down there!"

Silence.

"You? You hear me?"

Nibble, nibble.

Is he eating something now? Maybe it's just a rat. Maybe it's a big sewer rat with beady eyes and giant pointy teeth and—AHHHH!

OK, I've got to get hold of myself. I've got to be brave. Surely he's just hungry. Maybe I should put some dog food down there. But we don't have any, and they only sell it in gigantic bags down at Walmart, and I can't afford it, and how would I carry it all the way up here, and what would I tell my parents, and besides, we DON'T HAVE A DOG! If we did, I'd send him to go under my bed and eat that thing!

"Hey, you!"

Maybe the worst time for feeling fear is at night when you're alone in bed. Somehow things that don't seem so bad during the day can be overwhelming at night. A verse from the Bible to remember is Isaiah 12:2: "See, God has come to save me. I will trust in him and not be afraid."

MYSTERY OF THE
THING UNDER MY BED

Silence.

Scritch, scritch.

Should I stick my hand out over the edge of my bed? No, wait! Not my hand. I should stick something else down there. My light saber, or that big foam tube my sister swims with. But what if he bites it? What if he claws his way up to my hand? What if I drop it? Will I have to fight?

"Hey? You listening down there? Come on out. Show yourself. I want to see you."

Silence.

Then: *click. Click. Click. Click.*

Claws! He's walking across the floor. He's got those big huge claws that can gouge your brains out. Help! Help!

No, I've got to be calm. OK, what to do?

"I'm going to stick my hand out now. See that, I'm sticking my hand over the edge of the bed. See it? It's just a nice little hand. It's not very juicy, so you shouldn't chomp into it. But if you're there, maybe you can just breathe on it or something."

I'm reaching down now. My hand is almost to the lower mattress. But what if I stick it out and he whacks it right off with a big crunch?

Worry has a way of multiplying, and taking control of your thoughts and emotions. God knows that—after all, he created you! But he doesn't want you to be consumed by worry. In his Sermon on the Mount Jesus said this: "Can all your worries add a single moment to your life? Of course not. And why worry about your clothes? Look at the lilies and how they grow. They don't work or make their clothing, yet Solomon in all his glory was not dressed as beautifully as they are. And if God cares so wonderfully for flowers that are here today and gone tomorrow, won't he more surely care for you?" (Matthew 6:27-29).

Where is he? Is he on the edge? Is he ready to pounce?

OK, this is it. I'm sticking my hand all the way down there to see what happens. If he eats it off, that's it. It's over for me.

I'm sticking my hand out. Down. Down. Down.

It's all the way there now. It's in the open space between the floor and the bed. If he's going to do anything, he'll do it— AHHHHH! He's licking me!

Eeeewww! That felt ooky. Could I catch some kind of disease from his spit? Could I be exposed to some sort of skin-eating bacteria? What if I can't wash it off?

What should I do now? I mean, he didn't bite off my hand. Maybe he's friendly. Maybe he can be trained to sit and stay. Maybe I should just stow it. Maybe I should just go to sleep and stop talking. Maybe I—

No! Wait! What if he's luring me in? What if he's trying to make me think he's friendly but he's really getting ready to trap me!

What should I do? I wish he would just come out and show himself. If I could see him, I would know what I was dealing with. Then I wouldn't be so afraid.

Or maybe, if I saw him, I'd be even more afraid.

It's true that worrying never solved anything. It just makes you feel bad. You don't know what the future holds, but you know who is in control. You can say with David, "Even when I walk through the dark valley of death, I will not be afraid, for you are close beside me. Your rod and your staff protect and comfort me" (Psalm 23:4). Being confident that God is with you can help you conquer your fears.

245

MYSTERY OF THE
THING UNDER
MY BED

OK, here goes. I'll stick my hand down again. Maybe if I touch him, he'll get scared and leave.

Oooo. He's licking me, with a rough tongue, like a cat's. But it couldn't be a cat, could it? Why doesn't it meow? Where would it be coming from?

OK, my hand's back. He just licked it. But I couldn't stand to touch him, so I still don't know how big he is. Maybe he's as scared of me as I am of him.

Get a grip! Just put your hand down there. If he was going to bite or attack, he would have already done so. Try to talk to him softly and gently like that guy on cable who trains dogs by sweet-talking them.

There. Down. Down. I feel the space. "Hey, you! Let me feel your fur. Rub up against my hand or something."

Hey, I feel his fur. It's soft, but there's a lot of it. This thing's pretty big—wow, really big. How can he fit under there?

Maybe I can get him to come out into the room. Then when he gets there, I'll turn on the light and really see him.

"Hey, would you come out for a second? I'd like to take a little picture. Come on, come out. Don't be afraid."

Click. Click. Clickety-click-click-click.

"I'm getting my camera. Just be still. Don't move. I can almost feel you out there. I know you're pretty big. But I won't be scared. I won't make any noise. All right, I've got the camera. I'm sitting up now. I'm aiming it. Are you ready?"

"Do not be afraid of the terrors of the night" (Psalm 91:5). Why should you not be afraid? Read Psalm 91:1-6 and find out. To what creature does this Scripture compare God? How does he provide armor and protection?

Flash!

What was that? Big red eyes. That's all I could see. He was sitting up, wasn't he? Looking at me. I'll have to get a flashlight.

"Stay right there, OK? Don't move. I want to see you better. Then we can be friends. Would that be nice?"

I can feel him staring back at me, licking his lips. He can taste me. He's ready to leap. He will bite into my throat. I hope it happens fast. I could stand it if it happened fast, if I didn't have to hear him chomping.

"Hey, you over there? Will you let me go get my flashlight?"

Grrrrrrrrrrr.

That doesn't sound good. How tall is he? Is he bigger than me? What if he is bigger than me? What if he's bigger than the whole room? What if he's here from another planet?

Oh, man. I have to risk this. I have to see him.

"Just be cool, OK? I'm just slipping over there to my desk to get my flashlight. Don't jump on me when I get off the bed, OK? That wouldn't be nice. You're nice, right? You don't want to eat me?"

Click click click.

How can you be sure that God will help you handle your worries and fears? The apostle John gave this reason: "the Spirit who lives in you is greater than the spirit who lives in the world" (1 John 4:4).

Do you have problems or concerns that keep you awake at night? You can rest easy because God is in control.

MYSTERY OF THE
THING UNDER
MY BED

Oh, man. Oh, man. He's coming toward me.

Get ready. Leap out of bed, grab the flashlight. Turn it on. Turn it on!

Oh, don't tell me the batteries are dead! Good grief! Could it get any worse?

Click click click.

He's coming for me! Hit the bed! Get back under the covers. He can't hurt you under the covers—they're like steel to a monster.

No, no! What am I doing? Just turn on the light. Just hit the switch. Quit being such a baby about it!

I'm going for it; almost there.

Click.

Close your eyes! Don't look! If you don't look, he won't leap on you!

OK, now open one eye. Just a little, go ahead.

Oooooo, I can see something. He's right there. He's looking at me. He has shiny white teeth. But they're not that big. He's not that big.

OK, open your eye more. And now the other one.

GRRRRRRRRRR.

AHHHHH.

"Dad, Dad! Hurry! There's a raccoon in my room!"

There will always be things to be afraid of, and there will always be circumstances beyond our control. But we can be sure that God will always be with us, and he will hear our prayers.

"In times of trouble, may the Lord respond to your cry. May the God of Israel keep you safe from all harm. May he send you help from his sanctuary and strengthen you from Jerusalem" (Psalm 20:1, 2). How will you respond when God gives you help?

Jamal and I walked along the street, looking for something to do. The wind kicked up and I grabbed my hat to keep it from blowing off.

"We could play catch," Jamal said.

"I'm tired of that." We'd played catch every day since the summer started. I kicked at stones and little piles of dirt in the road.

"We could go up to the store," Jamal commented.

"I don't have any money, do you?"

"Nah."

"We could go climb some trees and look out over everything."

I sighed. "I skinned myself up pretty bad last time we did that," I answered, remembering how it had stung when I took a bath that night.

A big gust hit and my hat blew off before I could grab it. "Hey!"

It rolled across the street. We both ran after it. I leaned down and almost had it when another gust grabbed and threw it even further away. We ran along, stooping and reaching, but always it stayed out in front. Then, with a swoosh, it whacked into one of the sewer drains and disappeared.

"Oh, no!"

We stood at the drain, looking down. There lay my hat on the dry bottom. It didn't move, and there hadn't been rain, so it was fine. All I had to do was go get it.

Have you ever lost a favorite hat—or coat, or game, or toy? It's sad and frustrating, even if the item isn't worth much money. It's worth a lot to you if it's your favorite.

Jesus told a parable about a woman who lost a coin that was extremely valuable to her. Find out what she did by reading Luke 15:8-10. According to Jesus, how are people like lost coins? —◎

MYSTERY OF THE
FLYING HAT

"Maybe I can slide into the hole here," Jamal said. He quickly slid in a foot, then both feet. He tried to push himself all the way through, but I held up my hand.

"Don't risk it," I said. "Let's see if we can lift the grate."

Jamal pulled out and we both got our hands on the back of the grate, heaving with all our might. It didn't budge.

"Again," I cried. We really got into it, but the thing was just too heavy. We stood panting.

"What do we do now?" Jamal said.

"Doesn't the drain pipe empty into the creek?" I asked.

"Yeah, I think so."

"Let's go down and look. Maybe we can crawl up the drain pipe to here and get my hat." It was my favorite baseball cap, a Phillies cap. Though we lived far from Philadelphia, my father had grown up there and was a big Phillies fan. He'd made me one.

It may sound strange, but all I could think about at that moment was to pray. "I want to pray about this," I said.

"Wow! You must be really stressed out over this," Jamal said.

I looked up at the sky. "God," I began, "I know this seems really silly that I should care so much about a hat, but that Phillies cap means a lot to me, and to my dad. I don't want to lose it. Will you please help us to think carefully about what to do, and make a way for me to get the cap back? Please keep Jamal and me safe. Thank you for listening. Amen."

Have you ever talked to God about something that other people would think is trivial? You don't have to be embarrassed. God loves you so much, he will listen to your every prayer. He may not give you everything you ask, but he will always listen to you. David was sure that when he prayed God would hear him. Read what he said in Psalm 5:1-3.

We hurried down to the creek and climbed down the steep banks to where the drain pipe came out. We both gazed into the pipe, a darkness in its depths like the eyes of a snake. The clouds in the sky darkened, and that culvert gave me chills.

I said, "I figure we can follow it all the way to the drain where the hat is. Maybe we can go even further. You just never know what we might find."

"How far will we have to go?" Jamal asked.

"I figure about three hundred yards."

"But what if it rains?" he asked, bringing up the question on my mind too.

"We have to hurry, I guess."

"Do the pipes get smaller as you go further in?" Jamal asked.

I hadn't thought about that. "I guess that's what we have to find out." I stepped into the drain pipe and suddenly wished I had a flashlight. "Come on, let's get going. This is the edge of adventure. This is the outer limits. This is the twilight zone."

Jamal gave me a quick push. "It's just a pipe," he said. "What do you think is in there? Stuff that goes in a pipe, that's what . . . and maybe a lair, hidden deep in the center of the earth . . . and a few monsters."

"Get out of here!" I said, and bent down to walk inside.

A drainage ditch or culvert can be a dangerous place. Unless there is some compelling reason to do so, you should not go into one.

How is life apart from God like a drainage tunnel? Find out by reading Proverbs 4:18, 19.

MYSTERY OF THE
FLYING HAT

Bending over at about three-quarters height, we walked along inside the pipe. Here and there, cobwebs hung down from the ceiling and I had to knock them out of the way to get by. Looking down, I suddenly saw something glinting brightly on the bottom. "Look," I said to Jamal.

I picked it up. It was a gold watch, very dirty, but it looked like it might work. I wound it for a second, but it didn't tick.

"It's probably one with a battery," Jamal said. "Probably dead by now."

I shoved the watch into my pocket. "Finders keepers," I said.

He suddenly bent down and pulled something out of the dirt and gravel. He held it up. "A nickel."

"I bet there's all kinds of money in here," I said, and began to speed up, watching the bottom as closely as I could. It had gotten darker inside the pipe, and I couldn't see much.

A big cobweb got into my hair and I looked up. A paper was caught in it. I reached up and studied it. "A five-dollar bill!" I almost screamed.

Jamal looked at it. "You're right. Pretty dirty, though."

I shoved it into my pocket. "Next time, we come down here with a flashlight."

I saw daylight ahead. Thinking this was the drain with my hat, we plunged on.

What's the most valuable thing you've ever found? Did you feel as though you'd discovered "hidden treasure?"

The book of Proverbs in the Bible tells you of something you should search for "as you would for lost money or hidden treasure." What is it? Read Proverbs 2:1-7 to discover the treasure God grants to the godly.

We reached the area where the light came in. It was a drain, but not the one with my hat. I looked up and could see the dark clouds clearly. "It's gonna rain," I said.

The first drops struck my face.

"Looks like it already is," Jamal said.

I glanced down at the floor of the drain and there lay a rubber baby doll, very dirty. I bent down to look more closely. There I found a quarter, two pennies, and a dime. Jamal found some coins too. I thought if we went to every pipe in the area, we'd be rich.

As I looked more closely, I saw something that stopped my heart: a dead bird. "Yuck," I cried. It looked gross.

"Don't step on it, you might hurt it," Jamal said.

"It's dead."

"That's what I mean. It might be a zombie bird, ready to bite into your shin if you step on it."

"Very funny." I gave him a shove.

We turned to continue, and suddenly I noticed that a few feet down, the pipe split. One section went to the left, and the other straight ahead. I looked back at Jamal.

A pipe that splits, like a fork in the road, forces you to make a decision. You can go one way or the other, but not both.

Following Jesus is a decision that requires you to choose one path over another. Jesus described it like this: "You can enter God's Kingdom only through the narrow gate. The highway to hell is broad, and its gate is wide for the many who choose the easy way. But the gateway to life is small, and the road is narrow, and only a few ever find it" (Matthew 7:13, 14).

"Which way should we go?" I asked.

"I don't know. But if it starts really pouring, we're going to have to get out. These drains fill up fast."

I thought about it. "I think it's just up a little ways. We should go straight."

We hurried on. A little water began to come in, and soon a small stream formed and went down the tube. I straddled it so I wouldn't get my sneakers wet.

We continued on, plodding harder now, our sneakers slapping the concrete sides of the drain with a whapping sound.

"It smells so bad," Jamal said after a while.

"Probably from people throwing garbage in the street. I bet there's someone up there right now—"

"Shut up," Jamal said, and his voice echoed mysteriously in the pipe, and then suddenly got swallowed up in silence.

"Sounds really crazy," I said.

The darkness was pierced by light again and soon we saw an end to the pipe. A moment later, we stood in a second drain and looked down. There was my hat, the little stream of water tugging at it. The drain was filling up fast now and I knew we had to go back quickly.

How many fears in life have you found that gripped you at one time, but now no longer affect you since you've grown up a little? In the past you might have been afraid of storms, but now that you're older you understand what lightning and thunder are. You may have been afraid of dogs, but as you got to know some dogs and were around them more, your fear evaporated. Sometimes knowledge or experience helps to dispel fear. John wrote about something else that conquers fear. Read 1 John 4:18 to find out what other force expels fear.

We hurried along, but above us the storm had really cut loose. We had to get out—now!

Soon the water sloshed around our knees and we couldn't straddle the flow any longer. Jamal said, "It's filling up fast."

"Hurry." But the stream slowed us down a lot. Slogging through the water was like trying to walk in the baby pool at the local community center, except worse because of all the debris floating in it. It was slow going. Soon the water began to approach our waists. The first drain we'd come to earlier loomed up ahead.

When we reached it, we looked up. It was really pouring now, and above us waterfalls rushed down into the drain.

"I have an idea. Swim in it," I said.

Jamal nodded. "That might work. You go first."

The water was now above my waist. I plunged into it and moved along at the same speed as the rushing water. I was just coasting, letting the water pull me. I heard Jamal plunge in behind me.

The water was filling up the tunnel, but I soon saw the end of the tube ahead. I doggie paddled to keep myself afloat.

Then with sudden force, I came out the end of the pipe into the creek. Jamal was right behind me. We laughed, until I went under and lost my hat again. This time I caught it, though.

This story has a happy ending, but it didn't have to end that way. Either of the boys could have been injured or even killed if they had waited any longer to get out of the culvert. God blessed them and answered their prayer for safety. He's an expert on water rescues. God words are recorded by Isaiah the prophet: "When you go through deep waters and great trouble, I will be with you. When you go through rivers of difficulty, you will not drown!" (Isaiah 43:2).

MYSTERY OF THE
SILVER DOLLAR

Rialta was at her usual spot, sitting on the stoop near the bar. For a homeless girl in Mexico, this was a good place to meet people and possibly get spare change. As she sat, Diego and Sargo, two regulars, left the bar. As they walked away, she heard a distinctive metallic *thunk*.

She crept over to the door. There on the ground lay Diego's shiny silver dollar. He must have dropped it. She snapped it up and put it into her pocket. A silver dollar could buy meals for two days, and maybe even a new shirt for her little brother Paco and a nice comb for her.

She nestled down by the bushes under the sign at the motel to think. Should she keep the silver dollar? Diego didn't need it, and she did. Rialta wrestled with her inner thoughts until she fell asleep.

Suddenly many people were shouting above and around her. Her eyes popped open. A crowd of people stood in a circle. From behind the bushes she could see two men in the middle of the circle, squaring off.

"You stole it! You've always wanted it!" It was a high, whiny voice. Diego!

"I took nothing!" Sargo's strong, hard-edged voice rang out.

They faced one another, fists raised. At least 20 people stood about.

"What is causing the quarrels and fights among you?" James wrote. Then he answered the question: "Isn't it the whole army of evil desires at war within you? You want what you don't have, so you scheme and kill to get it. You are jealous for what others have, and you can't possess it, so you fight and quarrel to take it away from them" (James 4:1, 2). In this story, Diego and Sargo are obviously fighting, but Rialta is fighting a battle of her own—with her conscience.

"Get him, Diego. He's always been a thief!" someone in the crowd yelled.

Diego pulled out a knife. "I'm going to cut you!"

Sargo stepped backward. "Not unless you can outfight this!" Sargo drew out an even larger knife. People in the crowd cried and laughed, the women looking fearful, the men grinning and clapping their hands.

Both men circled. Rialta got up. Still half asleep, she stumbled to the motel door, and felt in her pocket for the silver dollar.

"Someone should call the police," a woman said to a man in front of Rialta. The man pointed across the circle of people, where a policeman stood in the crowd, his arms crossed, grinning.

Rialta saw Violetta and slipped around the crowd. Violetta was a waitress at the bar who had shown kindness to Rialta, so she knew she was safe with her. Violetta put her hands on Rialta's shoulders and stood behind her. The volume rose, as the crowd jostled for position around the two fighters.

Sargo began to close in. He was a brute, said to have killed several men during his life. Diego was young and foolish, and his knife looked like a toy next to Sargo's.

Turning, Rialta tugged on Violetta's sleeve.

"They are fighting over the silver dollar?" she asked.

Violetta looked down and smiled, obviously not understanding.

Rialta can do something. She knows about the silver dollar. But what can—and what should—she do?

It's always right to do what's right. The Bible says, "See that no one pays back evil for evil, but always try to do good to each other and to everyone else" (1 Thessalonians 5:15). Ask God to help you do the right thing, even when it's not easy.

Rialta yelled this time. "The silver dollar!"

Violetta's eyes fixed on the two men. *"Sí,"* she said, without emotion.

Behind Rialta, one man took bets. He offered two to one odds for Sargo. Several of the onlookers grabbed their wallets and paid.

Rialta had to stop it. But how?

Calling forth all her strength, she yelled, "Stop! Stop! I have it!"

No one responded. With everyone milling about, all bellowing encouragement to Diego or Sargo, no one even noticed her. Rialta stamped her foot. Could she make them listen? What should she do now? Just walk away? That wasn't right.

She held the silver dollar up. "Look!" she cried. "Here it is."

No one gave her a glance. She felt invisible.

Another roar went up from the crowd. Diego had cut Sargo on the hand. Sargo waved it back, saying it was nothing, and droplets of blood flew into the crowd. Violetta ducked, but a droplet struck her cheek and splattered. *"Mi madre!"* she cried.

Rialta looked Violetta in the face as the small woman wiped the blood away. "I have it!" Rialta yelled, waving it in her face. "The silver dollar."

Violetta pushed her aside. "Go bet then!" she cried.

When things in your life are spinning out of control, what can you do? You can look to God. "As for God, his way is perfect. All the Lord's promises prove true. He is a shield for all who look to him for protection. For who is God except the Lord? Who but our God is a solid rock? God is my strong fortress; he has made my way safe" (2 Samuel 22:31-33). Remember the times God has kept you safe, and give him thanks.

Desperate, Rialta lofted the coin into the air. It plunked down to the ground directly between the two men.

The crowd gasped as one. Then everything went silent.

"The coin!" someone cried.

First Sargo looked down. Then Diego. They dropped their arms.

Both men turned to the crowd.

"Who threw it out?" Sargo asked, his face dark with anger.

Rialta's heart pounded against her rib cage. She looked up at Violetta, but the woman turned to someone else, whispering. Should she tell them?

Rialta stepped forward. "I threw it out."

"You, the beggar girl?" Sargo screamed. "We could have killed one another."

"I tried to stop it!" Rialta protested. "But everyone wanted blood."

Several in the crowd shifted uneasily on their feet. Sargo glared at Rialta, his small black eyes hard and hateful. He couldn't hold the stare, though, and turned away.

"Thank you, *niña!*" Diego said, snapping up the coin. "You saved someone's life, probably Sargo's."

Sargo glared at her, then pushed past the people back into the bar.

Rarely does an individual have the opportunity to save another's life. But God is in the lifesaving business. The psalmist wrote, "Though I walk in the midst of trouble, you preserve my life; you stretch out your hand against the anger of my foes, with your right hand you save me. The Lord will fulfill his purpose for me; your love, O Lord, endures forever" (Psalm 138:7, 8, *NIV*). Even in the toughest times of life you can depend on God. Take your troubles to him in prayer.

MYSTERY OF THE
SILVER DOLLAR

Rialta slumped under the motel sign. Why couldn't something, just one thing, go right?

Violetta approached, and reached down to pat her on the shoulder. "You did a good thing, little one," she said.

Rialta returned her gaze. Violetta's eyes reminded her of her name: violet and beautiful.

"You saved a life today," the small woman said again. At 12 years old, Rialta stood only an inch or two shorter than her. Behind them, the last of the crowd filed into the motel. "That is not something to forget."

"But everything goes wrong for me," Rialta said. "Everything."

Violetta nodded. "I know. But one day it will go right. When you do right, in the end, things do you right. Like the Golden Rule."

Rialta blinked and smiled resignedly. "I guess so."

"Here," Violetta said, reaching into her purse. "One new peso." She handed it to Rialta. "Draw a picture of me when you have time. I have gotten some good tips tonight."

Rialta had done something good, but no one seemed to acknowledge it. And then Violetta spoke up.

Jesus told his disciples that recognition is not the greatest thing in the world. He said that people who do good things may wait a long time for their reward. How long may you have to wait to be rewarded for the good you do? Read Luke 14:12-14 to find out.

Rialta stood there, watching the tiny woman walk back toward the bar. Violetta's life was hard too, even if not in the same way as Rialta's. "Everyone has some problem," she murmured. "Maybe that's the way of the world."

She got her backpack from under the bushes and took out some paper. "I will do the best I can do for Violetta—the best."

She began drawing, getting the outline of Violetta's jaw and hair perfect. Then, as she always did, she moved on to the part of a person's face that most thrilled her. "Her eyes," Rialta murmured as she concentrated. "Her beautiful violet eyes."

Deep down, she wished for paints to show their brilliant color. Rialta worked quickly, putting in just the right strokes to make the drawing beautiful. She didn't look up. Suddenly, two boots she recognized stood by her and a hand gripped her shoulder. She knew who it was, but she was afraid to look up.

"You did a good thing, little one," the voice said.

Slowly, Rialta looked up. Diego stood there, grinning. He held the silver dollar. He pressed two pesos into her hand.

"Gracias," he said. "Sargo is cruel, but I am not. I remember who my friends are."

Rialta smiled. *"Gracias,* Diego. I will draw you a picture."

"Two more pesos for such a thing," he said, and walked away.

Suddenly, good things are happening. As a direct result of her good deed, Rialta is being rewarded. Paul the apostle wrote this: "Remember this—a farmer who plants only a few seeds will get a small crop. But the one who plants generously will get a generous crop" (2 Corinthians 9:6). What does this verse teach you about how God chooses to bless his children?

Finishing the picture of Violetta, Rialta turned to Diego's portrait. Again she worked quickly and soon had a great likeness of him in a cowboy hat, flipping his silver dollar into the air and holding out his hand to catch it.

Just finished, Violetta walked out with Diego behind her. He had his hand over her shoulder. Rialta had never seen them like this. They were both singing a famous country song. Then they stood beside her.

"Show us Violetta's picture first," Diego said.

"No," Violetta said. "Yours."

"*Si,*" he said. "The handsome cowboy!"

Rialta held it up. Violetta took it. "Ah, this is wondrous, handsomer than Diego is, if that could be possible."

They both laughed.

Rialta held up the second picture. The two adults stared for a moment, clearly astonished.

"She is a movie star," Diego whispered.

"How?" Violetta said, almost weeping, "How did you do this?"

"It is my gift to you," Rialta said.

Violetta and Diego hugged and he gave Rialta a five-peso note. "For you to eat a good meal with your little brother," he said. And they walked away.

Rialta held the note, staring at it. Then she sobbed, "*Gracias,* God. *Gracias!* Some things do turn out right, after all."

When we are obedient to him, God promises to reward us. Look at this verse from Galatians 6:9: "So don't get tired of doing what is good. Don't get discouraged and give up, for we will reap a harvest of blessing at the appropriate time." How can you apply this now to your life?

"Help!" Holly cried as she stood near the fence. "Someone's trying to hurt the llamas!"

Mrs. Gaston looked up from her work in her lavish garden. She was a skinny lady, with sharp, angular features, a small nose and a tired, unhappy-looking mouth. "What's the matter, child?" she called to Holly.

"The llamas!" Holly cried. "Some men are trying to shoot them. They have a big gun. I don't know who they are."

"My stars!" the widow cried. "That's awful. I'll call the police."

Mrs. Gaston came out of her garden. When she saw Holly standing on one foot, she reached out to steady her. "What's wrong with your foot, child?"

"I twisted my ankle as I was running. It really hurts."

Mrs. Gaston helped Holly as she hopped up the stairs to the house on her good foot. "It's starting to swell, too. Let's get you inside." She smiled, but not in a friendly way. It made Holly feel uncomfortable.

Inside, Mrs. Gaston motioned toward a chair, and Holly sank into it. A large Doberman gave her a sniff, then lay down on the floor. Holly had seen the dog before.

The room was clean, dust-free, and full of antiques and expensive-looking furniture. It was much nicer than the rental house where Holly and her family were staying.

"Can I get some ice to put on your ankle?" Mrs. Gaston asked.

Not everyone is as they appear. Sometimes people appear to do good, but they have evil intentions in their hearts. Jesus condemned people like that and called them hypocrites. He said to them, "You try to look like upright people outwardly, but inside your hearts are filled with hypocrisy and lawlessness" (Matthew 23:28). Have you ever known a hypocrite? Have you ever been one?

"No, I'll be OK," Holly said, though her ankle continued to throb. "Could you just call the police? Please, I'm afraid the llamas—" She wanted to say she needed to call her parents. But they were blocks away, and she didn't know the phone number at the house where they were staying.

"Oh, of course," Mrs. Gaston said, and she went into the kitchen.

The Doberman watched Holly with menacing eyes. She felt him studying her. Something was wrong, she sensed. But what?

Holly listened as the widow dialed the phone number. She only hit three buttons. So it had to be 911. Mrs. Gaston began to talk: "Yes sir, this is Mrs. Gaston of 664 Pine Woods Lane. Apparently there's something going on in the Preserve right now. A child observed some men trying to hurt the llamas. . . . Yes. Thank you. All right, I'll wait outside."

Mrs. Gaston smiled and walked back in. "The police will be here. But it'll be a few minutes. Do you want something to drink? I have some orange juice, soda, and grape juice. You look a little flushed."

"Yes, orange juice, please," Holly answered. She was feeling thirsty and a little weak after her frantic run. And she needed to be able to show the police where the men with the gun were.

You always have to be on the lookout for trouble in our world. Even when you are cautious, however, trouble may come. And in those times, the best thing you can do is call on God. "My God, rescue me from the power of the wicked, from the clutches of cruel oppressors" (Psalm 71:4). How can you use God's help today?

Holly watched Mrs. Gaston pull open the refrigerator door. She was a slight woman, but her grip when she'd helped Holly up the stairs had been strong. She was a tough old lady, for sure. Even though she seemed to be nice, there was something about her that made Holly squeamish. And it didn't help any that the Doberman continued staring at her like she was a hunk of beef.

Holly had talked with Mrs. Gaston the previous year when she stood looking at the flowers in the garden. The woman had scowled and not been real nice, but maybe she'd just had a bad day. Another time, she showed Holly some of the flowers. Mrs. Gaston was certainly friendly now. Except for her dog, everything looked pretty normal.

Still, Holly felt uneasy. Her parents had told her a thousand times never to go into a stranger's house. Even though Mrs. Gaston wasn't really a stranger, Holly and her parents didn't really know her.

Mrs. Gaston produced a glass of orange juice and set it on the table next to Holly. "Drink up," she said. "I'll be right back."

Holly decided she should get away as soon as she could and still be polite about it. She had to tell her parents. Now. She flexed her ankle back and forth to see if she could tolerate the pain.

A few minutes later, Mrs. Gaston came back. "You drink your juice, honey. I'm going to look outside. I'll be right back."

Holly scissored her feet back and forth, caressed and kneaded her ankle, and drank the juice, waiting uncomfortably. The dog watched her with unblinking eyes.

In stressful times, you need to be alert and think ahead. That's true in your spiritual life as well. Take Paul's advice: "Be on guard. Stand true to what you believe. Be courageous. Be strong" (1 Corinthians 16:13).

MYSTERY OF THE
LLAMAS IN DISTRESS

Why did Mrs. Gaston go outside? And why didn't she take Holly with her? Suddenly Holly realized that for all her friendliness, the woman seemed very nervous. It was weird. Holly slowly stood, leaning on her good leg.

Immediately, the dog growled.

She froze.

"I'm just looking is all," she said.

She sidestepped to the window. The dog rose menacingly, but didn't advance.

Out the window, Holly saw Mrs. Gaston get into her car. She sat inside, doing something—a phone. She had another phone. She was calling someone.

Holly stared, trying to make sense of this. Mrs. Gaston was talking to someone. But why was she doing it in her car, and not in her kitchen?

Because she doesn't want me to hear.

Holly peered at the phone, then at the dog. "I'm not doing anything," she said, as she sidled toward the kitchen. The dog suddenly barked and growled.

"OK, I'm just picking up the phone."

She scrutinized the different buttons until she found Redial. She pressed it. The dog growled. The redial beeped. She waited. Nothing happened. She hung up and hit the button again.

Holly's getting more frightened by the minute. But she, and you, can be sure that God doesn't change with circumstances. Look at Psalm 46:1: "God is our refuge and strength, always ready to help in times of trouble." What does it mean to you that God is "always ready"?

She read the display: "number incomplete."

Holly hung up. Something was wrong. Now she knew she had to get out of that house. How she wished she knew the phone number of their rental house! Then she could call her parents. That would solve everything.

She edged toward the porch, but the dog stalked her.

Then suddenly, she heard a voice behind her. "You won't get out that way, Missie."

She turned around. It was Mrs. Gaston. She walked directly toward Holly and motioned to the dog. The Doberman bared his teeth and stood beside her. This was serious!

Before Holly could react, the woman had her by the arm. She was strong, not one of those dried-up grandmother types. She had an iron grip. The fingers dug in Holly's biceps to the bone. It hurt.

For the first time, Holly noticed how powerful Mrs. Gaston looked, and she felt a sudden terror. Looking up at her face, Holly screamed. "That will do you no good, young lady. Just be quiet."

She dragged Holly to the chair. "You'll just sit here and Roscoe will watch you," she said. "You'll be quiet as a mouse. Correct?"

Holly looked into her eyes with panic: "It's you! You're after the llamas!"

Mrs. Gaston committed a crime. By depriving Holly of a way to leave safely, she broke the law. The situation has gone from inconsiderate and improper to illegal, and Holly needs to do her best to get out of the situation and get help.

You can be confident that when you are in danger, God is able to rescue you. Psalm 68:20 says, "Our God is a God who saves! The Sovereign Lord rescues us from death." What does it mean to you that God is "sovereign"?

MYSTERY OF THE
LLAMAS IN
DISTRESS

"Those blasted llamas! They disturb my garden! Preserve, my eye! My son needs that land for development. So there!" Mrs. Gaston snapped her fingers in Holly's face. Then she went out again.

Holly sat terrorized as realization washed over her. The police weren't coming. Mrs. Gaston never called them. Nobody knew where Holly was, and she couldn't run. She stared at the dog.

"How can you do this? What kind of dog are you?" she said. "Don't you know the llamas are in trouble?"

A growl rumbled in the dog's throat. Holly started to stand. Immediately, the dog stood, baring its teeth.

"OK, OK. Don't get in an uproar about it!"

She looked around the room. On the ocean side there was a porch with a door down to the dunes. But if she did manage to get that far, there was no door to stop the dog.

She glanced around and saw the stairs to the upper level.

Maybe that was the way.

If she could grab something to hit the dog with, maybe it would back away.

She looked on the table. Saltshakers only. "Crumballs!"

Suddenly, there was a loud banging at the door. Roscoe whipped around and ran to the door, barking. That was her chance. Holly bolted for the stairs.

Holly was able to see an opportunity and take it. The ability to think quickly and clearly in a stressful situation is a blessing. The Bible says, "People can never predict when hard times might come. Like fish in a net or birds in a snare, people are often caught by sudden tragedy" (Ecclesiastes 9:12). Have you experienced sudden trouble? How did you deal with it?

MYSTERY OF THE
LLAMAS IN DISTRESS

Holly heard the dog scrabbling on the stairs. She looked wildly around the top level, then sped for the end bedroom.

The dog came around the corner, speeding directly at her. She slammed the door in his face and locked it. The dog hit the door at full speed.

Holly stepped back. The door held. She sat down for a second, her heart pounding. She ran to the window and pushed it up. She looked out. She couldn't jump, but maybe if she hung from the sill . . .

The dog barked outside the door. Mrs. Gaston would be back in moment. Holly had to make her move.

She pushed the screen out of the window. Behind her the dog slammed into the door with a boom. She climbed out onto the porch. At the edge, she backed over, hanging onto the gutter. She hesitated a moment, then later she dropped to the ground, and pain seared her ankle.

Holly got up, her ankle hurting worse than ever. She had to get to Mr. Zembra. He would help.

She hobbled along as quickly as she could, looking over her shoulder to make sure Mrs. Gaston wasn't following. Soon she was at Mr. Zembra's door pounding with her fists. When he opened the door, she couldn't hold back the tears any longer. She leaped into his arms, crying.

"Help me, please! Call the police!" Holly cried.

Without hesitating, Mr. Zembra dialed the phone. "You're safe now," he said.

Holly found a way to escape the trouble she was in. The Bible says that under certain circumstances God always provides Christians a way to escape. What are those time? Read 1 Corinthians 10:13 to find out.

MYSTERY OF THE
MISSING FRIEND

The phone rang about seven o'clock, and Jennie's mother asked her to answer it.

"Brelsforts," she said into the phone.

"Jennie, this is Mrs. Sanders."

"Oh, hi."

"Something's wrong. Karen didn't come home from school today. Do you know where she could be?" Mrs. Sanders's fast breathing told Jennie she was scared.

"Let me take a look at our favorite place," Jennie said, trying to sound reassuring. She, Karen, and two other girls had found an old tree house in the woods and had started a club meeting there. She thought Karen might have gone there and fallen asleep.

"Please hurry," Mrs. Sanders said.

Jennie hung up and walked into the family room. "Mom, would you mind if I went to the tree house to see if Karen's there?"

"Is something wrong?"

"Mrs. Sanders called. Karen never came home from school."

Mrs. Brelsfort looked up at Jennie. "Should Dad go with you?"

"No, I'll be fine."

"Well, take Jasper just in case. Keep him on the leash."

For what reasons might a fifth grader be gone from home for a few hours? There are plenty, but usually responsible kids let their parents know where they'll be in advance.

Probably Mrs. Sanders did the right thing by not panicking and calling a friend of her daughter's. But what would you do if a friend went missing—really missing?

Jesus said, "I command you to love each other in the same way that I love you. And here is how to measure it—the greatest love is shown when people lay down their lives for their friends" (John 15:12, 13). Think about what you would do for a friend. And what would your friends do for you?

Jennie got Jasper's leash and they headed out. It was still light and birds twittered in the trees. A squirrel shot across the path, and a small bunny jumped out of a clearing when it saw Jasper.

"I hope she's there," Jennie whispered under her breath, her heart pounding a little faster. "I don't like this."

Jasper woofed as if he understood. He led the walk, pulling on the leash so hard Jennie could barely hold on. She tucked her blonde hair behind her ear as she hurried along. Soon she saw the tree house up ahead. It was made of boards and nails. The girls found it the summer before while exploring. No one else seemed to know about it.

"Karen, you here?"

No answer.

"Karen! Hey!" After tying Jasper to the ladder, Jennie climbed up into the rickety contraption nailed to the thick trunk of the oak.

She stepped through the trapdoor and looked around. Everything was covered in shadows. Karen was not there. But on the floor of the tree house, she noticed something. Stooping to pick it up, she saw it was Karen's backpack and lunch box.

"Oh, no!" she cried.

Many dangers lurk in the world today. Bad things happen to people. However, you have to remember what God says about fear: "I command you—be strong and courageous! Do not be afraid or discouraged. For the Lord your God is with you wherever you go" (Joshua 1:9).

These words were spoken by God to Joshua, the leader of Israel after the death of Moses. He had good reason to be afraid about the future. But God assured him, and he succeeded. So will you if you trust God.

MYSTERY OF THE
MISSING FRIEND

Where would Karen go? There were no signs of a fight or a fast exit. So Karen must have left it without fear. But why would she leave the backpack and everything?

Jennie mulled this over. She decided to stop by Lizbeth's house. If Lizbeth didn't know where Karen was, she would stop at Carranda's. Surely one of them knew something.

She took the path toward Lizbeth's home and soon came out of the woods in her backyard. Lizbeth appeared when Jennie knocked on the sliding glass door.

"Have you seen Karen since school?" Jennie asked.

"We walked a ways, but I had to turn off. Is something wrong?"

"Her mom called me. She hasn't seen her at all after school."

"Oh no," Lizbeth said. "Karen told me she was real mad at her mom. They had a fight yesterday. Do you think she would run away?"

Jennie held up the backpack and lunch box. "Wouldn't she have taken these if she did?"

"Oh, wow," Lizbeth said. "Let me get my sweater on. Do you want one? You look cold."

"Sure."

The two girls headed out. "Where to first?" Lizbeth asked.

"Carranda's."

Many times young people react in anger to a fight or argument with a parent. They may resort to hurting the person they're mad at to get attention or to send a message. Some kids will even run away.

How does God want children to relate to their parents? Read Ephesians 6:1-3 to find out.

As Jennie and Lizbeth walked, they talked about Karen. "You know how mad she gets," Lizbeth said. "How many times has she told us as soon as she's able she's going to leave home?"

"But she's only 12! That's stupid," Jennie answered.

"Sure. But it makes sense to her."

Up the street, they saw Carranda and her brother throwing a ball in the front yard. They hurried up to her.

"Wanna play?" Carranda asked.

Jennie shook her head, holding back Jasper from licking Carranda. "We're looking for Karen. She's disappeared."

"Oh, man!" Carranda answered. "She told me last week she was leaving for good this time."

Jennie's eyes widened. Lizbeth looked horrified. "Why didn't you tell us?" Jennie asked.

"I thought it was another threat," Carranda said. "Let me take this inside. I'll come with you. She couldn't have gotten far."

While they waited, Jennie looked through Karen's backpack. She found a wallet with $20 in it; also Karen's ID card, and a bunch of photos. Jennie held them up. "Would Karen run away without taking these things, especially the money?"

The three girls all looked worried. Jennie said, "Maybe we should pray about this."

Prayer should always be our first response to a need or a problem. Too many Christians wait until they're desperate or it's too late.

Jesus connected prayer to forgiveness in Mark 11:24, 25: "Listen to me! You can pray for anything, and if you believe, you will have it. But when you are praying, first forgive anyone you are holding a grudge against, so that your Father in heaven will forgive your sins, too."

Is there "anyone you are holding a grudge against," even a parent? Take steps to forgive.

"Dear God," Jennie prayed, "Please help us to find Karen. More important, please keep Karen safe, wherever she is. Amen."

She looked at Lizbeth and Carranda. "Where do we go now?"

"The bus station?" Carranda suggested.

"But she doesn't have any money," Lizbeth said. "How could she go anywhere?"

Jennie thought about it. "You know, Karen reads all those *Goosebumps* books all the time. Maybe she thought of some weird scenario that would throw everyone off."

"Like what?" Carranda asked. She flipped the dreadlocks out of her eyes and stared at both friends.

"What if she wants to make us think she was kidnapped?" Jennie said. "Leaving everything there at the tree house was a clue."

"You think Karen is that smart?" Lizbeth asked innocently.

The other two laughed.

"What if she wants to make us think she went with someone she knows? That would keep people looking in all the wrong places until she had the time she needed to escape."

Jennie sucked her lip. "Would Karen be that nasty about it?"

People will surprise you at the ways they come up with to hide something—a trail, a precious item, information. God, though, wants us to lead open and honest lives.

If Karen had a bad home situation, she should talk about it to a counselor or trusted adult, not take matters into her own hands. Find out what the Bible says about handling anger and telling the truth in Ephesians 4:25, 26.

Do you have any ideas about where Karen might be?

The three girls headed to the bus station. At the same time, Lizbeth pulled out her cell phone and told her mother what they were doing. Her mom said she would pick them up there at eight o'clock and get them home.

They all got more nervous as they saw the *Trailways* sign up ahead. When they reached the bus station, it was virtually deserted. It was a small building, with one clerk selling tickets.

"I'm gonna ask the guy in the window," Jennie said and walked over. The other two followed.

The clerk looked up. "Can I help you?"

"We're looking for a friend," Jennie said. "She's about five feet tall, with long reddish hair; kind of pretty. Did she buy a ticket?"

The clerk thought about it. "For security reasons I'm not allowed to tell you who bought tickets," he said, "but I may have seen a young girl approaching people asking for handouts."

Lizbeth rolled her eyes. "I think you nailed it, Jen," she said. "She left the money and things to throw us off, then came here and tried to talk people into giving her money."

"But where would she be now?"

Jennie thought a moment. "Hold it. I've got it."

People can get lost. Sometimes fugitives disappear and are never heard from again. But God never hides. Isaiah 55:6, 7 says, "Seek the Lord while you can find him. Call on him now while he is near. Let the people turn from their wicked deeds. Let them banish from their minds the very thought of doing wrong! Let them turn to the Lord that he may have mercy on them. Yes, turn to our God, for he will abundantly pardon."

God awaits. If you need him, go to him now. Even if you don't think you need him, go to him, because some day you will.

Across the street from the bus station, Jennie spotted the ice cream shop. They all ran across, opened the door, and looked inside. In the booth farthest back, they saw some red hair. There sat Karen, eating a banana split.

She dropped her spoon when all three girls ran up.

"Where have you been?" Jennie asked angrily.

"Here," Karen said. "Want some ice cream?"

"Karen," Jennie said, sitting down with the others, "everybody's been terrified you were taken—you know, kidnapped. You made it look that way on purpose, didn't you?"

Karen hung her head. When she looked up, there were tears in her eyes. "I can't take it anymore," she said.

"What is so horrible about your mom?"

Karen sighed. "I just wanted to scare her this time."

"Why? If she didn't care about you, she wouldn't have called me when you didn't come home."

"I know." Karen nodded as tears dripped off her cheeks. "I'm sorry."

"Come on, let's get you home. Your mom is freaking out."

As they waited for Lizbeth's mom, they talked about how to help Karen work out her problems so this wouldn't happen again.

Christians are called to be peacemakers in a troubled world. Helping people get along can save many lives from bitterness and hate. Jesus said, "God blesses those who work for peace, for they will be called the children of God" (Matthew 5:9).

Work for peace in your home, in your friends' homes, and everywhere you go, and you truly will be called a child of God.

Jake Cutler stared into the shadows searching for the trap. "Shhhh!" he whispered to his twin sister, Sarah. "We're almost there. This time we'll get one of our own."

As they crept through the woods toward the creek, Jake listened for every noise. Little sounds told him of nearby animals—and danger. On the Ohio frontier in 1798, anything could happen. Their home was only a few hundred yards down the creek. They could shout, but they were now too far into the dense undergrowth for Papa to hear.

Papa had often told Jake and Sarah, "Be careful in the woods. If you see Indians, get moving. Run, if necessary."

"What will we call it?" Sarah asked, bringing Jake's thoughts back to their search.

"I'm calling him Joshua if he's a boy. And . . ."

"If only Petey hadn't died. We should call him Petey."

"Petey is a cat's name." Jake turned to look at his sister. "Do you still feel bad?"

"I think if we catch a raccoon, I might feel better."

Petey, their mama's cat, came with them to Ohio five years ago. She had grown old and died. Jake's father often said, "Petey was the only member of the family that never did anything wrong."

In a perfect world, Jake knew he'd most like a dog, even a puppy. But this far out in the wilderness, only the Indians had dogs. And some folks said they ate them!

The pioneer days were dangerous times. Having a solid faith helped a great deal. Knowing God was with you probably gave you more courage in situations like this. Perhaps a verse like 1 Corinthians 16:13 was worth memorizing: "Be on guard. Stand true to what you believe. Be courageous. Be strong." Those are powerful words all Christians should count on in perilous times.

Jake kept his eyes fixed on the trees, looking for the slightest movements. If they had to run, he felt ready. But what about Sarah? What would he do if she fell behind?

"I liked Petey, though." Sarah moved along. Jake worried she wasn't watching like he was. "I liked to pet Petey and—"

"Be quiet," Jake said.

"What is it?" Sarah whispered.

"The shadow. Someone is following us." Jake squinted and stopped, listening hard. The two waited. Jake raised his hand to shade his eyes. "I think it's nothing."

"I'm not scared." Sarah patted her blue bonnet in place and then folded her arms.

"You're never scared."

"Maybe it just eats boys," she teased.

Jake glared at her. "Don't start with that." He grabbed the hilt of his knife that hung at his side. He wore buckskin pants and shirt and moccasins. Sarah wore a cream-colored muslin dress. Why had he allowed her to come out here in a dress? He wished they could run back and get her boots. But night would soon fall. They couldn't turn around.

"You're scared, aren't you?" Sarah asked him.

There's nothing wrong with being cautious in a tight spot. Thinking through an action, preparing what you will say or do is always wise. But you should learn not to fear when you're doing something right and in God's will.

Moses encouraged the people of Israel when they were afraid. Discover what he told them in Exodus 20:20. Remember to keep looking to God no matter how bad things get.

"I am not. Let's find the trap. I wish I had brought my gun."

They hurried up the creek. The sun was low in the sky. Trees and branches hung over their path. Jake and Sarah knew these woods like their own fields of corn and wheat. Their papa had taught them both what to watch for, what to run from. No one lived past their farm in the nearby forest, except bears, deer, mountain lions, and the Indians.

Jake stopped again. "Look!"

Up ahead stood a doe and a buck. With them, a fawn pranced about, ducking its head and nibbling at leaves and patches of grass.

"Oh, they're so beautiful." Sarah eyes went wide with awe. "And you'd probably want to shoot them!" She turned and glared at Jake.

Jake shrugged. At that moment, something whizzed by.

Jake pulled Sarah to the ground. They both looked up, shaking. An arrow stuck in the trunk of a tree just a few feet from the deer.

The deer leaped away.

"Who shot that?" Jake whispered, his heart drumming hard.

"I don't know." Sarah breathed more quickly.

They both waited, listening. No sound but the breeze and the call of crows broke the silence. That arrow might have struck one of them, right in the heart. He had to do something. And fast.

Jake took a deep breath and thought about what to do. Then he stood. "Hello! Is anyone there?"

The Bible says this about those who trust in God and live for him: "You will not fear the terror of night, nor the arrow that flies by day" (Psalm 91:5, *NIV*). Today, God might say, "Do not be afraid of the AK-47, biological weapons, or suitcase nuclear bombs. I am in charge. Keep trusting me."

MYSTERY OF THE
FOREST SHADOW
PART 1

No one answered. Sarah rose beside him and grabbed his hand. "Let's find the trap and get back. That was an Indian."

"The Shawnee are friendly. Papa says they won't hurt us."

"He said to run."

"If there were a bunch of them. This might only be one."

"They have bows and arrows. We have nothing but your knife."

"I'm ready," Jake said. Once again, he gripped the knife his father had given him. "Anyway, if that Indian wanted to hurt us, he probably would have by now."

They hurried to the pine tree with the arrow stuck into the bark. Jake pulled it out, held it up for whoever was out there to see, and dropped it to the ground.

"Break it," Sarah said.

"No." Jake stared into the trees, trying to fix where the Indian hid. "No reason to make them mad."

When he saw no movement, they ran along the creek until he could see the glade where they'd left the trap up ahead.

Jake spotted the trap, set up against a large boulder jutting from the grass. "We should show Papa this place," Sarah said.

"Oh, he's seen it. He says he hopes to turn it into a field someday."

A minute later they stopped and surveyed the area again. Jake's heart still beat hard. What would he do if the next arrow struck Sarah? Or him?

Leaves rustled in the slight wind. Jake licked his finger and held it up, letting the breeze dry it.

No matter what danger lurks, remember that God knew long ago what you would face today. Second Peter 2:9 says, "So you see, the Lord knows how to rescue godly people from their trials, even while punishing the wicked right up until the day of judgment." Never give up on God. As long as you walk with him, he will never give up on you.

After giving the trees one more look, they stole toward the trap. "It'll be dark soon," Sarah said, looking up into the golden sky.

Jake figured the Indian had gone by now. He kept his hand on his knife, but nothing indicated the Indian meant harm. He scurried to the boulder and stooped by the trap. "Nothing." He threw up his hands. "We didn't catch anything."

"Maybe we will tomorrow." Sarah obviously meant to brighten his mood. She put her hand on his shoulder.

"I thought we might catch one of those little raccoons we saw. That would make a good pet to keep."

Sarah squeezed Jake's shoulder. "Not like Petey, though."

"Even a mouse would be better than nothing." Deep down, he felt more depressed than ever. "I'll even take a muskrat."

"Phew!" Sarah answered, grinning.

Behind them, a twig snapped. Both of them froze.

The floor of the forest was almost dark. "It'll be night, Jake." Sarah crouched beside him. He noticed her hand shook.

Jake knelt and pulled the trapdoor open. He fixed the stick that held it up back in place. He placed a scrap of jerky in the middle of the trap. In the woods, an owl hooted. "That should work," he said and stood. He searched the woods one more time. He saw no one lingering in the shadows. "Let's go home."

They started back through the meadow to the darkening woods. Moments later, Sarah stopped. "He's following us, Jake."

Sometimes you can sense danger, even if you don't know for sure what it is. It's called "intuition." Jesus told us, "Be sure of this: I am with you always, even to the end of the age" (Matthew 28:20b). Wherever you are—even in danger—Jesus is there too.

MYSTERY OF THE
FOREST SHADOW
PART 1

Jake took her hand. Someone was out there watching with a bow and arrow. Whoever it was had shot it once. Had he meant it as a warning? Or had he just missed shooting at the deer?

Indians hunted deer all around the area. That was the whole problem. They considered all the land everyone's land. But the settlers paid for parcels of land, and considered it private property.

"Let's go faster," he said to Sarah.

They hurried along. The sun threw a few last golden rays across tops of the pines and up in the sky.

"Do you see anything?" Sarah whispered.

"The shadows," Jake answered. "He stays in the shadows."

"Is it a person or an animal?"

"A person for sure." There were Delaware and Shawnee in the area. Everyone told stories. A tribe lived not far down the creek. They wore paint. They dressed in deerskins. They traded furs. Jake had never met an Indian in person or tried to talk with one. He'd seen them, though, at the trading post and in the forest. They always seemed secretive and never showed any interest in children.

Plenty of people talked about them, though. At the general store in town, Jake listened to the elders talk. A week before, Mr. Stepps warned everyone that "time is comin' when we'll need more land. More people movin' in. It's almost time. Who's with me?"

Jake's father sighed and turned away, putting his hand on Jake's shoulder. "Remember, son," he said quietly, "all a man has is his word. When he goes back on his word, he becomes just like the rest of the world."

Much trouble in the world comes from people who won't follow the rules. They don't care what God or anyone else says. The Bible tells us what God says about such people. Read Hebrews 2:2 to find out what happened to people who refused to listen to God.

As they ran along the creek back to home, Jake thought about these things. Would there ever be peace between the settlers and the Indians? What if a war started again?

The shadows grew long and dark. Jake looked back many times. He was sure he heard the Indian moving behind them. Soon he saw smoke rising into the yellow-tinged air, and he knew the cabin was just up ahead.

"What will we tell Papa?" Sarah looked back with wide eyes. "Jake, look!"

Jake turned and stared.

"The trees there!" Sarah pointed.

Jake waited. He thought he saw someone standing there. "Turn around slowly. Don't look now."

Both of them turned.

"Walk a couple of steps."

Jake waited several long seconds, then whispered, "Turn around quick!"

They both whirled around.

This time they saw him. Someone jumped between two trees. Jake knew instantly it was an Indian. Did he have on paint? Why was he following them?

Jake did a wise thing by trying to catch a glimpse of the person following them. Psalm 119:98 says, "Your commands make me wiser than my enemies, for your commands are my constant guide." If you want to defeat your enemies, learn, memorize, and meditate on God's Word. It will make you wiser than the shrewdest opponent.

Sarah called, "Who are you?"

No one answered.

Jake lifted his fist. "We're not afraid of you!"

The person in the trees didn't move.

Jake took Sarah's hand. "Let's hurry."

When they reached the edge of their field, he stopped. The corn was already picked. The September days were getting shorter and soon winter snow would cover the forest and everything else. The family had to be ready. Ohio winters could be brutal. In their settlement, several people had died the previous winter of various sicknesses.

Now the field lay flat and pale yellow with shucks.

He heard a sound of metal clanging. It was a trap snapping shut!

And then a cry of pain, a high-pitched shriek: "Oooooooooo!" It sounded like a girl to Jake.

"Come on," Jake yelled. "She's hurt."

Jake and Sarah found an Indian girl about their age desperately trying to pull her foot out of one of their father's strong metal traps. Jake knew she needed help. Blood ran down her foot into her moccasin.

As Jake stood there, catching his breath, the girl looked up, then down. She pointed to her foot. "Sall-a-tee," she said.

Jesus said, "If you love only those who love you, what good is that? Even corrupt tax collectors do that much. If you are kind only to your friends, how are you different from anyone else? Even pagans do that. But you are to be perfect, even as your Father in heaven is perfect" (Matthew 5:46-48). God wants us to treat everyone with love and kindness, even our enemies, because that reflects God's love.

Jake didn't know the words, but her voice showed pain. A little brown dog stood at her side, looking afraid but ready to fight. For a second, a pang struck Jake's heart. What would he give to have a dog like that? But then he turned to the girl. She was pretty and looked as terrified as he felt.

She bent over her foot, trying to get free. A bow and quiver of arrows hung over her back. Clad in buckskin like Jake, colorful beads covered her shirt.

Jake moved closer, holding up his hand. The girl's lips twisted with fright, she said, "Sa-ma! Sa-ma!" The dog growled, but Jake stepped toward them.

As the girl's eyes seemed to plead to be gentle, Sarah took her hand while Jake grabbed the two sides of the trap. It took all his strength to open it enough for the girl to slide her foot out.

When she was free, Jake let the trap snap shut. "I'm sorry," he said. "It wasn't meant for you." Her dark eyes didn't show understanding and he tried desperately to think of a way to communicate.

Her eyes were coal black, as was her hair, but she had a pert nose and thick red lips. He smiled. "Let me look at that foot," he said, pointing to her foot as she held it up to put no weight on it.

Have you ever tried to communicate with someone who didn't speak your language? It can be difficult. There are many misunderstandings. But ultimately, love communicates best. Think on this truth: "I command you to love each other" (John 15:17). When we do that, we may make friends of our enemies.

She nodded. There were jagged gashes in her leg, and her blood flowed. It struck Jake almost as funny. Some of the young people in town had told him Indians had "black blood," proving they were "from the devil." Now he knew for sure. This girl's blood was as red as his own and Sarah's. She was just like them.

Jake touched her foot and felt all around the heel, instep, and toes. "Nothing's broken," he finally said. He reached into his leather pouch and pulled out several strips of muslin that his mother always made him take on treks into the forest. He gently pulled off the girl's moccasin and handed it to Sarah. Then he began to bandage the girl's wounds.

When he finished, he looked up. The girl eyes glimmered with tears and she nodded again. "Ha-ta-say," she said.

"You're welcome," Jake said.

The girl smiled. Jake knelt and let the dog lick his face. He stroked it gently as Sarah knelt beside him.

"What I wouldn't give for a dog, a real dog," Jake muttered.

The girl said something to the dog and it jumped up. She hobbled back toward the woods. The dog darted after her.

As Jake and Sarah watched, the girl stopped. She turned and smiled, then nodded. "A-wa-ta-no," she said, lifting her hand in peace. Jake raised his hand and nudged Sarah, who raised hers.

The girl nodded again, then hurried into the shadows.

It's easy to reach out to someone if they have something you want. This Indian girl had a dog, and Jake wanted a dog. But he didn't show love based on that; his love, as it should always be, had no conditions attached. The Bible tells us, "Love does no wrong to anyone, so love satisfies all of God's requirements" (Romans 13:10). Who can you love today, no strings attached?

That evening Jake and Sarah told their parents what had happened.

Papa simply said, "You did the right thing, but be careful. The Indians in this area mean no harm to us . . . at least not for now."

"Mister Stepps says—" Jake added.

"I know what he says," his father snapped. "And if people go with him, there will be trouble."

"Will there be a war?" Sarah asked meekly, as she lifted some venison stew to her lips.

"We need to keep our word," Mr. Cutler said. "That's all I have to say about it. But no one will listen to the likes of me."

"Yes, they will, dear," Jake's mother said, patting his hand. "You have much influence in this community."

Mr. Cutler grimaced, and Jake could see by the darkness reflected in his features that his father was worried.

After dinner, his father said, "Next time you go into the woods, take your gun, Jake. But don't shoot. Just show that you're not afraid."

"I will, Papa," Jake answered. He was glad his father hadn't said he couldn't go back into the woods.

As long as Jake lived in dangerous times, he was wise to take precautions. But that doesn't mean you can't be friendly from the start. Hebrews 11:31 tells about a person who saved her life and her family by showing friendliness. Read that verse to find out who she was, and read her story in Joshua 2:1-23; 6:20-23.

MYSTERY OF THE
FOREST SHADOW
PART 2

The next morning Jake watched for the Indian girl, but she didn't appear. As evening came, Jake found Sarah in the main field. Their chores were done. It was time to check the trap.

"Let's go," he said to her. His flintlock rifle hung from a strap on his shoulder. It was heavy and powerful.

"Did you see the Indian girl today?" Sarah asked.

"No."

"Maybe she'll be friends with us." Sarah's blue eyes looked bright and hopeful. "Maybe she's just curious. Like us."

"Maybe." Jake led Sarah past their house. They told Papa they wanted to check the trap.

"Be careful," Mr. Cutler said. "Be back before supper." He stared at Jake with his sharp gray eyes. "Remember, these Indians are peaceful. So don't point that gun at one of them. They could easily take it the wrong way. You don't point a gun at a friend."

"I won't."

"Good. Hurry then. Supper's less than an hour away."

Sarah picked up her little bag. Inside she carried some clothing and a corncob doll she played with when she was younger. Jake also saw the edge of her book, something she read in the mornings as their mother taught them their lessons.

The two of them jogged bravely through the woods. Jake said if they didn't look afraid, the Indian girl might appear again.

Jake and Sarah were building a friendship. How do you make friends with someone? By a lot of small things: nice words, kindness, helping, offering to pray for someone. Friendship may start with a little thing, but it can lead to great things in your life if you build on it. Proverbs 17:17 offers this counsel: "A friend is always loyal, and a brother is born to help in time of need."

Make many friends. They will be there when you need them.

Soon they reached the meadow. Jake could already see the trap was sprung, but empty.

"It got away." He placed his hands on his hips and shook his head. "See, it chewed its way out." He showed Sarah the broken knot. "It was probably a raccoon, too."

Crack! A branch broke! Both of them whipped around.

"Jake, watch out!" Sarah cried.

Jake raised his gun.

At the edge of the clearing stood the Indian girl. She had her bow in her hands, but was not pointing the arrow. She smiled at them. The little dog sat at her side.

"Who are you?" Jake said, lowering his flintlock.

The Indian girl shook her head. "Watawi-ah!"

"She can't speak English." Jake said, "and we can't speak her language." He lifted his hand, making the sign for peace again.

The Indian girl made the same sign. She turned to go, stopped, looked back, waved for them to follow. Then she started off again. The dog barked.

"She wants us to go with her," Sarah said.

"Maybe it's a trick."

"I don't think so."

The girl smiled as they followed. Heart pounding, Jake grabbed Sarah's hand. They stepped onto the trail. He saw the Indian girl had wrapped her foot in deerskin.

The Indian girl had shown she had no evil intent, so Jake and Sarah felt safe in following her. A good Bible verse for them, and you, to remember is Leviticus 25:18 (*NIV*): "Follow my decrees and be careful to obey my laws, and you will live safely in the land."

MYSTERY OF THE
FOREST SHADOW
PART 2

Jake said to her, "My name is Jake. What's yours?" He pointed to his chest when she looked. "Jake," he said.

The Indian girl just waved to them to follow. The dog pranced along next to her.

Soon they walked next to her. He patted his chest. "Jake," he said again.

Then he pointed to Sarah. "Sarah," he said. "Jake, Sarah."

The Indian girl looked at them. Her big dark eyes widened, and she smiled. "Ramana," she said, and pointed to herself.

Jake grinned. "Your name is Ramana?"

The girl nodded. "Sama-na cado culrasa." She waved her hand again, turned, and they followed.

Soon they reached the creek. Sarah and Jake both heard barking.

Two puppies burst through the water. Ramana picked up one wriggling puppy and held it out. "Suluta," she said.

Jake took it and the furry dog licked his cheek.

Sarah pulled her bag off her shoulder. "We should give her a gift," she said. Sarah looked in her bag and pulled out a comb.

"It's your best comb!" Jake said.

"For you," Sarah said. She pulled back her hair and showed how to hold it with the comb. Then she handed it to Ramana.

The girl smiled and took it, then bowed. She drew the comb through her hair. "Ah!" she said with pleasure.

She spoke again, then crossed the creek. The other puppy and the big brown dog followed. Soon they were out of sight.

What a gift! But that's what friends do, isn't it? God is a God of gifts too. The most important gift of all is revealed in Romans 6:23. Read that verse. Have you received God's greatest gift of all?

Sean walked down to the mailbox to get the mail for his mother. When he opened the box, he was surprised to find a small metal statue of a Shawnee brave standing at the front. He stared at it, at first a little wary, then picked it up and took it in with the mail.

"Mom," he cried as he ran into the house. He showed her the little figure. "Who could have put this in our mailbox?"

She looked at it. "I have no idea, honey. You know we have those two new neighbors. Do either of them have kids?"

"I don't know. I never see them."

"Well, look around. See if anyone comes out of that house and walks our way."

"Mom, I know how to nail someone."

"Nail them?"

"Well, you know."

"No, I don't. Don't talk like a gangster, honey."

"Yes, Ma'am."

Today we use the word *neighbor* to refer to the people who live next door or very near to us. In the Bible, neighbor means far more. Your neighbor is anyone who is not you—any other human being, the rest of humankind. And God has a lot to say in his Word about how to treat your neighbor.

Of the Ten Commandments, four deal with people's relationship with God, and the other six deal with relationships with people—two with parents and spouses, and the others with everyone else. Can you say which of the Ten Commandments concern your neighbor? If you can't, read Exodus 20:13, 15-17 to find out. —⊙

MYSTERY OF THE
TRADED TRINKETS

The next day when Sean planned to go to his mailbox, he saw a mysterious figure walk up the street. The person was wearing an outfit like Yoda from *Star Wars*. Sean held back and watched the person walk up the street past the mailbox and then back, and disappear into the house next door.

He hurried out to the mailbox and found a stone with a happy face painted on it. He took it in and showed it to his mother. "Interesting," she said. "Seems like a nice person, I'd say."

Sean kept a watch out. He decided to do something unusual. He took the two items and placed the rock in Yoda's mailbox, and the Shawnee brave in the neighbor's across the street.

He waited nervously all night, wondering what would happen.

The next day he ran to his mailbox. There to his astonishment lay the stone he put in Yoda's mailbox and also a political button. So was this mystery person Yoda?

He thought about it and decided what he would do next.

After the Ten Commandments, God gave additional more detailed instructions for how he wanted his people to live. One of these is recorded in Leviticus 19:18: "Never seek revenge or bear a grudge against anyone, but love your neighbor as yourself. I am the Lord." What does it mean to love your neighbor as yourself? Think about it, and talk to God about what he wants you to do.

Sean had a plan. He put the stone and the button in Yoda's mailbox this time. He put a dirty penny in a third neighbor's mailbox across the street, and an ace of diamonds playing card in the mailbox where he'd put the Shawnee.

His heart was really beating when he watched and saw the other two neighbors come out the next day and take their mail. Neither of them looked weird. Just for fun, he named one Joe and the second Moe.

He now had several items out there: the Indian with Moe, the playing card with Joe, and two items with Yoda, the dirty penny and the stone. This would solve the mystery, he was sure.

The next day Sean was totally amazed. Inside his mailbox were the two items from Yoda, AND the political button and the ace of diamonds. What on earth was going on now? Could all three neighbors be playing some sort of joke on him?

He piled up everything he had received, and decided not to do anything for the next day. He would just go to his mailbox and see what was there.

Once when Jesus was teaching, someone asked, "'Of all the commandments, which is the most important?' Jesus replied, 'The most important commandment is this: . . . "You must love the Lord your God with all your heart, all your soul, all your mind, and all your strength." The second is equally important: "Love your neighbor as yourself." No other commandment is greater than these'" (Mark 12:28-31). Are you loving God and others? When you are, you are doing what God wants you to do.

At school, Sean told some of his friends about the mysterious mailbox game. Trey and Josh thought it sounded like fun. Marcus said it was lame, and Taylor thought that it was a practical joke being played by Sean's parents.

When Sean came home on the bus his friend Carlton went with him to the mailbox. There inside was a penny nail, copper in color. Underneath it was a note that said, "This is fun. Will you continue?"

Sean stared at it. He handed the note to his friend Carlton. Carlton rolled his eyes and said, "This whole thing could be solved if you'd just talk to your neighbors. Why don't you just ask them?"

"That's the easy way out. I'm not going to give up yet," Sean said. "I have another idea."

He put all the items—the penny, the ace, the Shawnee, the stone, and political button, plus the nail—in Yoda's mailbox. He put a queen of hearts in Moe's mailbox with "I know it's you" written on it. He put a three of clubs that said, "Gotcha!" in Joe's box.

When Sean got home from school and opened his mailbox, there were all the items from Yoda's box, plus the playing cards from the two other boxes.

Paul encouraged Christians with the freedom they have in Jesus. Because of Jesus' sacrifice we don't pay the penalty for breaking all the laws God gave in the Old Testament. Because of Jesus, we don't have to earn our way to Heaven. Paul said, "The whole law can be summed up in this one command: 'Love your neighbor as yourself'" (Galatians 5:14). That's a simple requirement, but it isn't always easy. Which of your neighbors do you have trouble loving? Ask God to help you treat them with his love.

This is too weird, Sean thought to himself. *I'm never going to figure this out. Maybe Carlton was right, and I should just talk to the neighbors. I hate to let someone get one over on me, though. I'll give it one more day, and this time, I won't put anything in anyone's mailbox.*

The next day Sean didn't even go to the mailbox. His mother walked in with the mail and handed him a note. "This was in the mailbox," she said.

Sean read it. "Don't you like me anymore?" it said.

"This person seems eager to have you for a friend," Mom said. "Or at least he or she is enjoying trading secret gifts. It seems as though once the mystery of the person's identity is solved, the game will be over."

"Yeah, maybe," Sean agreed, "But I'm ready for it to be over now." He went upstairs to his room and thought of writing the mystery person his own note. He tried all sorts of different things to say. Finally he wrote, "I'd like to know who you are. But then will our game be over? Give me a hint."

"It is a sin to despise one's neighbors; blessed are those who help the poor" (Proverbs 14:21). Even when you're trying to love others as God loves them, you may not like them, and they may not like you. Your personalities may grate on each other, or others may have habits or values that you don't condone. Keeping your distance from someone you don't get along with is not a sin; in fact, it may be the best way to live peacefully. But you must do so with respect for the other people, not wishing them harm or gossiping behind their backs. Think of someone you don't like, and ask God to bless that person.

MYSTERY OF THE
TRADED TRINKETS

Sean placed the note in the mailbox and prayed over it. He went to school that day convinced he would get an answer. Marcus asked, "Do you think he'll give you a real hint?"

"Why not?" Sean responded. "It's been a fun game so far."

Trey asked, "Which one of your neighbors do you think it is?"

"Not Yoda, I've decided. Either Joe or Moe."

"How about your father?"

"Nah," Sean said. "I've eliminated my parents as suspects."

"How about a cousin or someone related to you?" Josh asked.

"All my relatives live too far away."

He climbed aboard the bus full of expectation. When he got to the mailbox, he prayed before opening it. "Let's get this worked out, Lord," he said to God. He thought a moment, then added, "Bless this person, God."

Then he opened the mailbox.

The object sitting in the mailbox was an envelope with a stamp. An arrow was drawn pointing to the stamp.

Sometimes modern neighbors compete with each other—whose lawn is the greenest, whose car is the coolest, whose outdoor Christmas lights are the gaudiest. Even in ancient times this was true, and Solomon wrote about it: "Then I observed that most people are motivated to success by their envy of their neighbors. But this, too, is meaningless, like chasing the wind" (Ecclesiastes 4:4). Friendly competition can be fun and bring out the best in people, but if you're competing in order to somehow prove that you're a better person than someone else, it's wrong. And as Solomon learned, it's pointless.

Sean ran into the house and showed the envelope to his mom. She looked at it and smiled. "Have you figured it out yet?"

"No. But the stamp has Elvis on it. Do you think that means something?"

"Your mystery friend is Elvis?" Mom asked innocently.

"Don't think so, Mom!"

"Then who?"

Sean thought. "Maybe it's an Elvis fan. But that doesn't help. There are lots of them."

"Maybe it's not the picture on the stamp that's the clue," Mom offered. "Maybe it's the fact that it's a stamp. Who produces stamps? Who uses stamps?"

"The post office." Sean smiled. "So it's the postman. Maybe he does this with lots of kids on his route."

"Write him a nice note, honey."

Sean wrote, "I think you're our letter carrier. An Elvis fan too. And I'm wondering how many kids you've done this with."

The next day he got a note in response. "Congratulations. You figured it out," the note said. "I listen to Elvis every day when I do my route. And I've done this with many people, even adults."

Sean waited at his mailbox the next day to shake hands with the man, and thank him.

The Bible is clear on how we are to treat our neighbors, and not just the ones who live nearby. But Jesus taught something else that many people find astonishing. He said, "You have heard that the law of Moses says, 'Love your neighbor' and hate your enemy. But I say, love your enemies! Pray for those who persecute you!" (Matthew 5:43, 44). How did Jesus show love for his enemies? How do Christians today live out this teaching?

MYSTERY OF THE
SOUNDS FROM THE BASEMENT

Tink-tink. Tinka-tink-tink-tink.

The weird noise was back. Probably no one else noticed in our sixth-grade science class. None of them would have their ears tuned to any and all possible strange sounds that could indicate the presence of an alien, monster, or evil creature bent on world destruction. But I had my ears at ten on the dial. Always. I learned through hard experience that no one should ever ignore a mysterious anything anywhere. It could mean your life.

I glanced at my best friend, Jenna Sabarino. "Hear it?" I whispered. Something about the sound suggested more than some kid tapping out a tune on a porcelain toilet bowl.

"It's creepy," Jenna said. "What do you think it is? A ghost?"

"Jenna!" Mrs. Coogan's voice rang out crisp and clear. "Do you have something to share with the class?"

"No, Mrs. Coogan," Jenna said, frowning at me.

I stared down at my desk hoping one of those gloop-holes would appear so I could tear off to another galaxy far away.

No such luck for me, though. The heavy-set science teacher bore down on both of us, swishing her giant behind down the aisle of desks, knocking several askew. I sometimes thought if she could just get control of her bottom, the world would be a safer place. She glared down at me. "I understand you fancy yourself to be an investigator of sorts, Mr. Kandall. Is that correct?"

Doug has quite an imagination! A vivid imagination can be a gift of God, especially if it helps you to form new ideas, or to be creative and resourceful.

Jesus appealed to his hearers' imagination when he told parables. Read one or two parables in Luke 8, and imagine what Jesus' hearers would have thought.

I gulped. No one was supposed to know about my new work as a creature-buster except Jenna. She knew everything about me and still talked to me—definitely not your average girl.

But I couldn't lie to Mrs. Coogan about the creature-busting thing, could I?

"Um, I'd like to be a C.B. when I grow up, Mrs. Coogan," I somehow stammered. "That's true. But it's a long way off, and—"

"C.B.?" Mrs. Coogan interrupted. "And what, pray tell, is that?"

"Um, uh, you see it's a little, well, OK, it stands for 'Creature-Buster.'" I pulled on my best smile, my lips drawn back till I thought one might split.

Her face crinkled. "A Creature-Buster? Hmmm. You bust creatures? Like the Creature from the Black Lagoon? Like from Creature Feature movies?"

"Sort of, I guess, but I'm not officially one yet. I'm learning to be one from my uncle."

She smiled sarcastically. "Ah, your uncle; the one who lectures all about the intruders among us and those hidden conspiracies."

Stevens Tuttle snickered. "Yeah, Doug Kandall, investigator of all things weird and wild. Got something spooky under your bed? Kandall will come and make it dead!"

The class erupted with laughter.

Sometimes in life, you will choose to do something that other people will laugh at. Don't let them get to you. When Gideon was called to save Israel from the Midianites, he had this conversation with God: "'But Lord,' Gideon replied, 'how can I rescue Israel? My clan is the weakest in the whole tribe of Manasseh, and I am the least in my entire family!' Then the Lord turned to him and said, 'I will be with you. And you will destroy the Midianites as if you were fighting against one man'" (Judges 6:15, 16). God plus you is a majority.

MYSTERY OF THE
SOUNDS FROM
THE BASEMENT

I gave him my best glare. Maybe next time a creature arrived on our doorstep, I'd let it play with Tuttle before I tried to get rid of it.

Mrs. Coogan stared at me like I was some nasty insect under a microscope. "If I catch you and Miss Sabarino talking again, Douglas, you will visit the principal! Do you remember him?"

"Yes, Mrs. Coogan."

"Then stop talking!"

She waved her bony finger in my face. For having such a giant behind, everything else about her was maximum skinny.

As that finger waggled, getting closer and closer to my nose, I noticed her fingernails. They looked black underneath the worn red enamel. Could some Nergs, tiny creatures from a volcano on the planet Bubar, be inhabiting her? They could eat their way right through you until you became a giant Nergle with really bad breath.

No, I thought, it was probably just a fungus, the kind old people like Uncle Ed got all the time.

While there are no monsters in this world, there are mean people, and sometimes people in authority can be mean. How do you deal with them? Paul the apostle wrote to the Christians at Colosse, "You slaves must obey your earthly masters in everything you do. Try to please them all the time, not just when they are watching you. Obey them willingly because of your reverent fear of the Lord. Work hard and cheerfully at whatever you do, as though you were working for the Lord rather than for people" (Colossians 3:22, 23). Even though it wasn't fair that people were held as slaves, Paul told them not to use that as an excuse for not doing their best. When you submit to an authority, even a mean one, you're doing it out of obedience to God.

Tink. Tink-tink. Tink-tinka-tinkety-tink.

There it was again. Was it sending a signal to someone? I knew about the Pony-People of the jungles of Caffica who spoke to each other in Hors-Code by tapping their nails together, but that seemed remote. These tinks sounded metallic.

Then I remembered that strange brown tooth I stepped on in the gym. It was a lucky find: brown, pointed. I believed it could be from a dog, wolf, or even—werewolf?

Then there were those thick, long hairs I discovered in the sink in the music department bathroom. Clearly, someone had shaved or cut those hairs in there, but who? I'd never seen hairs like that except on Barrel Gorillas from Mozam-bunk, an unknown world under Mozambique in Africa that only creature busters know about.

I scribbled a note to Jenna and passed it to her while Mrs. Coogan stood at the board.

"I saw that note," Mrs. Coogan said, without turning around.

Several kids gasped. About 10 other notes were passed at the same moment, so I couldn't be sure if Mrs. Coogan referred to mine or the others.

I homed in on the soft plinking sound until it suddenly stopped.

Do you think Doug's imagination is running away with him? While a creative imagination can be a blessing, it can also be a distraction. You need to know when to focus your attention on important things, and when you can allow your imagination to run wild. There's godly advice in the Bible for your thought life. Read it in Proverbs 4:25-27.

MYSTERY OF THE
SOUNDS FROM
THE BASEMENT

Jenna's eyes widened. "Why did the noise stop?" she whispered.

"If it's a Graybody, it might have had a seizure."

"Another epileptic Graybody?" Jenna almost yelled it.

"They're increasing."

"How come?"

"Too many of them sniffing art class paint these days. It gets them hyper and then they go nuts. Usually while lying on the floor with their eyes blinking a million times a second. Listen, will you help me about the noise? This could be my first big case."

"Sure."

"Mr. Kandall!" Mrs. Coogan yelled. "What are you doing now?" Her eyes looked like fire erupted from them.

I shot up in my seat, eyes forward. "Nothing, Ma'am."

"You are going to have to report to the principal about this."

"Please, not again."

"Gather up your things."

The bell rang. "Saved by the bell," I whispered to Jenna.

"I will overlook it this time, Douglas. But no more," Mrs. Coogan said, her eyes squinty shut and looking weirder every minute. Was I having some kind of seizure?

No, just the normal problems of being kind of crazy.

At this time in his life, Doug's imagination is getting him into trouble. But when he grows up, his imagination may enable him to do things that nobody has thought of before.

Whenever you try to do a great work, there will be opposition. Paul wrote in 2 Timothy 3:12 that "Everyone who wants to live a godly life in Christ Jesus will suffer persecution." Expect to be opposed whenever you attempt something for God. Be on the lookout.

Naturally Mrs. Coogan frowned. "All of you—out! You too, Mr. Kandall."

I hurried through the doorway. Jenna caught up to me in the hall. "I think the sound might be coming from the old basement," I said. "Our classroom is right above it—that room past the storage room."

We reached the stairs down to the lower level that led to the basement. The big green door at the bottom of the stairs loomed ahead like a black hole into terror.

We pushed open the green doors. The white cinderblock hall stretched before us. It looked like a tunnel in the low light. We would first walk through the storage room, which was eerie enough, then to the janitor's office at the end. That was where I thought the tinking sound originated. But there was no telling what we might find on the way. Graybodies galore? A rat or two? A dead body?

We hurried down the hall, our sneakers creaking on the linoleum floor. I glanced behind me, then ducked into an alcove outside the door to the storage room. A water fountain was there. I grabbed the handle.

Pop! I shot up, my mouth filled with water. "Whaaaaaa?"

"My gum," Jenna said. Another *pop*.

I pulled Jenna into the alcove. "Be quiet," I seethed.

I heard something. A scratching noise.

"What's that?"

Often when you're doing something, there is a point of no return. Will you continue, or turn back? Jesus said that "Anyone who puts a hand to the plow and then looks back is not fit for the Kingdom of God" (Luke 9:62).

Jesus meant that when you take on a job for God, be ready to keep going even when things get tough. God will give you the strength you need.

MYSTERY OF THE
SOUNDS FROM THE BASEMENT

I took out my Ghost-and-Creature-Busting-Get-Everything-Down-First tape recorder. It not only records human voices, but also other creatures' voices that normal tape recorders miss. That's what Uncle Ed says it does, anyway.

I listened for the scratching noise. It had stopped. I spoke into the recorder. "We're standing at the corner next to the storage room. We are about to descend into the pit. God be with us."

I followed Jenna to the door.

"Ladies first," I said as we stood at the door.

She snorted. "You just want me to go first so you won't be eaten."

"Fine." I set my hand on the doorknob. I admit it, I felt scared. You just never know what can happen in this creature busting business.

I shivered as I pushed the door all the way open, then stepped back as if I expected something to shoot out at us.

Something came toward us, and it was dragging a dead body! Jenna screamed. But I stared, unwilling to move.

"Dieter?" I asked.

Dieter turned around. He was a sixth grader who flunked last year, but still hung around.

"Yeah," he said. "I'm painting this for the art contest." He showed us the mannequin made up to look like it had its throat slit.

Jenna looked at me and shrugged. "So much for ghosts, vampires, and werewolves," she said, and left.

I stood there feeling like an idiot. But what could I do? Sometimes I am an idiot. I can't help it. It's in my genes.

Doug wanted to do something great and spectacular. But most of us aren't called to be "spiritual superheroes." What does the Lord require of us? Read Micah 6:8 to find out.

As my dad pulled into our townhouse parking lot, I glanced at my watch: 3:00. The mail had come. Time to see if anyone had responded to my latest pen-pal letters.

Normally, Dad would park the car around the island at the top of the lot away from the mailboxes. But for some reason, he stopped in front of the mailboxes at the foot of the island. It was October, a Wednesday; a cool, cloudless, beautiful Indian summer day. I got out.

"I'll get the mail, Dad, if you want."

"Go ahead, Lou." He handed me the key to the box.

I took out the letters and looked them over. Nothing caught my attention. I murmured, "Well, maybe tomorrow."

Suddenly I heard a strange scraping sound. I stepped back instinctively as a man's scream broke through the quiet: "Helllllpp!"

I turned, my heart hammering, trying to spot what and where the problem was. A red Honda rolled backwards toward me on the pavement. The scraping sound got louder, like a rubber mat being pulled across concrete.

"Help me! Help me!"

I yelled to Dad, "Get out! Get out! Something's wrong!"

Accidents happen all the time in our world. Disasters, from Hurricane Katrina to 9/11 and many others make the news each evening. But the smaller ones, the ones we don't read about, are what we see in our lives.

What would you have done in that moment when that car came careening down toward Lou and his father? The Bible assures us that in such moments God is with us. Second Peter 2:9 says, "So you see, the Lord knows how to rescue godly people from their trials, even while punishing the wicked right up until the day of judgment." When has God rescued you?

MYSTERY OF THE
INCIDENT AT
THE MAILBOX

Two old people I recognized as neighbors hobbled down the lot toward me. The man cried, "Under car! Under car! My son! Caught under car!"

The car drove straight toward the curb and I could see there was no driver. In fact, the door on the driver's side was open, and so was the trunk. Dad came out next to me.

"What is it?"

"Someone's under the car."

I bent down and saw that someone was pinned under the rear axle of the car. I knew the man's name was Khin and he had recently moved here from Myanmar. One of his kids was my age and in my school. Clearly, he couldn't move.

I froze and watched in horror as the car moved in reverse with Khin screaming under it. Everything seemed to be in slow motion, and I felt anxious, yet ready for action. Maybe it was adrenalin.

The next instant, I dropped the mail and Dad and I ran to try to stop the car, but we couldn't. I was not afraid, though I wasn't sure of what to do.

The car hit the curb just behind us and stopped. The elderly woman caught me by the arm and yelled, "Please help him! Please get him out!"

An emergency is not a time to panic, but it's easy to lose control. There's barely time to think, pray, or plan. You have to take action immediately. One of the great Scriptures tells us to call on God in such moments: "Call to me and I will answer you and tell you great and unsearchable things you do not know" (Jeremiah 33:3, *NIV*). Do you know how to look to God in such a moment? What could you do now to be better prepared for an emergency that might occur?

The elderly man gestured and shrieked. Dad hurried around the car and jumped in. He called, "He must have forgotten to put it in park, gotten out, and walked behind it to place something in the trunk. It must have rolled backwards."

"What will you do?" I cried.

Khin wheezed, "Please! I can't breathe."

A younger woman, apparently Khin's wife, came running, screaming, "Please hurry! Hurry!"

Was Dad going to drive the car off him? I stooped down to look at Khin. "It'll be OK," I told him. "I'm praying right now."

Dad shouted out the window, "I'm going to start the engine. I might be able to move it off your chest."

I wasn't sure it would work. The old man yelled, "My son!"

The engine turned over and started. Dad started forward.

"Aiee!" Khin's wife was frantic.

As the car eased slightly forward, Khin screamed. I knew instantly it wouldn't work. He was pinned. Dad would only drag him back.

"Stop, Dad! It won't work," I yelled.

Dad stopped, jammed the stick back into park and jumped out.

There had to be a way. The wife shouted again, "He will die! Please hurry! He can't breathe."

Often in such a situation, you have to try several methods to solve a problem. You have to think fast and not make any errors. People's lives may depend on your quick thinking. What does God offer us in such a moment? He says in James 1:19, "be quick to listen, slow to speak, and slow to get angry." Are you a person quick to hear and learn? Are your ears open to the voice of God when you most need him to speak?

MYSTERY OF THE
INCIDENT AT THE MAILBOX

Khin's face was white and his cheeks quivered. "I . . . can't . . . get any air," he wheezed again.

Dad hurried around the car and motioned to me and the older man, "Help me try to lift it off him." It was a small car, a Honda, and I thought it might work.

I yelled to Khin, "See if you can pull out as we lift."

Khin shook his head, gasping, "It's crushing my chest."

We all heaved with all our might. But we couldn't budge the car. "On three!" Dad cried.

He counted and we tried again. But the car was too heavy. To get the axle off him, we needed to lift the back rear tire off the ground. I knew it was impossible with only the three of us, probably even with several more.

Dad let go and we all rested, breathing hard. "What do we do now, Lord? Show us!" I prayed silently.

A neighbor ran down toward us. "I called 911!" he shouted. "They'll be here in minutes."

But in minutes Khin might be dead. He said he couldn't breathe, and that had been more than a minute before. How long could a person go without air?

We had to do something, and quick. I searched in my mind for something. "God, help us!" I whispered.

> In a dangerous situation, ideas must come hard and fast. Where do you turn for such ideas? Ask God for them. Even if you don't really have time to form a prayer in your mind, lift your heart to God. He knows what you need, even if you can't put it into words. Jesus said, "your Father knows exactly what you need even before you ask him!" (Matthew 6:8).

Time was running out.

Khin choked again, "Please . . . Please."

Dad and I searched the lot for something. My eyes came back to Dad's car. Just a week before we'd had a flat tire. After changing it, Dad threw everything on top in the trunk. It was all right there in easy reach. "Dad! In the car—the jack!"

He sped to the car, opened the trunk and whipped the jack out. I took it and put it under Khin's car. The neighbor who called 911 was already at the car, telling Khin what we were doing. Dad positioned the jack while I stuck in the handle and began twisting it as quickly as I could. Dad stood next to me. "Faster. Faster," he said.

Khin's wife jumped anxiously next to me. "Will it work?"

In less than five seconds we knew. Khin gasped. "I can breathe," he said.

The weight began to come off him. Soon he wiggled a little. Then he got his hands up and started pushing against the axle.

"More, more," he cried, and I kept turning the handle.

Dad yelled, "As Lou lifts, pull yourself out. I'll help you. Give me your arm."

I wound the jack higher and higher. Dad grabbed Khin under the armpits and began tugging on him. Slowly, he moved only inches. But as I raised the car with the jack, Dad and the neighbor pulled him out from underneath the axle.

Isn't it amazing the way God works at times? The Bible says, "God is our refuge and strength, an ever-present help in trouble" (Psalm 46:1, *NIV*). God is always there, available in an instant, and powerful enough to do things greater than we can imagine. He can work through willing servants, even kids. How can God use you?

MYSTERY OF THE
INCIDENT AT THE MAILBOX

In another few seconds Khin stood shakily next to the back of the car, grinning. His skinny body was soaked with sweat. The accident had shredded his shirt in the back. Five huge patches of rubbed-off skin were visible on his shoulders, with flecks of gravel imbedded in them. I winced. It looked raw and painful. But Khin gave me his hand. "You saved me. You saved my life."

I laughed as tears burned my eyes. Dad clapped me on the back. "Thank the Lord for that one. I didn't know what to do. I thought you were gone. But Lou here saw it. God must have put the idea into his mind."

I nodded. Yes, that's exactly what happened.

We all shook hands, then I let the jack down, noticing for the first time the sweat under my shirt and my pounding heart. As I watched Khin hug his parents and shake his head with emotion as people asked questions, I fought back my own rush of emotion.

He didn't seem to be in pain. His face shone with gratitude, and his wife gripped his hand, weeping. Moments later, an ambulance, a fire truck, and then a policeman arrived. Khin was taken to a nearby hospital and bandaged up. Someone else drove the car back to its slot.

Dad and I grabbed our equipment and walked back to the car.

A near encounter with death. Had Lou and his dad not stopped at the mailboxes with their jack ready in the trunk, what might have happened? Read what David wrote about God: "You saw me before I was born. Every day of my life was recorded in your book. Every moment was laid out before a single day had passed" (Psalm 139:16). What does this say to you about how God is preparing you for the situations you will face today?

INCIDENT AT THE MAILBOX

Later, Dad said, "Did you notice that before they took Khin away in the ambulance that someone told him he was the luckiest man alive?"

"Yeah, I heard," I answered. "But I don't think it was luck."

"You're right," Dad said. "God had it all figured out."

That afternoon I found Khin's broken glasses by the curb and took them to his house. His father came out, thanked me for saving his son's life, and bowed several times. I said, "I think God was watching over the whole thing." I tried to explain my idea, how Dad had just happened to park at the mailbox instead of driving around; how I was able not to panic; how my thoughts remained clear throughout the whole rescue; how the jack was easily available at just the right moment.

He didn't seem to understand. But as I walked away, I thanked God. A rush of emotion filled me as I returned to our house.

Later that night, Khin came by my house and thanked me and Dad again for saving his life. I answered, "Thank the Lord, Khin. He's the one who did it."

He smiled and bowed. Maybe in the days ahead Dad and I would be able to tell him and his family more about God. I went to bed that night with confidence that God had not only helped me today, but that I could depend on him for the rest of my life.

Do you have a sense that God is with you always, wherever you are? Do you believe he is there to help, to offer wisdom, and to lead you through every circumstance of life?

When God called Isaiah to do a job for him, how did Isaiah answer? Read Isaiah 6:8 to find out. Is that the kind of response you'd like to make to God today?

MYSTERY OF THE
MONKEY'S PAW

Juan had just come home from a trip to Mexico. When he got together with his friends, he was eager to show them his latest souvenir. He pulled it out of his pocket and lay it on his hand.

"What is it?" Shanara asked. It looked like a small hand with five fingers and long fingernails.

"A monkey's paw," Juan said. "You can make wishes with it."

Quig looked at Zulu and rolled his eyes. "Yeah, sure."

"No, it's true. The man in Mexico told me when he sold it to me. He told me a story about a monkey's paw just like this one."

"Tell us!" Shanara said.

They all sat down on the picnic table. Juan began, "It's an old story. This sailor brought home a monkey's paw from the shores of Araby. He told his family about the wishes, and everyone wanted to make one. His father wished for a new hat. His sister wanted a dozen roses. But his aunt wished for five hundred dollars, 'To get us through this hard time,' she said.

"Strangely, the father found a new hat in his attic in a new hatbox. He'd never seen it before, so he said it had to be from the monkey's paw. The sister received a dozen roses the next day from her butcher. He said she was his one-thousandth customer."

"What about the aunt?" Zulu asked.

Making wishes is different from praying to God. A wish is asked to the air, fate, the stars, whatever. A prayer goes to God, the only one who can answer prayers. When you know God, you can say with David the psalmist, "Listen closely to my prayer, O Lord; hear my urgent cry. I will call on you whenever trouble strikes, and you will answer me" (Psalm 86:6, 7).

Juan took a deep breath. "The next day, the aunt heard a knock on the door. The man there told her that her husband had been killed in an auto accident. He had taken out a five-hundred dollar insurance policy some time earlier, and the man was there to deliver it."

"Oh, that' s awful!" Zulu said, and the other kids groaned.

Juan went on. "The aunt fainted right there. When she awakened she cried and screamed and wanted to take the wish back. Everyone was shocked. But then she said, 'Give me that monkey's paw! Give it to me.'

"Someone did, and immediately, she fell to her knees and cried, 'I wish for my husband to come through that door in the next two minutes.'

"Everyone gasped. They all sat very still. Nothing happened. Then they heard footsteps and the front gate opened with a squeak."

"This is stupid," Quig said.

"No, it's not!" Shanara argued. "Let him go on with the story."

Juan nodded. "They all froze. There were more footsteps, but they sounded funny, like the person walking had a strange sort of limp. Then there was a knock at the door."

Before television, even before books, storytelling was a major form of entertainment. Fantastic stories were a way for people to use their imaginations and interact with each other. Today, people don't tell many stories, but you can see outrageous things on TV, read them in books, or find "urban legends" on the Internet. As long as you know what's true and what's fiction, stories are harmless. Ask God to lead you in truth: "Lead me by your truth and teach me, for you are the God who saves me. All day long I put my hope in you" (Psalm 25:5).

"The aunt started toward the door," Juan continued, "but her son grabbed the monkey's paw out of her hand, ran to the door, and cried, 'Please make that thing at the door go away!'

"The aunt screamed, 'Nooooooo!' and threw open the door. There was no one there."

Juan looked around at the group and said quietly, "And that's the end of the story."

Several of the kids groaned. Quig said, "I told you it was stupid."

But Zulu said, "I think we should try it." He gestured to the monkey's paw in Juan's hand. "We should make wishes to see if it works. Just as a, you know, a scientific experiment."

Juan looked around at the group. "Think so?"

Several shrugged. Shanara said, "Yes, yes. Let's do it."

They took turns making wishes: Zulu wished for a BB gun, Quig for a moon ring, and Shanara wanted a new boyfriend. Nothing was too dramatic.

As they passed the paw around, everyone was soon laughing at the foolish wishes everyone made. Several got angry when others laughed.

At last the paw came back to Juan. "What do you wish, Juan?" asked Quig.

Have you ever made a wish when blowing out candles on a birthday cake? How is that like, or unlike, wishing on a monkey's paw? What would you say to a friend who asked you if wishing is wrong?

Jesus said, "If you remain in me and my words remain in you, ask whatever you wish, and it will be given you" (John 15:7, *NIV*). What do you think about wishing in light of that verse? Ask your parents and friends what they think.

MONKEY'S PAW

"Come back tomorrow and I'll tell you my wish," Juan said.

"Is it going to be an amazing one?" Zulu asked.

"Totally."

"What will you wish?" Shanara asked. "Come on, tell us."

"I haven't thought about it enough."

"Then it's not that amazing," Quig said.

"You'll see."

Juan went to bed that night thinking. What did he really want to wish for? What would be so amazing everyone would be totally stunned?

The next day, there was exciting news. Zulu got his BB gun. He'd found it in someone's trash on the curb. It was broken, but he was confident he could fix it.

Quig found a skull ring in his father's jewelry box, and his dad said he could have it. He said, "It's almost as good as a moon ring."

Shanara had met a new boy she liked. Well, not so new. It was Zulu, but she kept smiling at him like they had something special going.

Every day you have decisions to make about how you will live. The Bible gives this instruction: "So be careful how you live, not as fools but as those who are wise. Make the most of every opportunity for doing good in these evil days. Don't act thoughtlessly, but try to understand what the Lord wants you to do" (Ephesians 5:15-17).

They all turned to Juan. "Well," said Quig, "What's your wish?"

Juan shook his head. "I have so many. First, I thought I'd like to get my driver's license. But that can't happen till I'm 16. Three years away. So I decided not to go with that one."

"Maybe the government could write new laws," Zulu said.

"Don't think so," Shanara answered.

Juan looked over the group. "Then I thought I would ask for a full set of baseball cards with Babe Ruth in it, plus Lou Gehrig. But I thought that was too valuable."

"Come on, Juan. Get to the real one," Quig said.

"Well, the real big one was that Shanara would fall in love with me forever."

Shanara covered her mouth with amazement.

"But then I realized I should wish that I would fall in love with her forever too, or it wouldn't be any good. And I didn't know if I had more than one wish."

Shanara reached over and gave Juan a playful slap on the arm. "You could still ask for it."

Quig rolled his eyes again. Zulu looked a little hurt.

You can't always get what you want, especially if what you want involves someone else's free will. You must learn to live in whatever circumstances you find yourself.

Paul did that, and he urged Christians to also. To the church in Philippi he wrote, "I know how to live on almost nothing or with everything. I have learned the secret of living in every situation, whether it is with a full stomach or empty, with plenty or little. For I can do everything with the help of Christ who gives me the strength I need" (Philippians 4:12, 13). Can you be content when your wishes don't come true?

Juan took a deep breath. "No, seriously. My wish was for whatever it was in the story that came to the door and then was wished away to come to our door."

Everyone sat stunned.

"At 3:00 tomorrow."

"Oooooo," everyone said, whistling.

"I want to see it," said Quig. "That would be awesome if it did come."

"I think I'll be hiding in a back room," said Shanara.

"It won't come," said Zulu. "It's impossible. That was just a story."

"How do you know that?" asked Juan.

"I looked it up. It was written in 1902. It's in lots of anthologies of short stories. But you told it a little differently."

Juan nodded. "I gave it my own special spin." As they went out the door, he added, "Remember: 3:00 tomorrow."

Is there any reason that you fear the future? Do you dread something that is to come? You can go to God with your concerns, and he will listen and help you. Remember what Peter wrote in 1 Peter 5:7: "Give all your worries and cares to God, for he cares about what happens to you." How does it make you feel to know God cares for you?

MYSTERY OF THE
MONKEY'S PAW

By 2:30, everyone arrived at Juan's house. Quig alone wasn't there.

"It hasn't come yet?" Shanara asked when she stepped in the door at 2:36.

"No," said Juan. They all sat in the living room. Several kids picked up magazines and read, but clearly no one could concentrate. Zulu had a clock in front of him.

"I'll do a countdown," he said.

Everyone looked nervous and worried. Soon it was 2:50. Then 2:55. At 2:59, Zulu began a count. "Sixty, fifty-nine, fifty-eight—" He went on and on, down to "Ten, nine—" A gate creaked out front. Footsteps were heard. Running.

Suddenly, Juan jumped up. "I can't do it," he cried. He grabbed the paw. "Make whatever it is go away."

There was dead silence.

Zulu said, "Three, two, one, zero."

The doorbell rang.

Everyone stared. Juan took a breath, then opened the door. There stood Quig. He said, "Did I miss it?"

Everyone laughed. "You *are* it," Juan said with a chuckle.

Why would people believe in things that aren't real? Since soon after creation, human beings have believed lies. Some have made up their own gods and worshiped them. Daniel confronted Belshazzar, king of Babylon, for believing in false gods: "You and your nobles and your wives and concubines have been . . . praising gods of silver, gold, bronze, iron, wood, and stone—gods that neither see nor hear nor know anything at all. But you have not honored the God who gives you the breath of life and controls your destiny!" (Daniel 5:23b). What are people tempted to worship today? Are you tempted to worship anyone, or anything, besides God?

MYSTERY OF THE
ROCK CLIMB

The instructor demonstrated how to tie in the belaying rope. He said, "This rope is your lifeline. It protects you as you climb. If you slip, or even fall completely, the person holding the line at the top will rope you in. You will never fall more than a few feet. No rock climber would ever climb without being tied to a secure point, either by a person at the top holding the rope, or by pins actually secured in the rock with pitons, bolts, and carabiners. We're just doing a hundred foot rock climb. Nothing here will be overwhelming, but it will be demanding."

Brad Longacre shifted his weight nervously as he looked up at the cliffs towering over his little group. He'd never done a rock climb like this before, but the junior high group had been determined. It was all new to him, and induced a nearly paralyzing fear.

"Scared?" Jenny Howard poked him in the ribs playfully.

"No."

"Yes, you are."

"A little."

In rock climbing, the person with the belaying line will tighten it every now and then. You have no fear of the climb, but you also have freedom to climb the way you want. It's a lot like walking with Christ. He gives you just enough slack to climb freely, but tight enough that you have no fear. It's like what Paul wrote in Galatians 5:1: "So Christ has really set us free. Now make sure that you stay free, and don't get tied up again in slavery to the law." Do you sense that freedom in your walk with Christ? Why, or why not?

Jenny grinned. She had long brown hair pulled back in a pony tail, and blue eyes. It was through her that Brad's sister had gotten involved in the junior high youth group at church. He'd finally come on a dare. When he met Jenny, he began coming eagerly. And in the last year he'd become a Christian, trying to walk with Christ by getting involved in worship, Bible study, and youth group.

When the group attended a "survival camp" in the Adirondacks, the culmination was the rock climb. Brad didn't want to look like a wimp in front of the group, and especially not in front of Jenny. But his heart was pounding in his chest like a drum.

Jenny poked him again. "Why don't you go first? Show us your stuff."

"I've never done this before, Jen."

"Neither has anyone else."

It didn't matter. The instructor pointed to Brad anyway. "All right, Longacre, let's see you do it."

Brad sighed unhappily, but stepped forward to be tied in.

The climb didn't offer any easy spots, though there were plenty of places to get handholds and footholds. The belaying rope dangled slightly below him as he started up the climb.

Brad didn't have to be afraid of falling, but he was afraid of failing. Look at Psalm 3:6: "I am not afraid of ten thousand enemies who surround me on every side." God does not want us to live lives of fear. Fear paralyzes us. We can't do what we want to do, what we need to do. But when we remember that God is on our side, we can forge ahead. How does knowing that God is with you help you to conquer fear?

"Look and plan your way," the instructor said. "Keep looking up and ahead. There's no right way to do it."

Brad stuck his hiking boot into the first toehold, reached up to a crevice and pulled himself up.

"Go! Go! Go!" the group began to chant.

But the instructor stopped them. "Quiet. He needs to think. Let him find his way in quiet."

Right, Brad thought. *Just what I need.* A lengthy crevice cut deeply along one horizontal layer about 14 feet up. Brad couldn't see the man above belayed in behind a big rock. "I hope he stays alert," Brad murmured to himself.

The rope tightened slightly as Brad climbed. It gave him a feeling of confidence. His belay man was staying right in there with each step. He began climbing without thinking about the rope. He knew he was not to use it to help himself up over a projection or tough spot, but just the fact that it was there was powerful assurance. He couldn't really hurt himself, he figured, even if he did slip, just as the instructor said.

He was now 10 feet up. A small chimney hung to his right, and to his left an outcrop that he could not go over. He decided to try to work between the two.

"Be careful," he heard Jenny call up to him. *I am, I am!* he said in his mind. *What do you think I'm doing?*

There are many Bible verses to remember when we come face-to-face with something or someone dangerous. God says, "Be strong and courageous! Do not be afraid of them! The Lord your God will go ahead of you. He will neither fail you nor forsake you" (Deuteronomy 31:6). God is always ready to help us when we have a need. Talk to God, thanking him for a time or situation in which he helped you.

MYSTERY OF THE
ROCK CLIMB

He scrabbled for leverage to pull himself up to a small ledge, then got a boot on it. Two more major rises and he would be over the outcrop. He was already tired, though. Each lift and step took all his strength.

In another two minutes he was over it. Standing on the outcrop, he shielded his eyes from the sun. He had another 30 feet to go. But the instructor called up, "The rest is easy. Go to it!"

Brad soon made his way up over the "easy part" and came up over the final rise. He was greeted by the smiling face of one of the assistants. "Welcome," the man said. "You just made history."

"Yeah," Brad said. It was a good feeling. The assistant threw the rope back down to the group and called, "All clear. Number two ready to go."

Brad worked his way back down in an area where the terrain was easier. He soon joined the group. One of his friends, Chuck Shirley, had begun to climb.

"How was it?" Jenny said.

"Exciting!"

They both watched Chuck mount the outcrop and get over it. In a half hour two others had gone, and two other climbers had gotten started at other points on the cliff.

"So when're you going?" Brad asked Jenny, giving her a poke.

Do you know where courage comes from? According to the Bible, God gives it to us when we need it: "You will be secure, because there is hope; you will look about you and take your rest in safety" (Job 11:18, *NIV*). Having hope will give you courage. Have you ever exhibited courage that could only have come from God? When?

"Maybe next year," Jenny answered, not looking at him.

"Hey, no way! I did it. Get with the program."

Jenny turned to him. "I don't feel so good about this, Brad."

"Oh, try it. You can't get hurt."

"Yeah, that's what they say. But I'm still afraid."

Brad squinted at her. He realized Jenny was seriously scared. "Relax, Jen. We're all afraid. That's what this is all about. Face your fear—lean into it, you know? We're all behind you."

"Yeah, I know." She smiled weakly; then stepped up to be tied in.

Jenny started up at one of the easier climbs on a pocked piece of rock that had plenty of handholds. She climbed with calm assurance and Brad settled down once she'd started.

Jenny stopped at a small ledge to catch her breath. "This is really hard," she called down.

"You're doing fine, though," the instructor said. "Just don't get in a hurry. Take your time."

Jenny set her foot in another notch and started up the rock face again. "Don't break a nail now," Brad called playfully.

Jenny answered, "I've already broken three. I'm giving up on them." She was breathing hard.

Just do it. That's not only a slogan; it's a way of life. Sharing your faith, speaking in front of a group, making a personal sacrifice—all those things require you to step up and do them even when you're afraid.

Peter once stepped out of a boat in a treacherous sea to do something nobody had ever done before. What was it? Read Matthew 14:25-31 to find out. What would have happened if Peter had stayed in the boat?

MYSTERY OF THE
ROCK CLIMB

The belayer was careful to keep the rope just tight enough to give Jenny confidence, but loose enough to give her full freedom as she climbed. Several times she looked down. Brad stared up at her and smiled. "You're doing all right."

"Yeah."

The most difficult part was ahead, a wall 10 feet straight up. Brad watched as she planted a foot, got a handhold, and—

The fall was sudden and harrowing. Jenny fell four feet and swung out wildly from the cliff. "Help!" she screamed.

A second later, Jenny smacked against the wall. Everyone seemed to stop breathing for a moment.

"You OK?" the instructor called.

No answer.

Jenny hung at an odd angle, not moving. She was caught on a ledge, her leg under her.

"Jenny!" the instructor shouted. "Are you OK?"

Again no answer. The instructor called for another two lines.

"I'm going with you," Brad said.

"Leave it to the pros," the instructor said.

"Please."

Giving him a hard look, the instructor said, "All right. Get tied in." He turned to one of the assistants. "Bill, you go up and belay Brad on the left. I'll take the right. I think she's just had a knock."

Bad things happen even when we exhibit the greatest of courage. That was true in Paul's life. Often challenged, sometimes beaten, he didn't stop preaching the gospel. He didn't know whether his plans would succeed. But he plunged ahead, believing God would come through. Paul wrote, "The Lord will deliver me from every evil attack and will bring me safely to his heavenly Kingdom" (2 Timothy 4:18). He will do that for you too.

Brad's heart was pounding as he began climbing on the left side. He watched for any signs of Jenny coming around, but she hung there, limp. "Please, God, let her be all right."

When they reached her, the instructor propped Jenny up against the wall and held some smelling salts under her nose. She awoke with a start. "Oh, my head!"

The instructor looked into her eyes. "You feel OK? No broken bones?"

Jenny took a quick mental inventory and said, "No, I don't think so."

"Then let's get you down. Just let him wind out the line and you'll go right down."

Jenny glanced at Brad. "No, I want to go on."

"You were knocked out, Jenny. You need to get on the ground."

"But if I'm OK, you'll let me try again?"

Brad said, "Jen, you don't have to do it."

"I know. I want to. It's a challenge."

The instructor said, "Let's get you down and make sure everything's all right."

Jenny had a lump on the back of her head, but otherwise she was all right. After a half hour of letting others climb, she went again. This time Brad climbed next to her. "We can find footholds and handholds together," he said.

Jenny laughed. "It'll be fun."

When they came over the top together, they hugged and celebrated.

What is God doing when we attempt great things in his name? Psalm 37:23, 24 has the answer: "The steps of the godly are directed by the Lord. He delights in every detail of their lives. Though they stumble, they will not fall, for the Lord holds them by the hand." What comfort does this Scripture give you?

MYSTERY OF THE
UGLY RUMOR

Karen Wheeler stared across the table at Linda Bavaro. The yearbook meeting was going as usual, with Karen and Linda disagreeing about everything from page design, to the poetry in the literary section, to the arrangement of face photos in the Eighth Grade Spotlight. They were discussing the layout of the Sports Slot, and Linda felt strongly that the school's football League Champions should be given at least three pages.

"They won the Middle School Championship. They should get a big splash in this year's yearbook," Linda said. "We shouldn't break with Hillsboro tradition anyway."

"It's not tradition!" Karen said angrily. "We just don't have to give them everything. It's a slap in the face to all the other teams at the school."

"I can hear you two all the way down the hall!" Miss Harris, the advisor said as she stepped into the room. "You'd think there wasn't enough to fight about in the world without the two of you beating one another up about a few pages in a yearbook."

How do you speak when you have strong feelings about something? Do you get mad and yell? Do you sit quietly and do a slow burn? Do you tell yourself you just don't care and to forget about it? Consider this verse from Proverbs 15:1: "A gentle answer turns away wrath, but harsh words stir up anger." How can you apply this verse in conflicts with others, including your parents, brothers and sisters, friends, and teachers?

When Linda walked out, Miss Harris looked at Karen and shook her head. "I've just about had it with you two, Karen. What is this all about?"

Karen sucked her cheek, saying nothing.

Grant shook his head. "We told you they'd never be able to work together."

Miss Harris's eyes narrowed. "I know you told me that, Grant. But—" She gazed at Karen. "I thought you two were mature enough to put aside whatever it is that's bugging you and work as a team."

Karen sighed. She looked at her knuckles and said nothing.

It was true, all of it. She and Linda had been best friends a year ago, in the same church and youth group. Then somehow an ugly rumor circulated about Linda. Karen had a role in starting the rumor because of something she'd said to a few friends. And she had a role in perpetuating the rumor by not correcting the misinformation that she heard circulated. It had caused them to distance themselves, and gradually the friendship died a slow death. Now they barely spoke to each other unless it was absolutely necessary—such as in yearbook meetings.

Miss Harris continued, "If you two don't settle your differences, I'm going to put you both off the staff. Understand?"

Karen said stiffly, "Yes, Ma'am."

How do you solve a dispute like this? What does the Bible say about making peace with someone? Consider this verse from Hebrews 12:14: "Try to live in peace with everyone, and seek to live a clean and holy life, for those who are not holy will not see the Lord." What steps might you take to make peace with someone in your life?

Yearbook staff meetings went forward. Karen made an effort not to fight with Linda and chose only those rare "important" issues that she thought were worth debating. Meanwhile, Linda kept a low profile. Then one Saturday when the staff came in to work on a deadline, things blew up over a spilled soda.

Miss Harris raised her voice. "Are you two at it again?"

Linda stopped. Karen turned red. Jon and Grant said nothing.

"It was an accident," Karen said, mopping at the puddle on the table.

"It's ruined the photo—the very one she didn't like in the first place." Linda held the picture out to Miss Harris.

"All right, girls, come with me."

Miss Harris led them to the faculty lounge down the hall and closed the door behind her. "Sit!"

Karen slumped onto one end of a couch, folding her arms. Linda hunched on a red plastic chair.

Miss Harris took the seat between the two girls. "I don't get this. Yearbook staff is a team. We have a lot of work to do to meet our deadlines, and you two are causing everyone a lot of tension. I can't have this. Do you both want to be kicked off the staff?"

Karen and Linda glared at each other.

After a few moments of silence, Miss Harris said coldly, "I understand you two are very religious, into church and everything."

Even Christians can have serious disagreements or personality conflicts. What should you do under such conditions? Look at this verse from Galatians 6:1: "Dear brothers and sisters, if another Christian is overcome by some sin, you who are godly should gently and humbly help that person back onto the right path. And be careful not to fall into the same temptation yourself."

Both girls looked up. Karen hadn't wanted to discuss this. But she said, "Yes," and glanced at Linda, who agreed without looking back.

Miss Harris shook her head. "I grew up in a religious environment too. That's why I'm an agnostic now. All I saw was fights. I suspect that there's something deeper here, beyond yearbook pictures and pages that's the source of your disagreement, but you've got to set it aside. I won't have it on my yearbook staff."

Karen stiffened. Linda was sullen. Then Karen said, "Miss Harris, I'm really sorry . . ."

But Miss Harris interrupted. "Doesn't your church teach that 'love one another' stuff? If they do, it's been lost on you two."

Karen gulped, and Linda looked as though she'd been punched in the stomach. Miss Harris went on: "I want you two to settle this. Do you understand? If you can't, you're both off the yearbook, even though I know it will be hard to fill your positions."

What effect do fighting Christians have on the non-Christians around them? Paul warned Christians to watch their witness: "In everything you do, stay away from complaining and arguing, so that no one can speak a word of blame against you. You are to live clean, innocent lives as children of God in a dark world full of crooked and perverse people. Let your lives shine brightly before them" (Philippians 2:14, 15). Is there anyone you need to reconcile with in order to improve your witness as a Christian?

MYSTERY OF THE
UGLY RUMOR

Karen had never seen Miss Harris so angry. But before either girl had a chance to say anything, the teacher turned and walked out of the room, leaving Linda and Karen sitting uncomfortably on the edges of their seats.

Karen looked up. Linda's face looked gray, with all the blood drained out. Karen felt heavy and close to tears. This was the last thing she'd expected out of Miss Harris. She didn't speak.

Linda's voice was strained when she spoke again. "I don't know about you, but I feel like a real jerk."

"Yeah."

"What can we do?"

"I don't know." For the first time, Karen looked up hopefully. Maybe the ice was melting.

Linda sat down and gazed at Karen. "What do we do?"

Karen answered, "Linda, about that rumor that got started . . ."

Anger crossed Linda's face, but she said nothing.

"I'm sorry that I, that—I mean, I should have done something, or said something to defend you. But I was worried about being dragged down with you—you know, that I wouldn't be popular. I thought I was just trying to protect myself, but I abandoned you."

Linda gazed at Karen, and tears spilled onto her cheeks.

Rumors are fed by gossip when something gets bigger and worse with each telling. People like to embellish and add their own details. It's pretty easy to see how this might have happened with Karen and Linda. Look at this verse from Proverbs 16:28 on gossip: "A troublemaker plants seeds of strife; gossip separates the best of friends." Why do you think God condemns gossip so pointedly?

"Did you know how much I was hurting?" Linda asked. "I could hardly get through school each day."

Karen shook her head. "No, I really didn't. You looked like you were doing fine. And as a matter of fact, I guess I was a little jealous of you. You were becoming closer friends with Brian and Celeste, and I thought you'd outgrown me."

"Oh, no!" Linda said. "They could never take your place." She wiped her cheek with her hand. "Why didn't you just tell me how you felt?"

"I don't know. I guess I was ashamed." Karen moved down the couch, closer to Linda. "I felt inferior and defensive."

"I never thought you were inferior," Linda said. She paused. "But I did think you were rejecting me. And because I hurt, I wanted you to hurt too. After we took our achievement tests and I found out that you hadn't done well on the math section, I made fun of you. I didn't really believe the things I said, but I just got caught up in my own misery, and I lashed out at you."

"Wow, that's brutal," Karen said. She put her hand on her forehead, and Linda thought Karen looked like she was about to faint.

When someone hurts you, do you feel like hurting them back? It's a natural reaction. But retaliation is never constructive, and it damages you every bit as much as the person you're retaliating against. Jesus is our ultimate example of how to respond to hurt. Peter described him like this: "He never sinned, and he never deceived anyone. He did not retaliate when he was insulted. When he suffered, he did not threaten to get even. He left his case in the hands of God, who always judges fairly" (1 Peter 2:22, 23). The next time you are tempted to lash out at someone who hurts you, remember Jesus.

Time seemed to stand still, and neither girl spoke. It was as though both of them finally acknowledged their own pain, and the hurt they had caused each other.

Finally Karen stood up. "Why do we do these things to ourselves?"

Linda raised her eyebrows. "And not just to ourselves—to people around us. People like Grant and Jon and Miss Harris. All they know about us is that we're both Christians, and we're at each others' throats constantly."

Karen nodded. "I wouldn't blame them if they think Christians are phonies. So, what do we do now?"

"Let's start with this," Linda said. "Karen, I apologize to you for the way I treated you. I should have tried harder to salvage our friendship and been willing to work through it with you."

"Me too," Karen added.

"And I think we should apologize to Miss Harris and the yearbook staff for making them put up with our fighting."

"Yeah," Karen agreed, "but it's not going to be easy."

"Except this time—" Linda reached out to Karen, "we'll help each other. It's been a long time since we did that."

They hugged for a moment, then walked out.

Getting straightened out with someone you're at odds with is always a beautiful thing. Think about how God feels when a lost person reconciles with him. Reconciliation is a job God has given those who love him. "God . . . reconciled us to himself through Christ and gave us the ministry of reconciliation. . . . We are therefore Christ's ambassadors, as though God were making his appeal through us. We implore you on Christ's behalf: Be reconciled to God" (2 Corinthians 5:18, 20, *NIV*). So many relationships are broken in today's world. What can you do to be an ambassador of reconciliation?

As Katie and her brother Kent helped their parents clean out Grandpa's home, Katie found two large water bottles full of pennies. Katie tried to lift one, but it was way too heavy. She found her father in the basement with her mother.

"Dad, do you know about those pennies in Grandpa's closet?"

Dad nodded. "Grandpa used to put all his extra pennies in those jars. They must go back 20 or 30 years."

"How many do you think there are?"

"Oh, maybe there's a hundred dollars worth in each."

"Should we take them to the bank?"

"Probably."

Katie returned upstairs. "Maybe Dad will let us buy something with them," she said to Kent.

"I'd like a new bike," Kent said.

Katie could think of plenty of things she would buy: new clothes, some nice pairs of jeans, a few stylish shirts for school.

There was so much cleaning to do they soon forgot about the pennies.

A penny won't buy much these days. Even in Bible times, a penny was a very small amount of money. Luke records a time when Jesus watched people bringing their offerings to the temple in Jerusalem. "Then a poor widow came and dropped in two pennies. He called his disciples to him and said, 'I assure you, this poor widow has given more than all the others have given. For they gave a tiny part of their surplus, but she, poor as she is, has given everything she has'" (Mark 12:42-44). It wasn't the amount of the woman's offering that pleased Jesus; it was her sacrificial attitude.

MYSTERY OF THE

JARS OF PENNIES

Grandpa had died suddenly a month before, so Katie's family had a lot of work to do to empty out his house. And it was a sad task. One evening when they drove into the driveway they saw that the glass in the front door had been smashed. Someone had reached in, unlocked it, and burglarized the house.

The only things that were missing, though, were the jars of pennies.

"Why would someone just steal those?" Dad asked. "There're plenty of other good things that are worth more."

They called the police and they came, taking fingerprints and walking about. "Are you sure that was all they took?" asked the officer in charge.

"The only thing we can find."

"Were any of the pennies valuable?"

"We don't know," answered Dad.

"We'll see what we can do," said the officer.

Money has been a source of controversy throughout history. Once some tax collectors confronted Peter to insist that Jesus pay temple taxes. Jesus used the event as an opportunity to teach Peter, and to provide money in a miraculous way. How did Jesus supply the money for the temple tax? Read Matthew 17:24-27 to find out.

Katie couldn't let it go. She began to research pennies and their value. She found that pennies had changed over the years. At one time, Indian head pennies were made. After them came the Lincoln penny with the wheat emblem on the back. The next was the Lincoln head penny with the Lincoln Memorial on the reverse side.

She also discovered that pennies minted in certain years had great value. Some were valuable because so few of them were made. Others had mistakes, but accidentally got into circulation. Still others had great value because the image was off-center when the coin was struck.

Katie wrote down all the years that were valued, and all the places they were minted. She went in to talk to her father.

"Do we know if Grandpa collected coins?" she asked him.

"Yes, he did. But it was a long time ago. Back in the seventies, he had to sell his coin collection to pay bills. Grandma was sick, and Grandpa lost his job for a while. I remember his collection was quite valuable. Since then, I don't think he ever made an effort to collect coins. I think he took the pennies he had in his pocket at the end of the day and put them in the jars."

Collecting coins in a worthwhile hobby. Being a good steward and saving money is wise. But hoarding money and amassing wealth without giving thanks to God for providing it is greed. Jesus said, "No one can serve two masters. For you will hate one and love the other, or be devoted to one and despise the other. You cannot serve both God and money" (Matthew 6:24). What role does money play in your life?

MYSTERY OF THE
JARS OF PENNIES

Katie kept thinking about it. Why would her Grandpa just keep the pennies? He would know which ones were valuable and which were not. Why just put them all in a big bottle?

It seemed most of her questions could only be answered by getting the pennies back. But how could she even find them?

Wait! What about coin dealers, people who sold these things? If Grandpa had sold his collection at one point, he must have dealt with a coin dealer. But that was 30 years ago. Would any dealer he could have dealt with still be in business? Besides, a thief might not know what he had and take the pennies to a bank.

No, she thought. That couldn't be it. Someone must have known that Grandpa had some valuable pennies. Otherwise, the thief would have stolen other items from the house.

Solomon was the richest king of Israel. The Bible describes his wealth: "During Solomon's reign, silver and gold were as plentiful in Jerusalem as stones" (2 Chronicles 1:15). Solomon had beautiful palaces, huge armies, and many family members and servants. He lacked nothing. Yet what did Solomon say about wealth? He said, "Those who love money will never have enough. How absurd to think that wealth brings true happiness! The more you have, the more people come to help you spend it. So what is the advantage of wealth—except perhaps to watch it run through your fingers!" (Ecclesiastes 5:10, 11). What role does money or material possessions play in your happiness?

Katie decided to call the local coin dealers in her area. She went to the Yellow Pages and made a list of them, then began calling. She planned her questions ahead of time so that she wouldn't ask the obvious things.

The first place she called, she asked for the store expert. That turned out to be owner.

"Hello, my name is Katie Wallace. I'm wondering if you have a good collection of pennies for sale?"

"Quite good ones," answered the man. "Any special ones you're looking for?"

She looked at her list. "A 1922-D."

"Yes, we have a couple of those."

"How much are they?"

"Well, I'll have to check. I'll put you on hold."

He returned and gave her the price. Then she asked, "You haven't had any big new lots come in the last week or so, have you?"

"Are you looking for a particular collection?" he wanted to know.

"Not exactly." She paused. "Did you ever meet Cliff Wallace?"

The man thought. "A collector, right? Probably in his seventies now? He used to come in. Bought some pennies as I recall."

Money doesn't buy happiness—nor does it buy a lot of other good things. When Peter and John were going to the temple to pray, a beggar who couldn't walk asked them for money. "Peter said, 'I don't have any money for you. But I'll give you what I have. In the name of Jesus Christ of Nazareth, get up and walk!'" (Acts 3:6). No money in the world could buy the man's healing. But God gave it for free. What free gifts of God do you value most?

MYSTERY OF THE
JARS OF PENNIES

Katie decided calling wasn't the best way to go, so she talked her mom into taking her to a couple of local stores that dealt in coins. The first one had all these coins in big cases, and there were plenty of pennies. But the man she talked to hadn't had any new collections come in.

The second store was pretty much the same. As they visited stores, they discovered that coins were big business, and they cost a lot. Katie felt very discouraged. She crossed off the first three stores on her list and they headed to the fourth.

"Do you really think you'll find anything, honey?" her mom asked at one point.

"I don't know. But I have to try. For Grandpa, I guess."

"How many more stores are there?"

"I'd hate to say. I've only been concentrating on the ones on our side of town."

"OK, two more today. Then it's your father's turn."

They walked into the last store for the day and Katie prayed that she'd get a clue—just one. The owner was nice and showed them a lot of coins. As they browsed the store, Katie edged back to a curtained-off area and looked in.

There on a workbench was a large pile of pennies.

Money earned honestly is God's provision for people. But money gained by dishonest means can be a curse. Three verses from the book of Proverbs sum it up: "Ill-gotten treasures are of no value, but righteousness delivers from death. The wages of the righteous bring them life, but the income of the wicked brings them punishment. . . . Dishonest money dwindles away, but he who gathers money little by little makes it grow" (Proverbs 10:2, 16; 13:11, *NIV*). When you view money in the proper perspective, you please God.

Next to the workbench were two large water bottles—Grandpa's bottles! Katie tapped her mother's arm and pointed.

"Let's go to the parking lot," her mother said quietly, and they thanked the owner and left the store. When they got in the car, Katie's mom took out her cell phone and called the police.

An hour later, with two officers going through the pennies, Katie, her mom and dad, and Kent stood watching.

"Look," one of the officers said. "This is one of the valuable ones."

The officers found others. Grandpa must not just have thrown all his pennies in the jars; he had put valuable collector pennies in with them.

In the end, the two jars turned out to be worth nearly $20,000. They found out the coin dealer had appraised some of Grandpa's pennies, so he knew what Grandpa had. When he read Grandpa's obituary in the newspaper, he decided to break in to Grandpa's house and take them.

Months later, when the matter was settled in court, the family celebrated with a nice dinner. Dad asked Katie, "So what's your next investigation?"

"I think I'll find out why Kent is such a nerd-burger."

Everyone had a good laugh at that joke—even Kent.

In Isaiah's day rich people were exploiting the poor, and the poor cried out to God for help. God promised that eventually he would save them, and he gave these words of prophecy to Isaiah: "Is anyone thirsty? Come and drink—even if you have no money! Come, take your choice of wine or milk—it's all free! Why spend your money on food that does not give you strength? Why pay for food that does you no good? Listen and I will tell you where to get food that is food for the soul!" (Isaiah 55:1, 2).

MYSTERY OF THE
THANKSGIVING TURKEYS

Benin lay in bed listening in the night. The subdivision he lived in backed up to a large farm with a tract of forest on one side. His house sat on the edge of the forest. He liked listening to the woods at night. It gave him a peaceful feeling.

He rolled over and closed his eyes. "Good night, God," he murmured, something he always did after praying and getting into bed. He started to drift, when he suddenly heard a strange noise.

Gobble gobble gobble.

He sat straight up. Turkeys in the forest? The farm behind his house raised turkeys for Thanksgiving dinners. At this time of year they'd be full grown. But they belonged in their pens near the barn, not loose in the forest.

He got up and went to the window. In the darkness, he couldn't see anything. The sounds, though, were unmistakable. Did the farmer let the turkeys come all the way over there? Or had they gotten loose? Couldn't someone just steal them?

He stood at the window, but finally he went back to bed. "Maybe tomorrow," he said.

What gives you a peaceful feeling when you go to bed at night? Do you like the sounds of the night? Do you listen to music? Do you mull over the events of the day? Do you pray?

Nighttime is a good time to feel close to God. David the psalmist wrote, "Through each day the Lord pours his unfailing love upon me, and through each night I sing his songs, praying to God who gives me life" (Psalm 42:8). Tonight when you go to bed, remember how God has showed his love to you, and you'll sleep peacefully.

The next morning Benin went out into the backyard to put some things in the trash. He didn't hear the turkeys again, but he looked into the forest. Where could they be?

After school, he decided to explore. He went out back, opened the rear gate, and stepped into the forest. He followed a familiar trail. He wished he had his dog along, but Jake would just scare the turkeys if he found them.

Following the trail, he soon came out on the back boundary of the farm. The corn they grew was long gone, just bare stalks left crushed to the ground. Turkeys ate corn, right? He wondered. That made sense.

He walked the edge of the field for about a hundred yards to his left, then went back to the right. He didn't hear anything or see any sign of turkeys outside the pens. So he found the trail and went back to his house. When did turkeys make noise? At night?

He didn't know. He thought he would do a Google search on the Internet. So he went into the house and sat down at the family computer, and soon came up with some info. Turkeys are not nocturnal.

So maybe they gobbled at night because they were scared?

At this time in your life, learning is something you do a lot. Gaining knowledge and wisdom is important for your future. Solomon wrote, "Choose my instruction rather than silver, and knowledge over pure gold. For wisdom is far more valuable than rubies. Nothing you desire can be compared with it" (Proverbs 8:10, 11). When you are discouraged by the schoolwork you must do, ask God to help you see the value of learning.

MYSTERY OF THE
THANKSGIVING TURKEYS

Benin lay in bed the next night, listening again. He was fully dressed, and he had his dad's big 14-inch flashlight. When he heard the turkeys, he got up and went outside. He didn't turn the flashlight on till he reached the path. Then he turned it on, and listened.

Sure enough, the turkeys spoke again, and he got a sense of where the sounds came from. He followed them till they quieted, then waited for the next outburst. Tracking them this way, he soon came to a small clearing. There was a little lean-to in the bushes, and three large turkeys pecking at a pile of corn in the middle. He stepped closer and saw that the turkeys each had a tether around a foot so they couldn't go far away.

The whole area was protected by a five-foot-high chicken wire fence so dogs and other predators couldn't get in.

Benin knelt down, his flashlight on the three turkeys. They didn't act frightened. "Why are these turkeys here?" he asked himself.

He finally stood up and walked back to the path, then home. He wondered why a farmer would hide three turkeys like this away from the main farm.

When he got home, he sat at his desk and took out a permanent marker.

Have you ever gone exploring at night? Things look different in the dark, and it's easy to get confused. The Bible compares not knowing God with being lost in darkness. Before Jesus was born Zechariah said, "Because of God's tender mercy, the light from heaven is about to break upon us, to give light to those who sit in darkness and in the shadow of death, and to guide us to the path of peace" (Luke 1:78, 79). Jesus is the light that shines in spiritual darkness.

Benin went out to the turkey cage the next morning and sat down and watched for awhile, to see if anyone showed up.

When no one did, he posted a sign on the fence. It said, "Please call Benin at 555-3407." He didn't think the person would, but he thought it might help. He went home whistling.

No one called, though, and when the evening came early, he took another walk out to the cage. The turkeys were fine, and pecking at a new pile of corn. On his sign someone had written: "Go away. Private property."

Below that, Benin thought about something new to write. Finally, he settled on, "I just want to be friends." He left it in place and hiked back to his house. That night no one called, but the turkeys kicked up a ruckus about midnight and a dog began barking furiously. He finally went out to investigate. He followed the path and reached the cage shortly. There was no dog nearby. He looked, and under his note someone had written, "I don't."

What to do now? Why wouldn't the person just talk? He wasn't going to steal the turkeys, or even tell anyone about them.

Have you ever wanted to be a friend to someone who didn't want to be a friend to you? It's hard when someone rejects your effort to be a friend.

When he was on earth, Jesus knew what it was like to be rejected. The prophet Isaiah described it like this: "He was despised and rejected —a man of sorrows, acquainted with bitterest grief. We turned our backs on him and looked the other way when he went by. He was despised, and we did not care" (Isaiah 53:3, 4). When you're feeling rejected, you can pray, knowing that God understands.

Discouraged, Benin was about to turn and go when someone in the dark said, "Why are you here?"

Benin turned. "Where are you?"

A flashlight went on, shining in his face. He didn't move. "I heard the dog barking and was afraid it would attack the turkeys."

The flashlight lowered. "Why do you want to be friends with me?"

Benin was stunned. "I just thought it would be nice." He tried to make out the person in the dark. He couldn't see anything. "Look, I'll leave you alone forever, if that's what you want. I just thought it was interesting that there's a huge turkey farm here and then I find three lone turkeys in the woods who are obviously protected by someone. So I wondered about it."

Benin heard rustling in the bushes. A boy appeared. He wore overalls and he looked familiar, like maybe he'd seen him in school.

"John Leverett," he said. "I live here on the farm."

Names are important. They identify us. That's why you usually start a friendship by telling someone your name. Names also define us. Your parents may have thought long and hard about what to name you before you were born. They wanted to give you a name that reflected who you are, and who they hoped you would become.

Names in the Bible were important. Some people even had their names changed after important events in their lives. Find out about some of them by reading Genesis 17:5, 15; John 1:42; and Acts 13:9. What were those people's names, and what else were they called?

MYSTERY OF THE
THANKSGIVING TURKEYS

The two boys looked in on the turkeys. "Do you want to meet them?" John asked.

"Sure," Benin said. John opened a gate on the far side and they stepped inside the fence. The three turkeys walked over to him immediately and he began feeding them pieces of corn.

They talked about the turkeys, and about school, and it seemed things were going well. Then John asked, "You haven't told anyone about the turkeys here, have you?"

"No," Benin said. "I just came to look at them."

"I wouldn't want them to be harmed. People have come to our farm at night and stolen turkeys. My father is very angry about it. He would not be happy if I showed him what I have done here."

"Why not?"

"During the season, we sell every turkey to the butchers, who get the turkeys ready for the market. We can't afford not to sell every one. But these three—"

He didn't finish the sentence. Benin was beginning to understand, though. "You didn't want these turkeys to get slaughtered?" he asked.

John nodded. "Turkeys are really stupid. But—" He looked away.

Is it possible for a boy like John to have turkeys as pets? Do you think that he not only wants to save them from being butchered, but that he may even love them? God has given all kinds of animals to bless humans. One story of a man and an extraordinary animal is found in Numbers 22:25-31. Read that Scripture to find out what kind of animal it was, and why it was extraordinary.

MYSTERY OF THE
THANKSGIVING
TURKEYS

"These turkeys are your pets?" Benin offered.

"I know it's stupid. My father won't allow me to have a dog or cat," he continued. "They both can kill young turkeys. I don't want a snake, or a hamster, so—"

Benin nodded. "So you made pets of these three?"

"One, actually, but the other two just kind of joined up. I would feed them and play with them a little. They're kind of fun in a weird sort of way."

Benin laughed. "It's great. I think it's great."

"My father wouldn't. I didn't dare tell him. One night, I sneaked one out, and then another, and then the third after I built this place here."

"What will you do with them?"

John shook his head. "I know I can't keep them here. Winter is coming. They'll need to be in the barn where it's warm. But my father would insist these turkeys be sold with the others."

Benin looked at the turkeys. "I'll help you build a turkey coop if you wish."

John looked at him hopefully. "You would?"

"Sure. Let's see what we can do. But for now, I'd better get home. I'll meet you here tomorrow."

John said, "Thanks . . . friend."

When you make friends with someone, it's always good to get involved in something they think is important. Look at what Jesus said in Mark 1:16-18. What did he say to the men he wanted to be his disciples? Why do you think those words appealed to them?

Whenever Grandpa and Grandma came visiting from Arizona, Travis always had a great time. He was only 10, but Grandpa played games with him and they had a lot of fun together. Many times, though, Mom said to him, "You should enjoy him now while you can, honey. He's not in great health."

Travis worried a lot about Grandpa getting sick. But he decided not to say anything about it because he was afraid that might make it happen.

One night, Travis said to Grandpa, "Can I comb your hair? It's so cool!"

Grandpa let Travis climb up on the easy chair and Travis combed it every which way. Travis's hair was tight and curly, but Grandpa's was straight and fine. So Travis had a lot of fun trying it all different ways—back, forward, to the side. It was so funny, Travis and Grandpa laughed and laughed.

When he was younger, Grandpa taught Travis to play catch. Sometimes, when neighbor kids came by, they played running bases. Grandpa could catch the ball behind his back, between his legs, over his head. He taught Travis to catch like that.

Sometimes Grandpa got out of breath. He had to stop playing, and Travis asked, "Is something wrong, Grandpa?" He thought, *Uh-oh, Grandpa's gonna get sick.*

Travis liked to comb his grandpa's hair, and his grandfather was a good sport to let him. For some people their hairstyle is a source of pride and identity. Your hair can remind you of God's love and of how valuable you are to him. How? Read Luke 12:6, 7. What does God know about your hair? How does he feel about you? Remember that as you brush or comb your hair today.

MYSTERY OF THE
GIFT FROM GRANDPA

It was cold out that Christmas. Grandpa said, "We don't see much snow where we live. Let's ask God for some snow." Travis prayed, and then Grandpa prayed. "Give us snow for Christmas," he said.

Two days later it snowed. Grandpa laughed so hard, he fell down!

Grandma said, "You're not a child, Abner." But Grandpa said, "I feel like one, though."

Before they left, Grandpa sat down with Travis for a talk. "Travis, one day I'll be gone for good. But I want you to know that when I get to Heaven, I'll be thinking about you."

"Don't say that Grandpa. I don't want you to go. You're my best friend."

"Don't worry," he said. "I'll leave you something that will always remind you of me."

"Nothing could ever take your place, Grandpa," Travis told him.

Grandpa and Grandpa went home after Christmas. One night, Travis's mom came to his bedroom with tears in her eyes. "Grandpa had something bad happen to him, honey," she told Travis. "It's called a stroke. It happens in your brain. He's in the hospital. He's very sick. He can't walk or talk. We need to pray for him."

Travis bowed his head and asked God to help his Grandpa.

When we are helpless, God is able. When bad things happen that we have no control over, we can be confident that God is in control. The Bible tells us that God is "always ready to help in times of trouble." Read Psalm 46:1-3, and thank God for his help, both in the past and in the future.

MYSTERY OF THE
GIFT FROM GRANDPA

49

Day 3

It was a long night. No one could talk to Grandpa because he was unable to respond. Though Travis prayed hard, and even with tears, it was many days before Grandpa seemed to get better. Over and over, his parents told him to be patient and give Grandpa time, but it seemed to Travis that Grandpa could die at any time.

One day he asked his youth pastor about it, and Glenn told him to keep praying and not give up, and God would work.

Travis couldn't talk to Grandpa on the phone because he was so sick. But Travis kept praying every night before bed, "God, please help my Grandpa. Please help him talk and walk again."

Nothing happened for a long time. Then one day, Mom called Travis to the kitchen. "Grandpa's on the phone, honey."

Travis said, "Hi, Grandpa. You can talk now. I prayed about it."

Grandpa said, "Maybe you can come visit Arizona and comb my hair. We can play ball again."

Travis felt so good inside he thought he could run around the yard a hundred times and not stop. He went immediately into his bedroom and thanked God for Grandpa's healing.

When a family member suffers through a serious time of trouble or illness, the family should rally around and give support. How can you give support? One of the things God says to do is offer comfort. Paul said in 2 Corinthians 1:4 that God "comforts us in all our troubles so that we can comfort others. When others are troubled, we will be able to give them the same comfort God has given us."

Have you felt God's comfort in your life in a sad time?

349

MYSTERY OF THE
GIFT FROM GRANDPA

It was a good time for Travis and his family. He talked frequently to Grandpa on the phone. Grandpa always seemed upbeat and happy. He always assured Travis that soon he would travel north to see the family.

It took a long time. Travis' mom explained, "Recovering from a stroke or other serious illness can take months, even years. Give Grandpa the time he needs."

Travis took that to heart and began praying for patience for himself as well as recovery for Grandpa.

In April, Travis and his parents flew out to see Grandpa and Grandma. To Travis, Grandpa looked tired and skinny, and he couldn't talk very well. Grandma said he was getting better, but Grandpa said, "We'll play ball again. You'll see."

Travis combed his hair, and everyone laughed. He and Grandpa talked many times. Grandpa said, "You know, Travis, even if I don't get better, that doesn't mean God has failed. And after I go, I have a big surprise for you."

"What do you mean?" Travis asked.

Grandpa took his hand. "God works in different ways in different people. I had this stroke and it's been really hard. God has a reason for that, even though he hasn't told me. Maybe it's so we'll talk more; I don't know."

"But I've been praying and praying, Grandpa!"

God has warned us that many times in life troubles will come upon us. Sometimes it's people opposing us for doing Christian deeds. Other times it's an illness, loss of money or home, or deep disappointment. Sometimes it's losing a loved one through death. We must always remember Jesus' promise in John 14:3: "When everything is ready, I will come and get you, so that you will always be with me where I am." Can you trust in that promise?

Travis kept praying. One day when he came home from school, Mom said, "I have a surprise." He stepped into the living room and there sat Grandpa and Grandma! Grandpa stood up and winked at Travis. He had a ball in his hand.

"Let's play," he said. "I'm not as good as I was, but I can still throw."

Grandpa got tired easily. He sat down with Travis on the lawn chairs. He said, "God answered your prayers for me, you know."

"I know," Travis answered, and gave Grandpa a big hug.

Travis spent a lot of time with Grandpa on that visit. It seemed everything was perfect for the first time in a long time. Even though Grandpa didn't move as well as he once did, he was alive, and happy, and ready for action. Travis told himself over and over that this would be a new beginning and Grandpa would just get better and better.

Grandpa sent him letters and called on the phone when they were apart. Each time, Grandpa reminded Travis of verses in the Bible that were encouraging and uplifting. It seemed Grandpa knew the Bible better than anyone. Often he said, "In it, you'll find the words that will keep you going no matter what happens to you in life."

No matter what problems we may face, a time of relief comes. God gives us a sense of hope, and we may believe nothing bad can happen again—at least for a time.

God tells us that we should not worry about the future: "So don't worry about tomorrow, for tomorrow will bring its own worries. Today's trouble is enough for today" (Matthew 6:34).

Are you able to trust in God so that you can stop worrying?

MYSTERY OF THE
GIFT FROM GRANDPA

Travis came home from school one day and Mom was crying. "Grandpa had another stroke. He might not make it, honey."

Travis knew what to do—he prayed every time he thought about it. He even prayed in the bathtub, and when he played baseball, and especially at night before he went to sleep. He called and left messages with Grandma. She always said, "Grandpa loves to hear from you, darling."

Travis was sure Grandpa would soon be well again.

But Grandpa didn't get better. Travis and his family went to see him in a nursing home. Grandpa just slept the whole time. Travis asked Grandma what was wrong. She said, "Grandpa is very old and maybe it's his time to go to Heaven."

"But I don't want Grandpa to leave us!" Travis said, and cried. He didn't think about that surprise Grandpa said he had for him. He just wanted Grandpa to live.

Travis prayed every day, but one afternoon Grandma called. She told Travis, "Your Grandpa died this morning very peacefully, darling. He wanted me to thank you for praying."

Travis cried and cried. Mom told him, "Grandpa is in Heaven with God now, and I bet they're having quite a party."

Travis asked, "Do you think someone is combing his hair and playing ball with him?"

Dad answered, "Sure. And he's probably thinking about you, too."

While death is something every person will face, God assures us that we can have hope. Read 1 Thessalonians 4:13, 14 to find out how Christians can look at death differently from other people.

After the funeral when Travis returned home with his parents, he began to think about Grandpa's surprise. What could it be? Why was Grandpa so mysterious about it?

Nothing happened for a while, but one day in the mail, Travis received a box from Grandma. Travis opened it carefully, wondering what could be in it.

He found there Grandpa's mitt, ball, and comb. Grandpa wrote a note, too. "I'll always love you, my wondrous grandson. One day you'll be with me in Heaven, and we'll play catch. You can comb my hair, too. That's the biggest miracle of all because God will make that happen. So always trust him, and I'll see you again one day."

Travis was still sad, and it was hard not to cry. But deep down he felt excited about seeing Grandpa again some day. He asked his youth pastor about it and he explained to Travis that was the great Christian hope. We do not perish. We do not cease. We do not end. Rather, we go to Heaven where life goes on and on forever with God in peace, love, and joy.

Today, whenever Travis feels bad that his Grandpa died, he picks up Grandpa's glove and ball. He remembers the good times past and that he'll see Grandpa again in the future. That's why he can't always be sad. And that's why he can always remember Grandpa with happiness in his heart.

In Revelation 21:3, 4, we read about what Heaven will be like: "I heard a loud shout from the throne, saying, 'Look, the home of God is now among his people! He will live with them, and they will be his people. God himself will be with them. He will remove all their sorrows, and there will be no more death or sorrow or crying or pain. For the old world and its evils are gone forever.'"

Are you looking forward to it even now?

MYSTERY OF THE
SNOW EMERGENCY

Lexie froze in the doorway. Her snowshoes clattered on the porch as they fell down from the place where she tried to lean them. Both dogs barked.

When she stepped into the warmth of the cabin, she could see Nadine's face white with fright. She wore her nightshirt, punching her hands together and stumbling about. "Where's the truck?"

"Stuck," Johnny said, ripping off his coat. "How are you?"

"The contractions are about every eight minutes. I—Oooooww!" Nadine's lips contorted and she closed her eyes. Johnny rushed to her side. Lexie stared.

Nadine wheezed, "Man, that hurts. I didn't know having a baby would be this bad." She breathed hard. She stood, pressing her hand into her back.

"We've got to do that breathing stuff," Johnny said. "Like the book said."

Squeezing her eyes shut, Nadine breathed steadily.

Having a baby is a wonderful thing. Giving birth, however, is difficult and painful. The Bible explains why. As a result of Adam and Eve choosing to disobey God in the Garden of Eden, God spelled out the consequences: "Then he said to the woman, 'You will bear children with intense pain and suffering'" (Genesis 3:16). Every time a baby is born there is a reminder of the consequences of sin. Why do you think God did this?

Nadine stumbled toward the bedroom. Her face contorted in pain. "I can't stand it!" she cried as she stood shaking in the doorway. "Aiiiiiiii!"

Lexie couldn't move. She looked from Johnny to Nadine and back to Johnny. He seemed rooted to his spot, halfway between the table and the bedroom. "I feel like my mind's just flown the coop."

As Johnny stepped back, Nadine climbed onto the bed and lay back, wiping her brow with a towel, then pulling up a sheet.

Johnny said, "I think I should—" He turned away.

"You're bleeding!" Lexie cried. "You're bleeding, Nadine."

Nadine felt with her hand, then stared at the red on her fingers. "What does that mean? Could something be wrong with the baby?"

Lexie swallowed. They needed a doctor, and her father was a doctor. She said firmly, "I'm going for my father."

It's the job of adults to protect and care for children. But in this case, Johnny and Nadine are adults in need of help, and Lexie is a girl with the ability to help them. More important, Lexie knows she can depend on God to help. Deuteronomy 31:8 says, "Do not be afraid or discouraged, for the Lord is the one who goes before you. He will be with you; he will neither fail you nor forsake you." Does this verse assure you?

The snow bit Lexie's cheeks. She tramped up toward the trail, able to spot the cut in the trees even in the dark. Repeatedly she asked herself if she could do it, if she could help Nadine and her baby.

The silence of the woods was overpowering. The wind had died down. It was only her and the eerie silence of a snow-filled wood.

She prayed silently as she walked. *Please, God, let me make it.*

As she stepped away from the light of the cabin, she looked at her watch one last time: 5:00 AM. The trees towered over her. In the darkness, she could feel their feathery stillness and nearness. But the trail? Even with the trees parted slightly at the point near the cabin, she strained to see where she was going in the dark.

She could see the wide space between the trees. But with the snow, everything looked the same. It made her feel as if she were inside a monstrous unlit cave. The silence sent prickles of fear up and down her back. She sensed that her forehead and her hands were sweating. She turned off the flashlight. "Got to save it," she told herself.

She bumped into boughs. Branches grabbed at her parka and sent showers of snow onto her face, down her neck. The sudden cold made her shiver. Where was she going?

Lexie's lost her bearings. She doesn't know where she is. Have you ever been lost? How did it feel? A Bible verse to remember when you're in a scary place is Psalm 23:4: "Even when I walk through the dark valley of death, I will not be afraid, for you are close beside me. Your rod and your staff protect and comfort me."

She flashed the light on the track ahead, then on her own trail behind her. "It's my own track!" she cried suddenly. "I'm going in circles."

She stifled a cry. "Please, God. Please!"

She pushed away from the tracks, thinking she had to run into something familiar. It was getting lighter now, and hopefully she would soon see something she recognized.

With the growing gray in the sky and the sun starting to shine gold far to her left, the east, it was easier now. In the distance she heard the whir of a snowmobile engine and wondered who might be out. Could she find them? Were they neighbors?

A moment later there was a loud report: BOOM! A gunshot!

Snow fell off boughs. Lexie dropped to the ground and flicked on the flashlight. "Don't shoot!" she called.

There was a silence. Then, "Who are you?"

"Lexie! Lexie Slade!"

"Thank God! We've been looking for you for hours!"

Lexie stood up and a man approached her. He was wearing a thick Russian-style fur cap with a badge in the front and a blue parka.

"Are you all right?" He shone a flashlight into her eyes. She winced, then shook her head, stepping forward.

Isn't it nice to know that when you are lost there are people who are concerned? That's one of the great things about being in a family. But what about people with no families? Look at James 1:27: "Pure and lasting religion in the sight of God our Father means that we must care for orphans and widows in their troubles, and refuse to let the world corrupt us." How does God intend for people to take care of those who have no families?

"Yes. I'm fine. I'm sorry. There's a woman—"

The officer smiled grimly. "All right. Let's get you home."

He waved her toward the freshly plowed road, extending his hand. "We've had two search teams out for hours."

In several minutes they reached the road. The first bright red of morning gleamed on the horizon. The clouds were clearing. The snow had slowed to flurries.

When they reached the Slade cabin, three snowmobiles sat in the road, steam rising off them. Lexie swallowed back her fear, praying that her father wouldn't be too angry.

Before she finished, she heard a cry behind her. Her father ran out of the house in his plaid hunting shirt with Uncle Josh. "Lexie! Lexie! Honey!" Lexie turned and leaped into his arms.

Her voice trembled, but she got out the words quickly. "There're some people who live in the old hunting cabin. Their truck's stuck in a ditch. She's in labor! Please, Daddy, we have to hurry! They need help!"

Throughout history there have been plenty of babies who were born in less than ideal situations. Even today on the news you occasionally hear stories of babies born in taxicabs, elevators, or other odd places.

The most important baby ever born came to earth under extraordinary circumstances: "She gave birth to her first child, a son. She wrapped him snugly in strips of cloth and laid him in a manger, because there was no room for them in the village inn" (Luke 2:7). Regardless of the circumstances, Jesus' coming forever changed the world. Remember to give him thanks.

Her father searched her eyes. "A woman having a baby? Now? Let me get my bag and some instruments. If the baby is breech, it could be real trouble." He turned to Lexie. "You can show us the way? You're not too tired?"

Relief swept over her. "Yes. In daylight I know it perfectly. The trail should be all marked by my tracks, anyway."

They sped to the cabin on snowmobiles. Johnny was already running out the door when they turned off the machines. "Less than a minute apart and she's really hurting, Dr. Slade."

"Don't worry." Lexie's father hurried past him to Nadine's bed. He gave some quick orders to the men, asked Johnny to stoke up the fire, and called Lexie to his side. Dr. Slade put on rubber gloves. "She's close," he said. "Thank the Lord the baby's not breech."

He called Johnny over. "I want you to hold your wife's hand, and when I tell her to push, I want you to encourage her. Got it?"

Turning to Lexie, Dr. Slade said, "Honey, you'll have to help me. Listen closely to what I tell you." He handed her a pair of rubber gloves. "Put these on."

Everyone's working together. Dr. Slade is in charge, but he can't do it alone. He needs the help of others. God intends for the church to work like that. He's in charge, but he uses people to help him. The apostle Paul compares Christians working together with how the parts of the human body work. "Now all of you together are Christ's body, and each one of you is a separate and necessary part of it" (1 Corinthians 12:27). What would a body be like if all the parts disagreed and rebelled? Read 1 Corinthians 12:15-26 to find out.

Lexie followed her dad's directions. She handed him a pair of bent medical pliers with a wad of gauze between the jaws.

Nadine yelled in pain, but Johnny gripped her hand and told her to be strong. Dr. Slade said, "Push, girl! Push with all your might."

Nadie let out a scream, and her baby slid into Dr. Slade's palms. "It's a girl," he cried. Lexie noticed the tears in his eyes as he worked.

"All right," Dr. Slade said. "Here comes the second one."

Lexie looked up, astonished. Johnny's jaw dropped. "The second one?"

Dr. Slade smiled. "Yes, two. Twins!" He smiled. "I guess you didn't know." He grinned sheepishly. "Another big push, Nadine!"

Moments later, the second baby—a boy—emerged.

Nadine's eyes teared. "They're so beautiful," she said. "The girl's name is Rebekah—Rebekah Fairlight Alexandra. And the boy—"

"John Junior," Johnny said triumphantly.

"Children are a gift from the Lord; they are a reward from him" (Psalm 127:3). You are God's gift to your parents. Are you grateful for them? How does your family reflect God's love?

MYSTERY OF THE
SUDDEN SNOWSTORM

51
Day 1

Shelly Ferrarra blinked repeatedly. The snow seemed right in her eyes, even though the windshield wipers batted the flakes away with a mesmerizing *shoosh shoosh*. "Caroline, please be careful. This is a back road."

"I know," her sister Caroline answered. "Isn't it great?"

"Just be careful."

"I am. I'm driving as slow as Mom."

"No way."

"I am." Caroline turned her eyes forward and grinned. Shelly saw the smile and shuddered. Sometimes she could be a complete ditz, she thought. Even though Caroline was 17 and had a driver's license, their mom often said Shelly had far more sense. Shelly decided not to think of that right now.

It was an unexpected snowstorm. They'd both gone skiing with the youth group in the Pennsylvania mountains, staying at their uncle's cabin far back in the woods. No one had been listening to the radio or TV, they were all so intent on skiing. The youth pastor and his wife had cleared out less than an hour before, getting assurances from Shelly that they'd be leaving in minutes. But one thing led to another, with little things to clean up here and there. She was not going to let Caroline leave the place a mess as they had the previous year.

Shelly listened to the whoosh of the snow around the car. It was a fearsome storm with the wind rising and splattering the snow in great swishes across the car and the windshield.

Consider this verse from Proverbs 25:11: "Timely advice is as lovely as golden apples in a silver basket." If you were in the car, what things do you think you could say to Caroline to help her in those perilous moments?

MYSTERY OF THE
SUDDEN
SNOWSTORM

"Watch it up here, Caroline. It's curvy."

"I know. I've been here more often than you."

"You don't have to get nasty about it."

"Shelly! Just be quiet and let me drive, OK?"

Shelly didn't like the feeling of being a nag. She'd seen enough of that in her mother. But Caroline was definitely going too fast.

"Caroline, please!"

"Oh no!"

There was a sharp rattle of stones and wood under the engine and the floorboards. Then the car crunched to a stop in front of a tree. The windshield wipers went on swishing. The headlights shone into the forest, illuminating the snowfall in an eerie glow. Everything else was silent.

"I'll check it."

Shelly didn't respond. She glumly thought of having to get out, dig out, and then push, snow splattering all over her jeans and her new ski jacket. Why did this have to happen?

"We're dead in the water," Caroline informed her after spinning the wheels in both directions. She couldn't even get it to rock. "I think we're caught on some stones."

"Now what do we do?"

The answer to the question, "Now what do we do?" is "Pray!" That's the first thing you should do in any situation. However, for all of us at one time or another, praying is the last thing we think of after exhausting other options.

Paul urged the Christians in Ephesus, "Pray at all times and on every occasion in the power of the Holy Spirit. Stay alert and be persistent in your prayers for all Christians everywhere" (Ephesians 6:18). Is praying a habit for you?

"Should I voice message central control?"

"Don't joke about this, Caroline. This is serious."

"Will you quit being our mother for one minute?"

Shelly sulked and stared into the night. It was past ten o'clock. No one would miss them till morning probably. It was a six-hour drive.

She pulled out her cell phone, though she didn't know why. NO SERVICE was on the display, as it had been since they came up the mountain. The cabin didn't even have a phone. It was disconnected for the winter. It was another mile or so to the main road. If the storm would just end, they could probably walk it and get a ride to a service station.

Shelly waited until Caroline came around and jumped back inside. "Man, it's cold," she said, rubbing her hands. "I packed my ski mittens and hat."

"What should we do?"

"Listen to the radio and dance the night away?"

"Caroline!"

"OK." She switched off the lights and then the engine. "We can't leave the engine running because of carbon monoxide. So that means no heat. I think we should get all our stuff out of the trunk and bed down. You want the back or the front?"

"We should bed down?"

These two are in a dangerous situation. When David was in danger, he called out to God, and he knew the comfort God gives. He wrote, "O my people, trust in him at all times. Pour out your heart to him, for God is our refuge" (Psalm 62:8). When do you depend on God as your refuge?

MYSTERY OF THE
SUDDEN
SNOWSTORM

"No use walking in the storm. We'll just get lost. It's at least eight inches now and we could lose the road real easy."

Dawn came with the snow still swirling. The car was cold, but covered up in their weekend clothes, pajamas, and a blanket and comforter that each had brought, they were warm. Shelly awoke first. She lay still, listening to the silence, and watching as daylight appeared through the fogged-up car windows. "Caroline?"

Shelly waited a full minute before speaking again. "Caroline?"

"Hmmmmm?"

"Are you awake?"

"Not yet."

"Well, get yourself in gear. We've got to get out of here."

"I'm hungry."

"Do we have anything?"

Shelly nodded. "I have a candy bar and some popcorn. And there was the stuff left over from the refrigerator—hamburger—frozen, I'm sure."

"I'll eat anything. Do you think we could make a fire?"

God created the world and controls the weather: "He sends the snow like white wool; he scatters frost upon the ground like ashes. He hurls the hail like stones. Who can stand against his freezing cold? Then, at his command, it all melts. He sends his winds, and the ice thaws" (Psalm 147:16-18). Thank God that he not only sends the snow, but causes it to melt, providing the water needed on the earth.

"With what?"

Caroline looked around. "The cigarette lighter, of course."

It took a long time to find loose sticks under the snow, but once she found some, she dug down deeper and got handfuls of dry pine needles. She added some scraps of paper that she found in the car. Holding the hot lighter to a tiny sliver of paper, she blew puffs of air until it finally started to flame. Gradually more and more of the fuel caught fire, and finally there was a fire big enough to heat the leftover hamburger.

Shelly rigged up a little cooking tin with some aluminum foil they had in the trunk. The two girls huddled over the fire while the meat cooked. The warmth felt good even though the smoke stung their eyes.

They were so hungry, the meat was delicious, but too soon it was gone. "I guess now we have to walk," Caroline said.

Shelly peered up the road.

Dressed in their skiing outfits, they made it to the road after a two-hour hike. But it wasn't even a state highway. The road wasn't plowed. Caroline and Shelly looked in both directions. There were no tire tracks, no sounds of cars or trucks, nothing in either direction for as far as Shelly could see.

It seems as if the girls are in an impossible situation. Have you ever felt you were facing the impossible? Moses thought he was facing an impossible situation when God called him from a burning bush: "'But who am I to appear before Pharaoh?' Moses asked God. 'How can you expect me to lead the Israelites out of Egypt?' Then God told him, 'I will be with you'" (Exodus 3:11, 12). No matter what situation you are in, God is with you, and he can do the impossible.

MYSTERY OF THE
SUDDEN SNOWSTORM

They started down the road toward the town. They had no idea what time it was, but it seemed as though they had been walking for several hours.

Suddenly Caroline stumbled and fell. Shelly grabbed her arm. "I smashed my knee in a pothole."

"Is it bad?" Shelly asked.

They stumbled a moment in the snow. "Just let me rest."

Shelly held her and they both settled down in a heap. After a few reassuring words, Shelly said, "Do you think you can walk?"

"I don't know."

"We have to, Caroline. We have to."

There was a fearful silence. Then Shelly said, "Let me help you over to the side of the road."

"What are you going to do?"

"Build an igloo."

"An igloo?"

"If you can't walk, we have to stop. It's late in the day. We need shelter before nightfall." Shelly began building a lean-to out of pine branches.

Shelley is smart to think ahead. Even though the situation is difficult and dangerous, it's better to take action than to delay. When Nehemiah found out that the walls of Jerusalem had been destroyed, he was devastated. He wrote, "When I heard this, I sat down and wept. In fact, for days I mourned, fasted, and prayed to the God of heaven" (Nehemiah 1:4). If you were lost in the snow, how would you approach God?

Shelley worked for over an hour on the lean-to. Caroline sat in the snow, getting colder by the minute. When it was ready and they finally crawled in, the wind was picking up. It swirled around them as they huddled together to preserve their body heat.

After hours of walking they were exhausted and quickly fell asleep. However, through the night they woke up many times and longed for daylight. They took turns praying.

Another dawn came with both of them cold, sneezing, and stiff. Caroline still couldn't walk. Before Shelly helped her up to the main road they prayed again, trying to make a decision about what to do.

"We can't sit here," Shelly said. "We've got to get moving or we'll get hypothermia."

They waded through mounds of snow in pockets and drifts on the road. They moved slowly, but kept moving as the sun rose higher in the sky. Around midday they were both so hungry and weak, Shelly sat down in a drift and closed her eyes. "Just let me rest," she murmured. "Rest."

"No!" Caroline screamed. "Wake up." She gripped her chin and pressed. "Get up, Shelly! Get up!"

Shelly leaned back and closed her eyes. She didn't care if she lived or died now.

And then she heard Caroline cry, "A plow! The plows are coming!"

Saved, and in just the nick of time! God is in the business of saving people. Look at the thief on the cross. When he came to believe in Jesus, even though it was at the last minute, what did Jesus say to him? "And Jesus replied, 'I assure you, today you will be with me in paradise'" (Luke 23:43). You too can be assured of God's help, and right on time.

MYSTERY OF THE
DISAPPEARING NATIVITY

Jaime came to church that Sunday with a big smile on his face. That Saturday, he, his father, and about 20 other people had worked to set up their life-size nativity in preparation for Christmas. When they arrived, Jaime showed their handiwork to his mom and his little brother, Raymie. Everything was perfect, and the life-size figures looked almost real. They were made out of a sturdy material so they wouldn't break easily, but were still lightweight enough to be moved in and out of storage each year.

Jaime explained, "There was a lot of dust on everything, so we had to clean off all the figures. I put the baby Jesus in the manger myself."

People coming into church smiled as they admired the arrangement. It was a proud moment for Jaime. He had just accepted Christ the previous summer, and this year the meaning behind the birth of Jesus was more real to him than ever before.

In church, the minister thanked the team and everyone clapped. Now that the nativity scene was in place, the countdown to Christmas could begin.

For many people, the Christmas story is a charming tale about a poor little baby born in a barn and laid in a manger. But for Christians, the Christmas story is the fulfillment of God's promise to send a Savior and reconcile people to him. When the angel came to Mary to tell her she would be mother to the Messiah, he said, "The Holy Spirit will come upon you, and the power of the Most High will overshadow you. So the baby born to you will be holy, and he will be called the Son of God" (Luke 1:35). What does Christmas mean to you?

The last week of school before Christmas vacation went quickly. There was the school Christmas party and play, and special activities and treats. But best of all for Jaime was the bus ride to and from school every day. As the bus went past the church, Jaime would look at the nativity scene outside, and he felt happy.

He told his friends on the bus about how he helped to put up the scene, and how now excited he was to celebrate Christmas this year as a Christian. Some of them thought he was strange, but most of them had grown up seeing the nativity scene each year and considered it an essential part of Christmas in their town.

That Sunday, Jaime's grandparents came to visit. After church the whole family stood next to the nativity scene for a photo. Mom said she'd put the picture on an ornament that they could hang on the Christmas tree. It was a happy time.

For Joseph, the news of Jesus' impending birth was a huge shock, and a problem for his reputation and Mary's. Yet an angel appeared to him in a dream and said, "Do not be afraid to go ahead with your marriage to Mary. For the child within her has been conceived by the Holy Spirit. And she will have a son, and you are to name him Jesus, for he will save his people from their sins" (Matthew 1:20, 21). For Joseph, for you, and for all people Jesus came to bring salvation. Express your gratitude to God for his Christmas gift.

MYSTERY OF THE
DISAPPEARING NATIVITY

The next week, startling news came from the church in a phone call to every member. The message said that one of the wise men had been taken from the nativity scene. It was hoped that the theft was just a practical joke, and whoever took it would bring it back immediately.

Jaime and his family drove past the church that afternoon to take a look. It was only one wise man missing, and yet Jaime felt a little pain in his heart. Someone had purposely messed up the nativity scene—and for a joke? He didn't think it was very funny. Didn't the joker have any respect for church property—especially at this time of year?

Jaime felt a little funny being so concerned for a statue. Surely there were more important things to brood about. Yet that night before he went to bed, he talked to God about how he felt. "God, I know the wise man's just a statue, but I'm angry, and hurt that someone would take him. Aren't you? Would you please help us to find the wise man and get him back? And, God, would you please bless the person who took him? Help that person to come to know you."

What do you know about the day you were born? Have your parents told you about where and when you were born, and what happened? How was Jesus' birth different from yours? "She gave birth to her first child, a son. She wrapped him snugly in strips of cloth and laid him in a manger, because there was no room for them in the village inn" (Luke 2:7). How did God provide for Jesus' birth? How did God provide for yours?

The next day another awful phone call came. What was thought to be a practical joke was turning into something worse. This time, several nativity figures were missing: Joseph, a cow, and another wise man.

Jaime went to the church that afternoon with his father as he talked to the minister. "How could someone do this?" his dad asked.

"Well," the minister told him, "I thought it was just a joke at first. But now I think this must be a person who's mad at God or mad at the church. Maybe he or she has hurt feelings about something involving a Christian, and wants to lash out in some public way without confronting anyone personally. Probably the best thing we can do now is to add lights to make sure the scene is so brightly lit that the thief will be discouraged from trying again. And in the meantime, the sheriff said he would increase the frequency of patrol cars past the church, so there's a greater chance of catching someone in the act."

"I've already prayed for the person," Jaime said.

His dad put his arm around Jaime. "That's the best thing you can do. But let's you and I go out to the shed and set up some additional spotlights for the figures that are left."

How did you first hear the news that Jesus came? Probably you don't even remember the first time you heard it. But on the first Christmas, the first to hear the news were "terribly frightened" (Luke 2:9). "But the angel reassured them. 'Don't be afraid!' he said, 'I bring you good news of great joy for everyone! The Savior—yes, the Messiah, the Lord—has been born tonight in Bethlehem, the city of David!'" (Luke 2:10). With whom can you share the good news of Jesus?

MYSTERY OF THE
DISAPPEARING
NATIVITY

Despite the extra lights and sheriff patrols, more statues were gone the next morning. This time it was the last wise man, two shepherds, three sheep, and a camel that were gone. Only Mary, the baby Jesus, and the lone angel remained. The whole church was shattered. Some people questioned whether God was punishing them for something.

On December 21, the minister called a big meeting and everyone came. He discussed the measures that had been taken, and asked the people for their ideas.

Jaime's dad suggested, "What if some of us camped out near the nativity tonight? We could stand guard all night and catch anybody who comes to steal something."

Other men agreed, and volunteered to bring their sons. They came up with a plan. They would take turns staying outside in a tent, and moving inside into the warm church building. If everyone took turns, no one would have to spend the entire night outside in the snow.

Late that night, the vigil began. The first father and son who stayed outside told about how a car full of teenagers went by several times shouting insults at the church. The second pair said they had seen a deer bounding across the road, but nothing else.

Then it was Jaime and his dad's turn. It was 3:00 in the morning, and Jaime's dad even let him sip hot coffee to stay awake.

While nativity scenes are serene, there was terrible violence associated with Jesus' coming. Herod was jealous at the prospect of a new king, and had his soldiers kill all the boys two and under in and around Bethlehem. "That night Joseph left for Egypt with the child and Mary, his mother, and they stayed there until Herod's death" (Matthew 2:14, 15a). Thank God that he saved Jesus from Herod's crime.

While the tent kept Jaime and his dad out of the wind, the air was bitterly cold. They sat in the doorway of the tent facing the nativity scene shivering. Even without the hot coffee Jaime probably wouldn't have fallen asleep, he was so cold. He snuggled as close as he could to his dad to preserve heat.

After about half an hour, Dad elbowed Jaime and pointed. Walking up the sidewalk next to the church building were two figures wearing black. They were careful to step only on the areas where the sidewalk had been shoveled, apparently because they wanted to leave no footprints. Jake opened his mouth to speak, but Dad gestured for him to be quiet.

The dark figures moved boldly into the spotlight, as though they didn't care if anyone could see what they were doing. Immediately Jaime noticed their faces—two boys, only a little older than he was.

Carefully, one boy lifted the Mary statue and wrapped his arms around it. The other took the angel. Awkwardly they moved back to the sidewalk, and started to leave.

Jesus did not stay a baby in the manger. He grew to teach about God, and to pay the sacrifice for sin, once and for all. The message of Christmas is summed up in John 3:16: "For God so loved the world that he gave his only Son, so that everyone who believes in him will not perish but have eternal life." Do you have eternal life in Jesus?

Jaime's dad motioned to him, and slowly they emerged from the tent. The boys didn't see them immediately, but as they approached the boys, Jaime's dad spoke: "Hey, fellas, you want to tell me what you're doing?"

The boys froze. One struggled as though he were about to drop the statue he was carrying, and turned to face Jaime and his dad.

"We didn't mean any harm—" he started to say, when the other boy started sobbing. He put his arm around him and went on. "I'm Luke Briscoe, and this is my brother James. Our mom died last year, and our dad's deployed in Afghanistan. We wanted . . . we just wanted . . . it's stupid, but we wanted a family like Jesus had for Christmas."

Suddenly Jaime wasn't mad about the missing nativity figures anymore. He felt sorry for the two boys and the sad times they were having. And he remembered his prayer, when he had asked God to help the thieves come to know him. Was God answering Jaime's prayer through Jaime?

"You want a family?" Jaime asked. He smiled. "Have I got a family for you!"

The book of Hebrews assures us that, because of Jesus' sacrifice, all who accept him as Savior are part of a family: "Both the one who makes men holy and those who are made holy are of the same family. So Jesus is not ashamed to call them brothers" (Hebrews 2:11, *NIV*). What does it mean to you to be a part of the family of God?

Jaime went and woke the other fathers and sons in the church building. They all came out and talked to Luke and James. Together the men and boys went to the garage where the boys had hidden the nativity figures. Because Luke and James had been careful, none was the worse for wear. They carried all the figures back to the church and reassembled the nativity scene. Then a couple of the men went back with Luke and James to talk to their grandparents.

At the Christmas Eve service, Luke and James sat next to Jaime. People came by to talk to the boys and their grandparents and make them feel welcome. Jaime's dad and the other men explained the situation, and the church members were willing to forgive the boys. Several of them even invited Luke, James, and their grandparents to their homes for Christmas dinner. They assured them that they would find family in the church.

On Christmas day, Jaime and his family stopped by to see Luke and James. They were very happy because they had found out they would be able to talk to their dad over a video phone. To them, it was a good Christmas because they had found a new family at the church to love them.

Before he left, Jaime presented them with a gift: a small nativity scene.

When we remember how much God loved us and gave his Son, we will find it easier to love others in response.
"This is real love. It is not that we loved God, but that he loved us and sent his Son as a sacrifice to take away our sins. Dear friends, since God loved us that much, we surely ought to love each other" (1 John 4:10, 11).

I'VE GOT A CLUE ABOUT . . .

Collect Your Clues Here!

Some devotions in this book contain this symbol: ➞◯. When you see it, do some investigating on your own. Use God's Word to find the answers to these questions, and write what you find out in the space provided.

Week 8, Day 1 (page 60). . . . . Luke 18:15-17
According to Jesus, if they want to enter the kingdom of God, how should adults be like children? _____
_____
_____

Week 8, Day 4 (page 63). . . . . 1 Samuel 17:45-47
As he faced the giant Goliath, what did David say about who would win the battle that day? _____
_____
_____
_____

Week 9, Day 7 (page 73). . . . . James 3:2-8
What small part of the body can change the entire course of a life?
_____
_____

Week 11, Day 1 (page 81). . . . . Joshua 10:11
God dropped objects from the sky to give Israel a victory over Gibeon. What were they? _____
_____
_____

Week 12, Day 6 (page 93). . . . . .1 Corinthians 2:9
What can't human eyes see? _____
_____
_____

Week 13, Day 1 (page 95). . . . . 1 Peter 1:3, 4
What has God reserved for his children, and where is it kept?
_____
_____
_____

Week 13, Day 2 (page 96). . . . . Luke 23:13-15
What two judges found Jesus not guilty? _____
_____
_____

. . . . .Luke 23:23, 24
Even though Jesus was pronounced not guilty, what was his sentence?
_____
_____
_____

Week 13, Day 3 (page 97). .Genesis 3:12, 13
Who did Adam and Even blame for their sin? _____
_____
_____
_____

Week 13, Day 4 (page 98). . . . . .Romans 12:19-21
What startling instructions does God have for those wanting to take
revenge? _____
_____
_____
_____

Week 15, Day 1 (page 109) . . . . Proverbs 20:15
What is rarer and more valuable than gold and rubies?

_____

_____

Week 15, Day 2 (page 110) . . . . Ephesians 6:13-17
What gear does the Christian need to do battle with the devil?

_____

_____

_____

_____

Week 16, Day 4 (page 119) . . . . Matthew 18:15-17
According to Jesus, what are three steps for confronting someone's
sin? _____

_____

_____

_____

_____

Week 18, Day 2 (page 131) . . . . 2 Samuel 22:5-7
Why did David call out to God? What did God do?

_____

_____

_____

Week 18, Day 3 (page 132) . . . . James 1:5-8
How will God respond when you ask for wisdom?

_____

_____

Week 18, Day 5 (page 134) . . . . Philemon 8-11, 14
How did Paul persuade his friend Philemon?

_____

_____

Week 18, Day 6 (page 135). . . . . .Luke 10:33
Why did the Samaritan help a person he didn't know?

_____

_____

Week 21, Day 2 (page 152). . . . . Ecclesiastes 4:9-12
What are four benefits of having a companion or friend?

_____

_____

_____

_____

_____

Week 21, Day 5 (page 155). . . . . .1 Corinthians 6:19, 20
Who does your body belong to? _____

Week 22, Day 1 (page 158). . . . . Hebrews 1:14; Mark 1:34
What two types of beings from another dimension exist in the
world? _____

_____

Week 22, Day 3 (page 160). . . . . .Ecclesiastes 7:11, 12
Which is better, being wise, or being rich? Why?

_____

_____

_____

Week 27, Day 4 (page 196). . . . . .Joshua 7:24-26
What was Achan's punishment for theft? _____

_____

_____

Week 28, Day 7 (page 206). . . . . .Numbers 21:6-9
How did God use an image of a snake as a tool for healing?

_____

_____

Week 29, Day 2 (page 208). Acts 19:13-15
What embarrassing (and painful) thing happened to the brothers
who were casting out demons? _____

_____

_____

_____

Week 29, Day 6 (page 212). . . . . Genesis 27:15-23
What disguise did Jacob use to fool his father Isaac, and what was
the result of his deception? _____

_____

_____

Week 30, Day 2 (page 215). . . . . Psalm 104:16-18
What animals does the psalmist mention, and what homes does
God provide for them? _____

_____

_____

Week 32, Day 1 (page 228). James 4:2, 3
What is one reason God answers "no" to prayers?

_____

_____

Week 32, Day 6 (page 233). 1 John 5:14
What is one essential characteristic of prayers God answers "yes"?

_____

_____

Week 33, Day 2 (page 236). . . . . 2 Kings 2:23-25
What had 42 boys done that caused them to be mauled by bears?

_____

_____

Week 33, Day 6 (page 240). . . . . Job 9:9
What constellations are identified in this verse?

_____

_____

Week 34, Day 5 (page 246). . . . . Psalm 91:1-6
Why should you not be afraid? _____

_____

_____

To what kind of creature does this Scripture compare God?

_____

What are your armor and protection? _____

_____

_____

Week 35, Day 1 (page 249). . . . . Luke 15:8-10
How are people like lost coins?

_____

_____

Week 35, Day 3 (page 251). . . . . Proverbs 4:18, 19
How is life apart from God like a drainage tunnel?

_____

_____

Week 35, Day 4 (page 252). . . . . Proverbs 2:1-7
What should you search for like lost money or hidden treasure?

_____

_____

What does God grant to the godly? _____

_____

_____

Week 35, Day 6 (page 254)........................1 John 4:18
What conquers fear? _____
_____

Week 36, Day 5 (page 260).................... Luke 14:12-14
When may you receive a reward for the good you have done?
_____
_____

Week 37, Day 7 (269).................... 1 Corinthians 10:13
Under what circumstances does God always provide a way of
escape? _____
_____

Week 38, Day 3 (page 272)................... Ephesians 6:1-3
How does God want children to relate to their parents?
_____
_____

Week 38, Day 5 (page 274)................Ephesians 4:25, 26
What does this Scripture say about handling anger and telling the
truth? _____
_____
_____

Week 39, Day 2 (page 278).................... Exodus 20:20
How did Moses encourage the Hebrew people when they were
afraid? _____
_____
_____

Week 39, Day 6 (page 282)...................... Hebrews 2:2
What happened to people who disobeyed God?
_____
_____

Week 40, Day 4 (page 287).....................Hebrews 11:31
Who saved her life by being friendly? _____
_____
_____

Week 40, Day 7 (page 290).....................Romans 6:23
What is God's free gift to all? _____
_____

Week 41, Day 1 (page 291)................Exodus 20:13, 15-17
Which of the Ten Commandments deal with how to treat your
neighbor? _____
_____
_____
_____

Week 42, Day 7 (page 304).........................Micah 6:8
What does God require of you? _____
_____
_____
_____

Week 43, Day 7 (page 311).........................Isaiah 6:8
When God called Isaiah to do a job for him, how did Isaiah answer?
_____
_____

Week 45, Day 5 (page 323).................Matthew 14:25-31
What did Peter do when he stepped out of a boat on a treacherous sea?
_____
_____

Week 47, Day 2 (page 334).................Matthew 17:24-27
How did Jesus supply money for the temple tax?
_____
_____

Week 48, Day 5 (page 344). . . . . Genesis 17:5, 15; John 1:42;
Acts 13:9

What were the people's names, and what else were they called?

_____

_____

_____

Week 48, Day 6 (page 345). . . . . Numbers 22:25-31

To what kind of animal did God give extraordinary ability, and
what was the result? _____

_____

_____

_____

Week 48, Day 7 (page 346). Mark 1:16-18

What did Jesus say to the men he wanted to be his disciples?

_____

_____

Why do you think those words appealed to them?

_____

Week 49, Day 1 (page 347). Luke 12:6, 7

What does God know about your hair? How does he feel about
you? _____

_____

_____

Week 49, Day 6 (page 352). . . . . 1 Thessalonians 4:13, 14

How can Christians view death differently from other people?

_____

_____

_____

_____